IMAGES
of America

BURNET

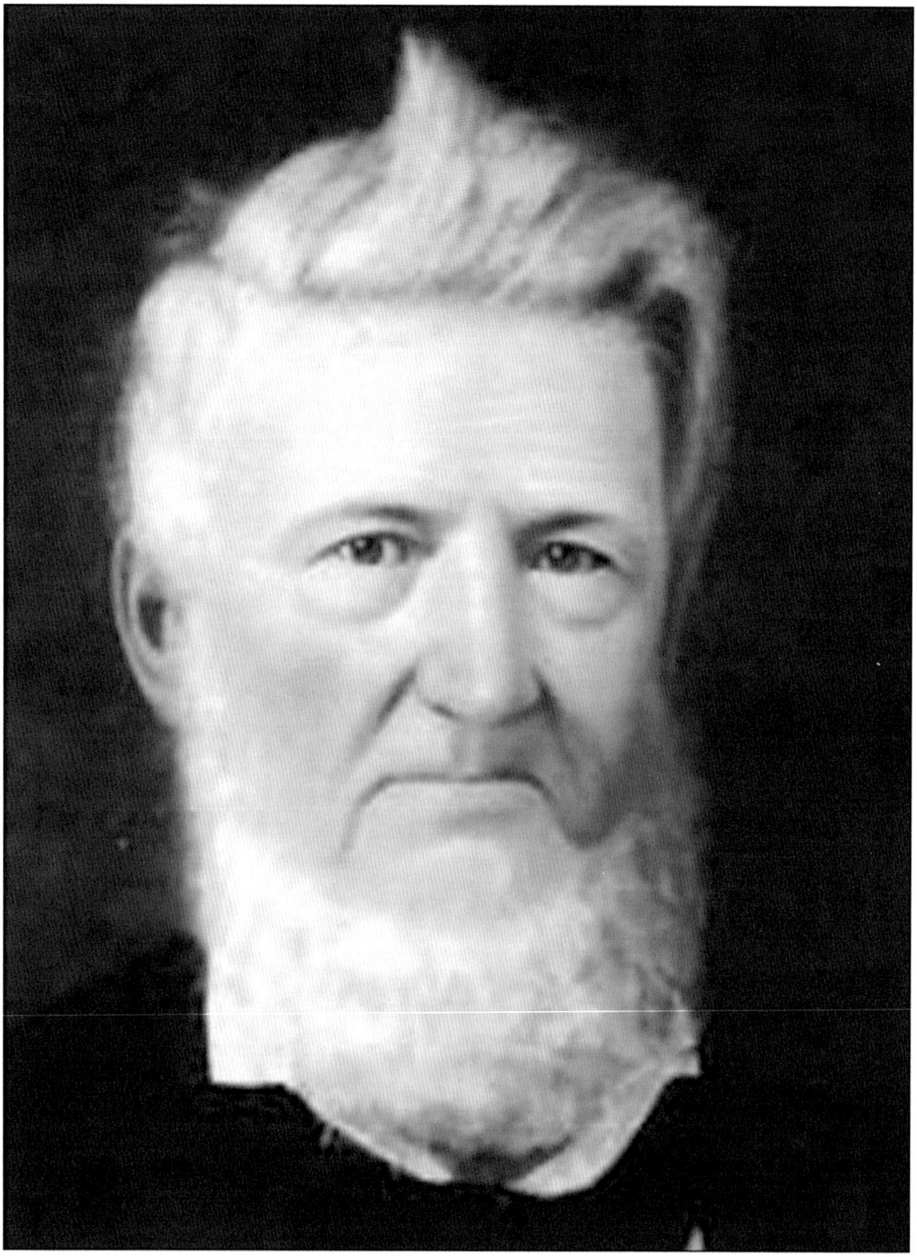

The county and the town of Burnet were named for David G. Burnet, who was the president ad-interim of the Republic of Texas in 1836 during the War for Independence from Mexico. Logan Vandeveer was one of the appointed organizers of Burnet County, and it is believed he chose the name because he knew and admired Burnet. (Photograph courtesy of Herman Brown Free Library.)

On the Cover: Burnet has had three courthouses. The first was of simple frame construction and burned under suspicious circumstances. The one in this photograph was of limestone and was completed in 1875. It served the county until 1935, when it was razed to build the present one of granite. (Photograph courtesy of Burnet County Heritage Society.)

IMAGES
of America

BURNET

Carole A. Goble

ARCADIA
PUBLISHING

ISBN 978-0-7385-7121-8

Published by Arcadia Publishing
Charleston, South Carolina

Printed in the United States of America

Library of Congress Control Number: 2009922900

For all general information contact Arcadia Publishing at:
Telephone 843-853-2070
Fax 843-853-0044
E-mail sales@arcadiapublishing.com
For customer service and orders:
Toll-Free 1-888-313-2665

Visit us on the Internet at www.arcadiapublishing.com

To my children, Sharol, Crista, Perry, Tina, Charles, John, Guy, and Jana, who encouraged me to write this book. Thank you.

Contents

ACKNOWLEDGMENTS

Most of my growing up years were spent on my grandparents' sheep ranch in the rural Burnet County community of Prairie Point. My grandmother's family came there in 1876 and my grandfather's in 1872. My grandfather Harris was known as the community historian. My parents, Charles and Fanny Normann, were famous historical artists. I grew up loving books, but hearing family tales of times past was what I loved most. Because of those stories, I sensed that we were actually living the history of tomorrow. Who people are and what they do constitutes the substance of history.

It has been a privilege to write this book about Burnet, the county seat of Burnet County. When the opportunity to do this book was offered to me, I had a lot of reservations. My family did not. They decidedly encouraged me to write it. So, thanks to them, here is my effort. Thank you to my son and daughter, Guy Goble and Crista Bromley, who constantly bailed me out of computer glitches and helped with scanning and photography. Thank you to my friend Darrell Debo, Burnet historian and author of *Burnet County History*, Volumes I and II. His books have been the ultimate source for historical fact. Thank you to the Burnet County Historical Commission (BCHC), the Herman Brown Free Library (HBFL), the First State Bank of Burnet (FSB), the Lower Colorado River Authority (LCRA), the City of Burnet (COB), and the citizens who have contributed photographs for use in this book. Without you, there would have been no book. Unless otherwise attributed, the photographs in this book are courtesy of the Burnet County Heritage Society. Thank you.

INTRODUCTION

The purpose of this book is to take longtime citizens on a nostalgic journey back to Burnet's beginnings and to educate young people and new citizens about how the town came to exist in the first place. It is a pictorial history, allowing the reader to see and read about its progression from a few cabins into a thriving city. The city of Burnet has a rich history that all of its citizens can be proud of. History is what happens every day, and what happens is brought about by the efforts of each person to make a good life for himself. Because history never ceases to be made, this book will include the city as it has evolved to the present day—that "day" being the time this book is published. As the author of this book, I hope that reading it will lead people to realize that each citizen's life is part of the future history of Burnet.

There were no settlers in what became Burnet County when Company A of the 2nd U.S. Dragoons established Fort Croghan on the western bank of Hamilton Creek. The year was 1849. The purpose of the fort was to make the area safe enough for settlers to come in. The land belonged to John Hamilton, who had served in the Army of the Republic of Texas. He was granted the land in 1838 for his military service. Although he never occupied it, the creek and valley were given his name. Hamilton Valley was a favored camping place for Native Americans because of the springs that constantly poured good clean water into the creek. Comanche chief Yellow Wolf and his tribe made central Texas their home and often used the site. When settlers moved into the area, the Comanches started attacking and stealing from them. Undoubtedly they felt they were defending their territory and considered it their right to do so.

The Texas Rangers directed Lt. Charles Tyler and the dragoons to Hamilton Valley. The Ranger camp was about 3 miles downstream on Hamilton Creek. The job of Capt. Henry McCulloch and his Rangers was to keep the Native Americans from raiding settlements to the south and east of the area. After the dragoons had taken authority over the area, the Rangers were offered discharges. Several of these Texas Rangers became the first citizens of Hamilton. The little settlement grew on the eastern bank of the creek, directly across from the fort. By 1852, the town was prospering and there were enough citizens to successfully petition the state legislature to organize a county. The new county was named after David G. Burnet, the first provisional president of the Republic of Texas. Hamilton was designated as the county seat. In 1852, the U.S. Postal Service registered the first post office as "Burnet Courthouse," but that caused confusion because the town was called Hamilton. Another problem was that there was already a town in Texas named Hamilton and the mail was often missent. Thirty-four citizens sent in a petition, and the Texas State Legislature changed the town's name to Burnet to correspond with the name of the county. This was in November 1857. By this time, there were enough settlers to protect themselves. Fort Croghan had been decommissioned, and the troops had moved farther west.

The town of Burnet was at the crossroads of east-west and north-south travel trails and soon became an important trade center. Grain mills were built on creeks and rivers, and communities grew up around them. These communities depended upon trade with Burnet and thereby contributed to its economy and growth. Rock quarries and lumber mills emerged to support the construction of buildings. Goods were shipped to surrounding communities by oxcart. The good economy was attracting a steady stream of people looking for a better life. Retail stores, livery stables, hotels, and saloons became abundant in Burnet. The area grew to become primarily a farm and ranching community.

There were two very significant things that spurred Burnet's economy and growth. When the State of Texas built its present capitol, the granite for it came from Burnet County. In 1882, a railroad had been constructed from Austin to the town of Burnet. Granite for the capitol was brought from the Marble Falls quarry to Burnet by ox wagon. There it was cut to specification and loaded for the train ride to the capitol site. The town's most significant progress was brought about by the damming of the Colorado River. That opened the area to tourist trade, and Burnet's citizens took full advantage of it. Restaurants, motels, and land developments arrived. Burnet called itself "The Gateway to the Highland Lakes" and began improving its amenities so people who visited would want to make it their home. The first Bluebonnet Festival was held 25 years ago and attracts some 30,000 visitors to the town each April. The state legislature dubbed the town "The Bluebonnet Capitol of Texas" in 1980. The city council has adopted the motto "Lakes, Hills and History."

The inhabitants of Burnet have always been an industrious lot, and they are some of the friendliest people one could find anywhere. Those attributes have combined to make the city of Burnet into one of the fastest growing areas in Texas. Hamilton Creek is now a waterway park just two blocks from the courthouse square. There are walkways, playgrounds, picnic areas, fountains, and a pavilion to enjoy. Historical attractions inside the city include Fort Croghan Museum and Grounds, the Highland Lakes Air Museum, and the Historical District, including the courthouse, old jailhouse, and store buildings from the 1800s. Burnet boasts a championship golf course, a full-service sports facility with indoor regulation swimming pool, game court, well-equipped workout gymnasium, meeting area, and a three-lane indoor tract. Outside are seven ball fields, pavilion, playgrounds, disk golf course, washer pits, walking track, spray-splash water park, and an RV park. A large courthouse annex and a state-of-the-art high school are the latest additions to Burnet's appeal. A new city park with soccer fields, hike and bike trails, and a performance-ready amphitheater will be open by the time this book is published. The Burnet Municipal Airport boasts a runway of 5,000 feet. The Industrial Park has a total of 236 acres available and is convenient to the highway, airport, and railroad. This is Burnet, past and present, for you to enjoy.

One

Fort Croghan and the First Settlers

There were no settlers in what became Burnet County when 2nd U.S. Dragoons, Company A, under the command of Lt. Charles H. Tyler, established Fort Croghan on the western bank of Hamilton Creek. The year was 1849. Hamilton Valley was a favored camping place for Native Americans because of the springs that constantly poured fresh clean water into the creek. Comanche chief Yellow Wolf and his tribe most often used the site. In 1848, Capt. Henry McCulloch had established a Texas Ranger camp about 3 miles down the creek from Hamilton Valley. The job of the Rangers was to protect settlements to the south and east from attacks. Several of these Rangers later became the first settlers in Hamilton Valley. Fort Croghan was established to provide protection, allowing settlers to come into the area. Chief Yellow Wolf and other Native American chiefs did their best to keep that from happening but, as history shows, lost out in the end.

The little settlement across the creek to the east of the fort was called Hamilton, and it grew steadily. None of its first settlers were born in Texas, but all of them were truly Texans with a deep love for their adopted home. They were intellectual, educated, and courageous. They had come to Texas to find fortune and adventure, and they were not disappointed. Logan Vandeveer, William Magill, and R. H. Hall had all been Rangers. Vandeveer and Magill had fought with the Texians for independence at the Battle of San Jacinto. Peter Kerr had brought news of the fall of Goliad to Gen. Sam Houston before San Jacinto. The desire of these first settlers to establish themselves laid the foundation for a successful settlement.

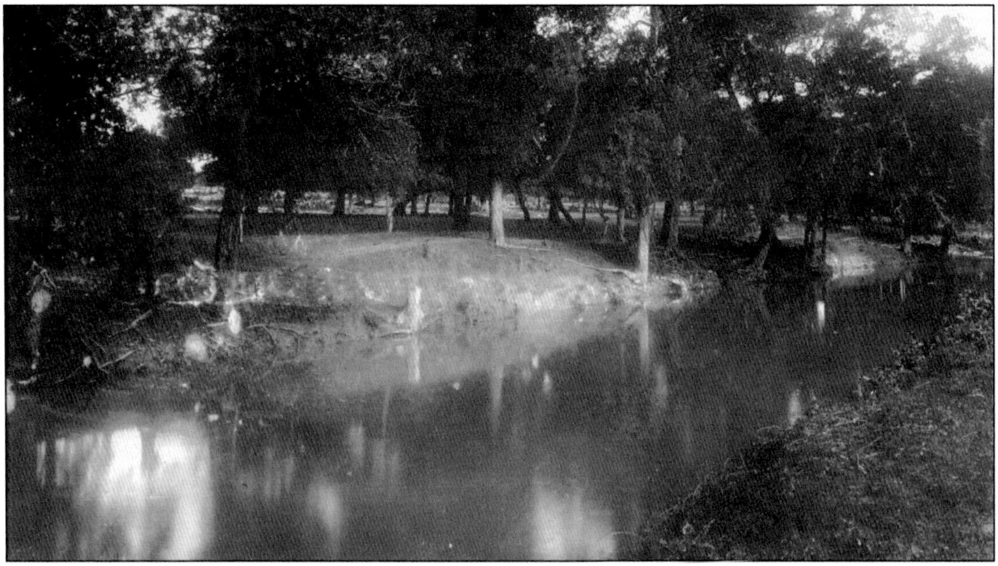

Hamilton Creek, a tributary of the Colorado River, meanders through Hamilton Valley, providing fresh water for plant and animal life. The valley was part of a land grant belonging to John Hamilton of Travis County and was a favorite camping place for Native Americans. Tribes who traveled through central Texas regularly were the Lipan Apaches, Tonkawas, Kiowas, and Comanches. The Comanches were constantly present and were fierce adversaries, making raids on settlers until the early 1870s. The tree in the photograph below is a Native American marker tree located near Hamilton Creek in Burnet. This tree is a result of having been bent and staked to the ground by Native Americans when it was a sapling. The direction in which it was bent marked the trail for others to follow. These trees are found throughout the United States.

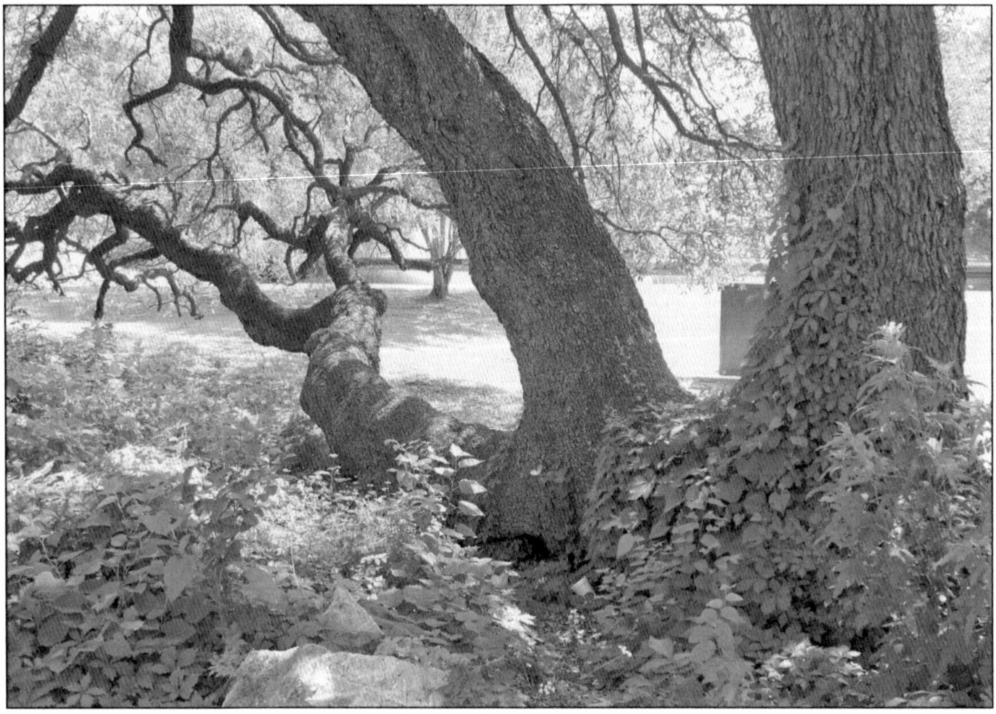

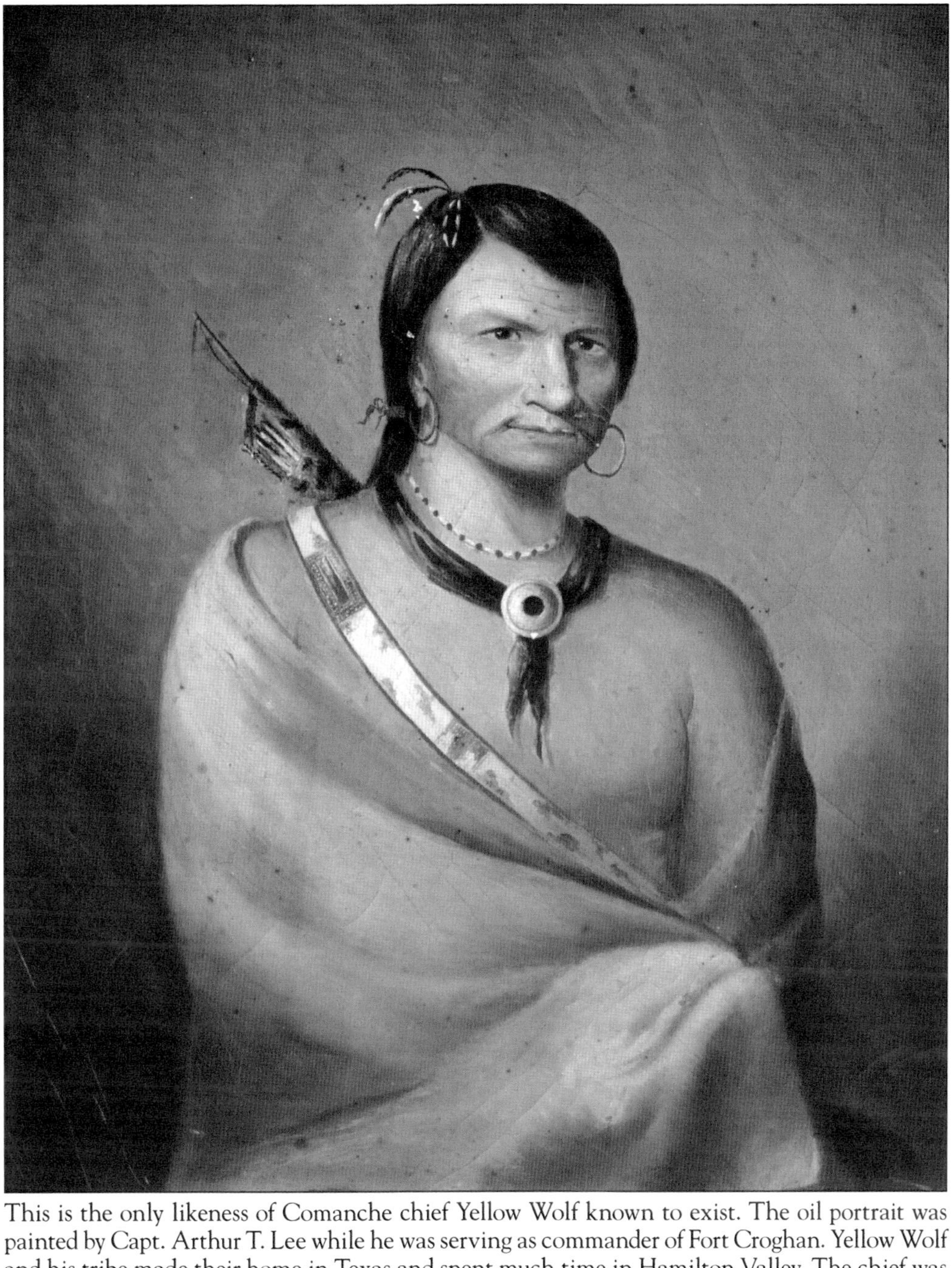

This is the only likeness of Comanche chief Yellow Wolf known to exist. The oil portrait was painted by Capt. Arthur T. Lee while he was serving as commander of Fort Croghan. Yellow Wolf and his tribe made their home in Texas and spent much time in Hamilton Valley. The chief was a staunch and fierce adversary before and during the time that the fort was being established. The Texas Rangers had frequent skirmishes with him and his warriors prior to that time. He was respected for his dignity, valor, and intelligence. Finally accepting terms of peace, he was issued beef and commodities from the fort. Chief Yellow Wolf never agreed to go to the reservation but led his people farther west to open land. He was killed in a battle with Lipan Apaches and is buried in Sanco Cemetery in Coke County. A Texas historical marker stands at his grave. (Photograph courtesy of the Rochester Museum and Science Center, Rochester, New York.)

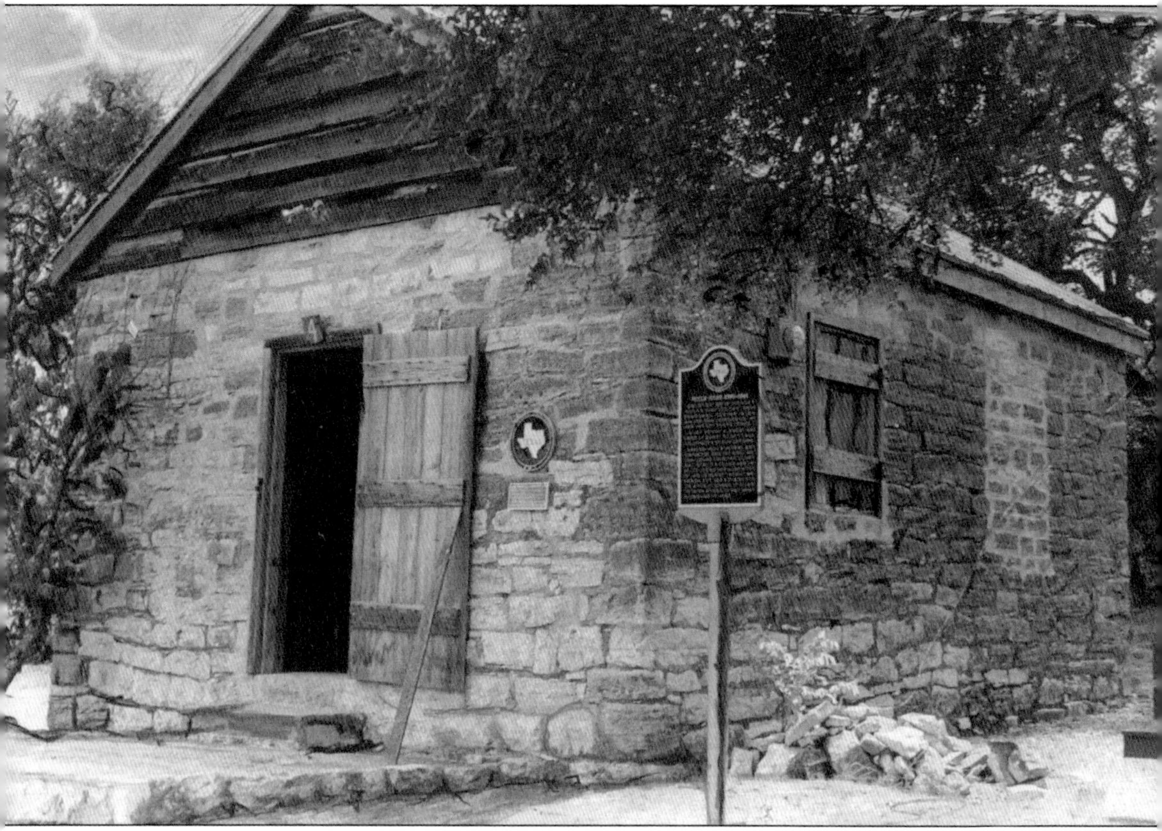

This rock building was the adjutant's office and headquarters for the 2nd Dragoon Regiment when Fort Croghan was active. Constructed of limestone, it is one of only two original buildings remaining. Three young officers, who served at the fort, later became noted generals during the Civil War. Henry Hopkins Sibley and Philip St. George Cook were fort commanders. Albert Sidney Johnston was the paymaster. During the Civil War, gunpowder was stored in this building, and it has since been known as the "powder house." According to legend, the building was later used as a school for black children. In 1966, it was restored and became a Recorded Texas Historical Landmark. It has been set up to represent a post exchange. Because forts were in remote areas, a merchant was usually contracted to operate a store on post to accommodate the troops. (Photograph by F. V. Normann, author's collection.)

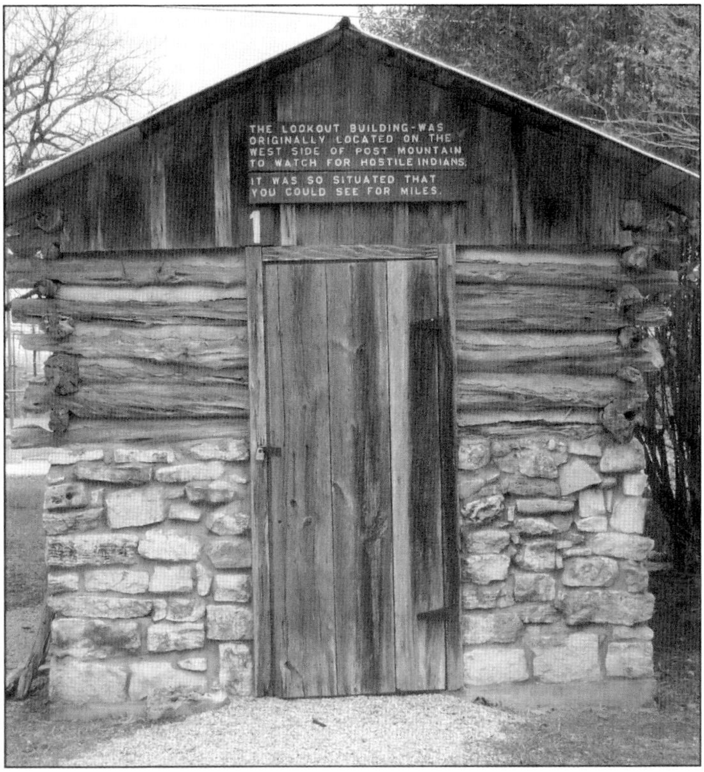

The sentry hut pictured here was originally on top of Post Mountain, where one could see for miles in all directions. It has been moved down onto the Fort Croghan Museum grounds and restored. Eight soldiers died while serving at the fort. They were buried on Post Mountain below the sentry hut, but their graves were eventually lost. The Burnet County Heritage Society has erected a monument, shown below, in their honor. The name, rank, and company of each soldier are listed so that descendants will know they are remembered and appreciated for their service to the country. (Both author's collection.)

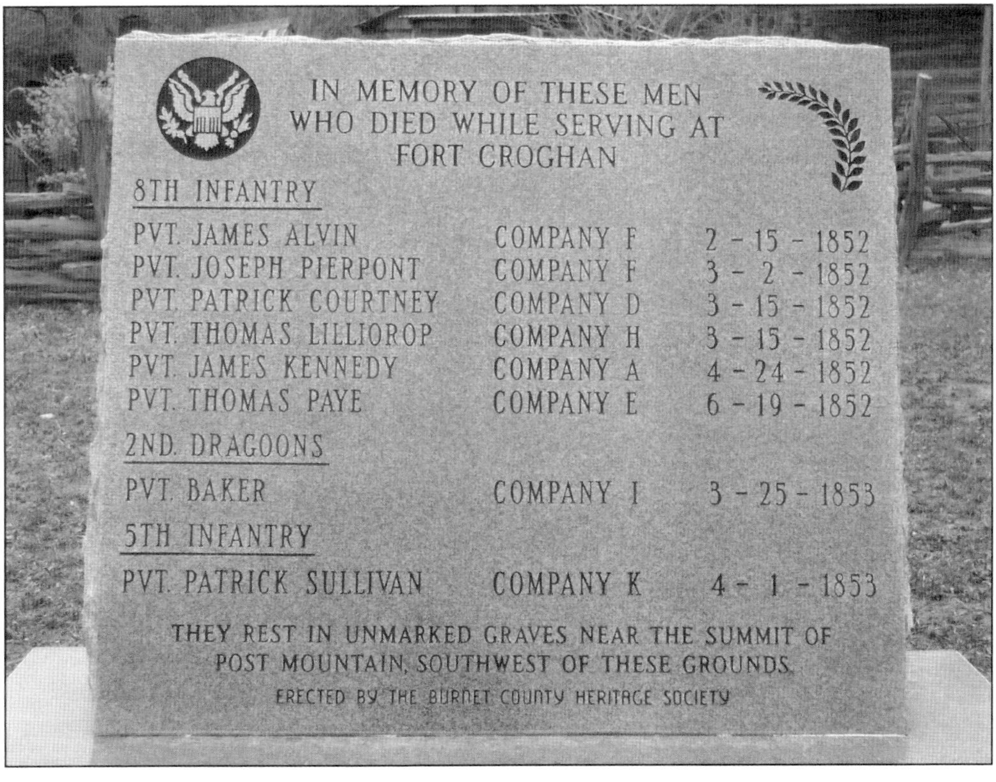

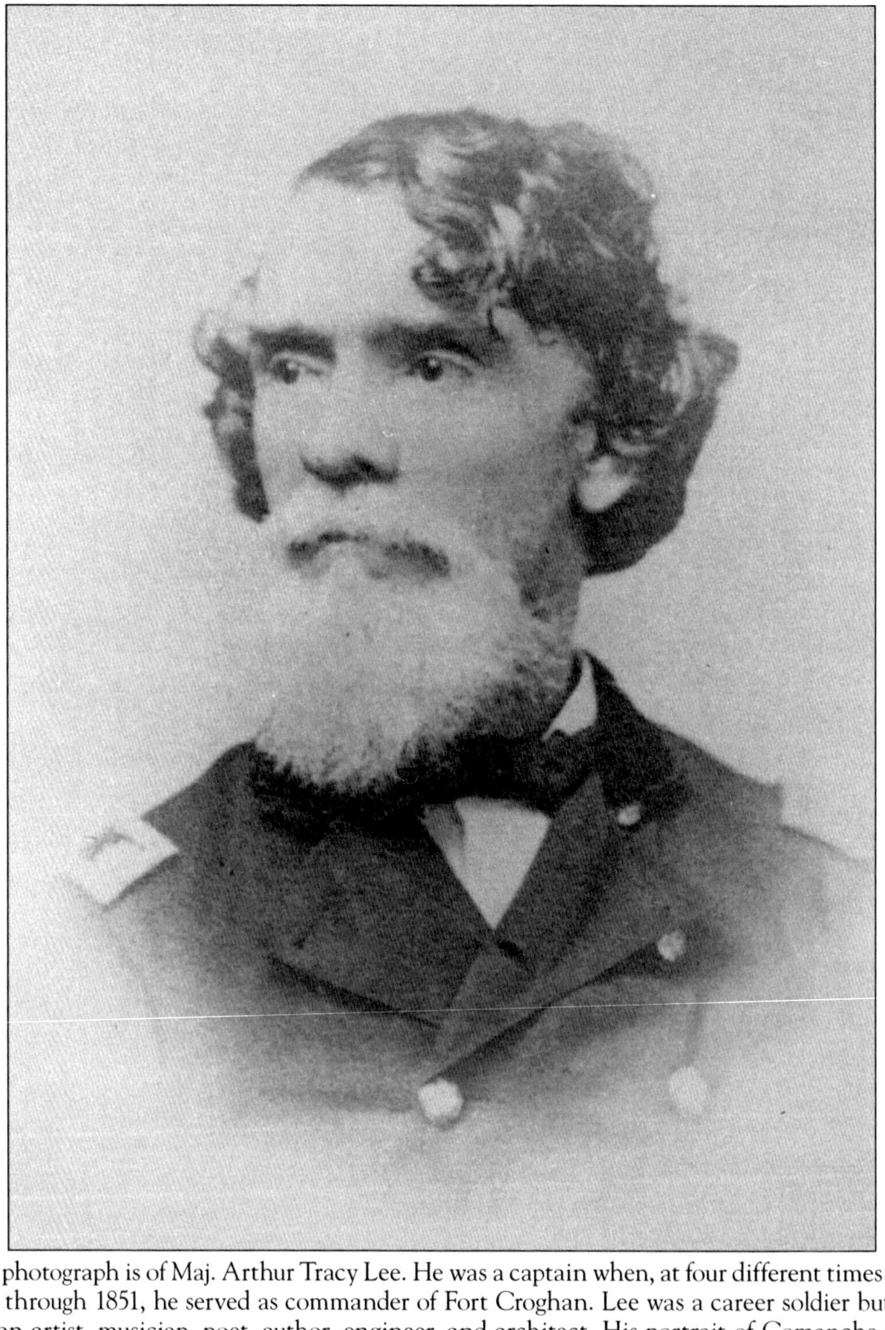

This photograph is of Maj. Arthur Tracy Lee. He was a captain when, at four different times from 1849 through 1851, he served as commander of Fort Croghan. Lee was a career soldier but was also an artist, musician, poet, author, engineer, and architect. His portrait of Comanche chief Yellow Wolf is the only likeness known to exist. His two published works are *Army Ballads and Other Poems* and *Reminiscences of the Regiment*. His last duty was as administrator of the Soldiers Home in Washington, where he served from 1867 to 1872. His reputation at Fort Croghan was one of a cordial gentleman who relieved the soldiers' boredom by inviting the town folk to the fort for occasional parties. A legend among old-timers was that he played his fiddle while the young ladies danced with the soldiers. (Photograph courtesy of the Rochester Museum and Science Center, Rochester, New York.)

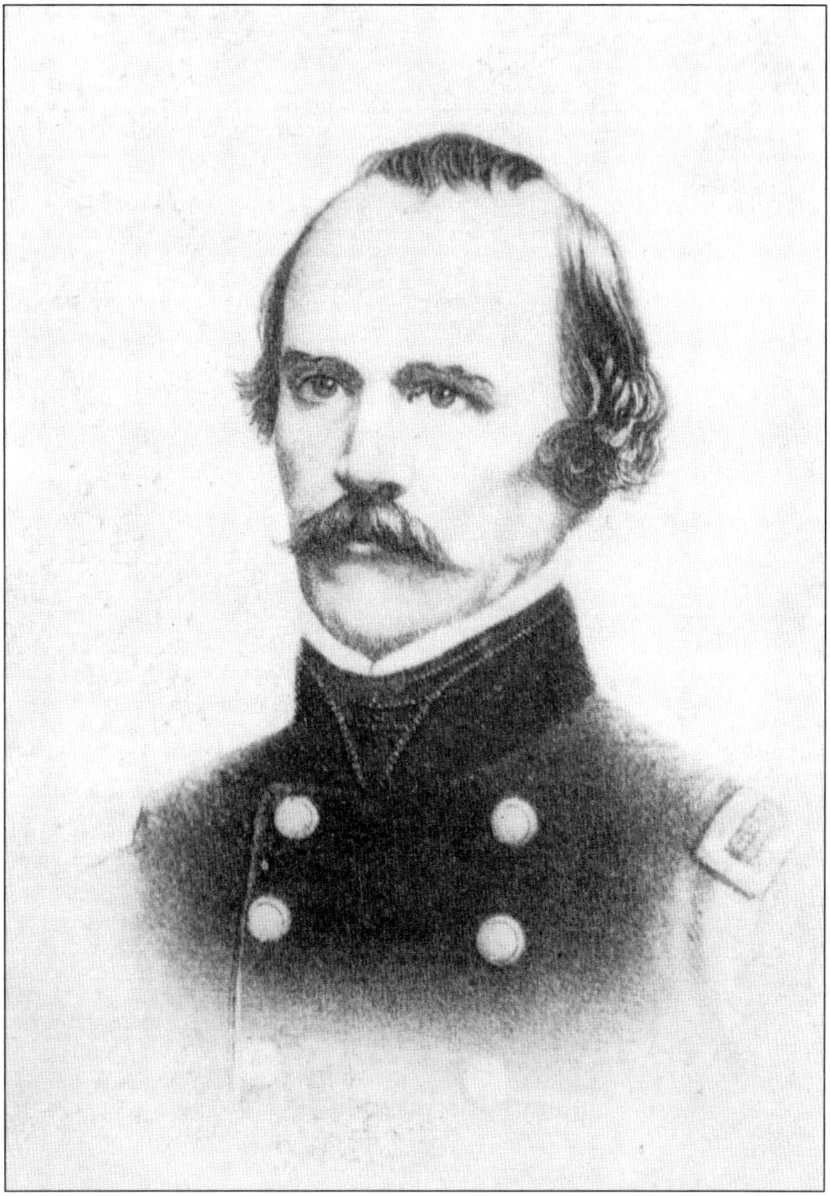

Maj. Albert Sidney Johnston was the paymaster at Fort Croghan. Major Johnston was a graduate of West Point with service in the Black Hawk War. He resigned from the army to seek his fortune in Texas. There he became a brigadier general in the Texas Army and was appointed Secretary of War for the Republic. When Texas was granted statehood, Johnston again joined the U.S. Army at the rank of major. When the Civil War broke out, he resigned again from the U.S. Army and joined the Confederacy. There he was given the rank of general, becoming the second highest ranked officer in the Confederacy. He was in command of troops defending Corinth, Mississippi, when Union troops sought to take it. He met the Union troops at Shiloh, where the battle lasted for two days and 25,000 men died. General Johnston was wounded and bled to death on the battlefield, becoming the highest ranking officer to be killed during the war. A monument stands at the site. (Photograph courtesy of the Center for American History, the University of Texas at Austin.)

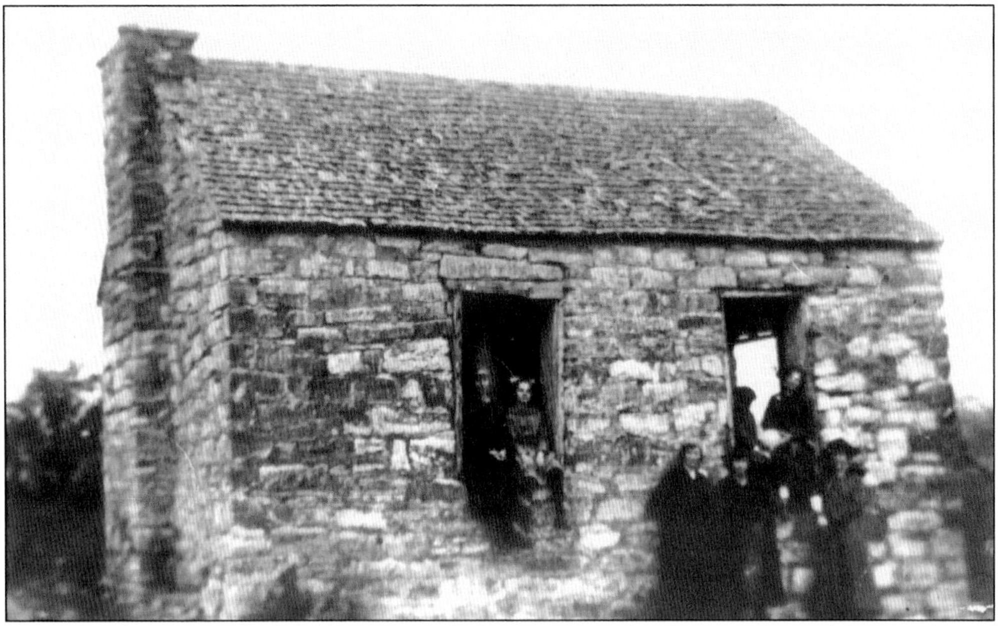

During the years after the fort became a ruin, the young people of Burnet enjoyed visiting the old "powder house" at Fort Croghan. Children played there often. This early photograph includes, from left to right, Lottie Chamberlain, Ruth Fry (both in the left window), Lucile Chamberlain, Nell Fry, Mabel Chamberlain (all standing), and Gordon and Lois Fry (both in right window.)

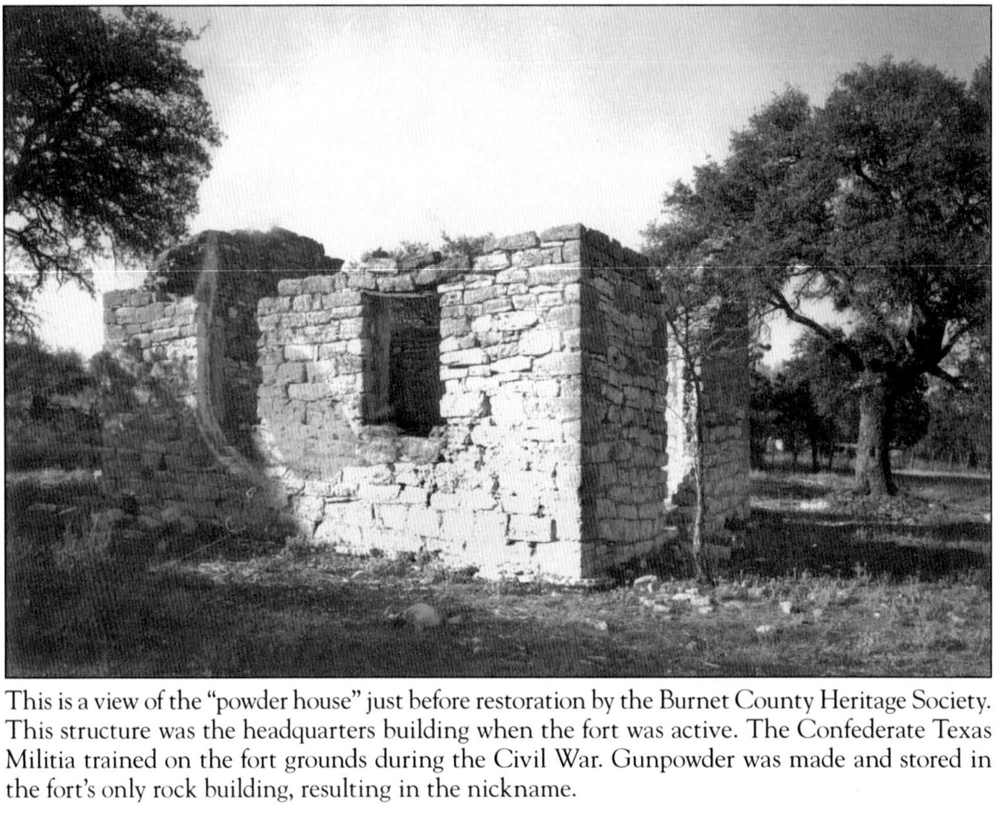

This is a view of the "powder house" just before restoration by the Burnet County Heritage Society. This structure was the headquarters building when the fort was active. The Confederate Texas Militia trained on the fort grounds during the Civil War. Gunpowder was made and stored in the fort's only rock building, resulting in the nickname.

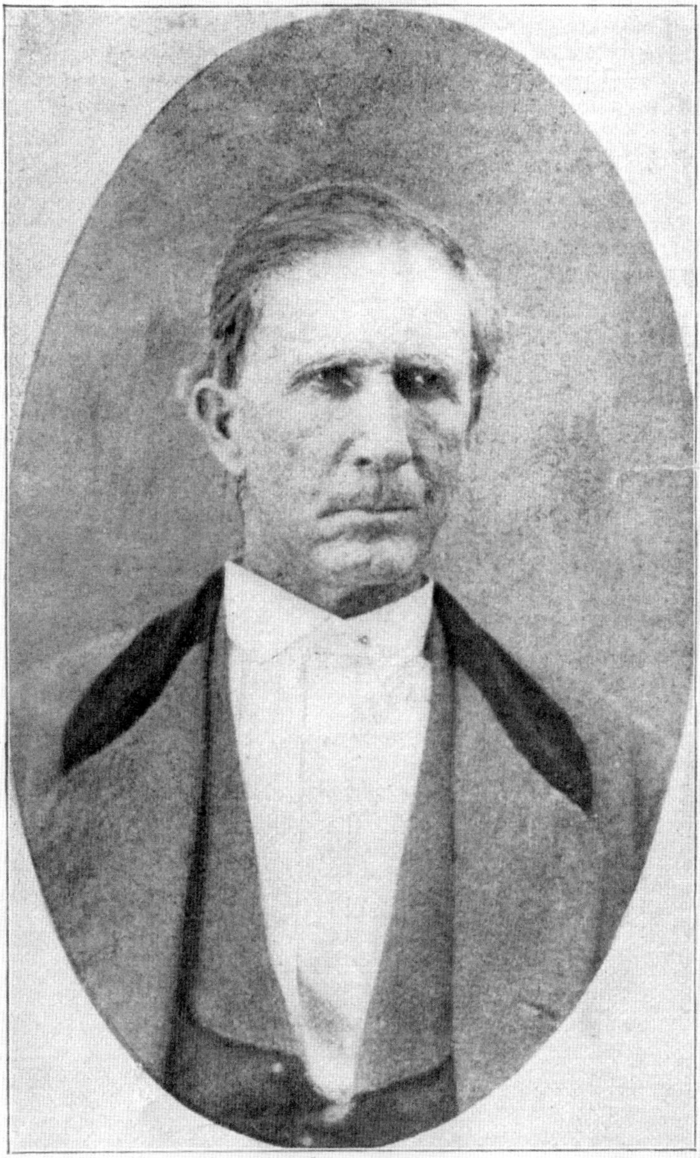

NOAH SMITHWICK—AGED 66.

Noah Smithwick arrived in Texas at the age of 19. He lived several places, including San Felipe and Burnhams Station, before he made his home near Hamilton Valley. He served during the Texas revolution with a detachment assisting in the "Runaway Scrape." After the war, he joined the Texas Rangers and served until 1839. During the time Fort Croghan was active, Smithwick was employed as the armorer there. After that, he bought and operated a gristmill on Hamilton Creek. He was not only a blacksmith, miller, and farmer but also played fiddle for dances. The community of Smithwick grew up around the site of his second gristmill. Smithwick moved to California rather than join the Confederates because both of his grandfathers fought for U.S. independence. His memoirs were published in a book titled *Evolution of a State*. (Photograph courtesy of the Center for American History, the University of Texas at Austin.)

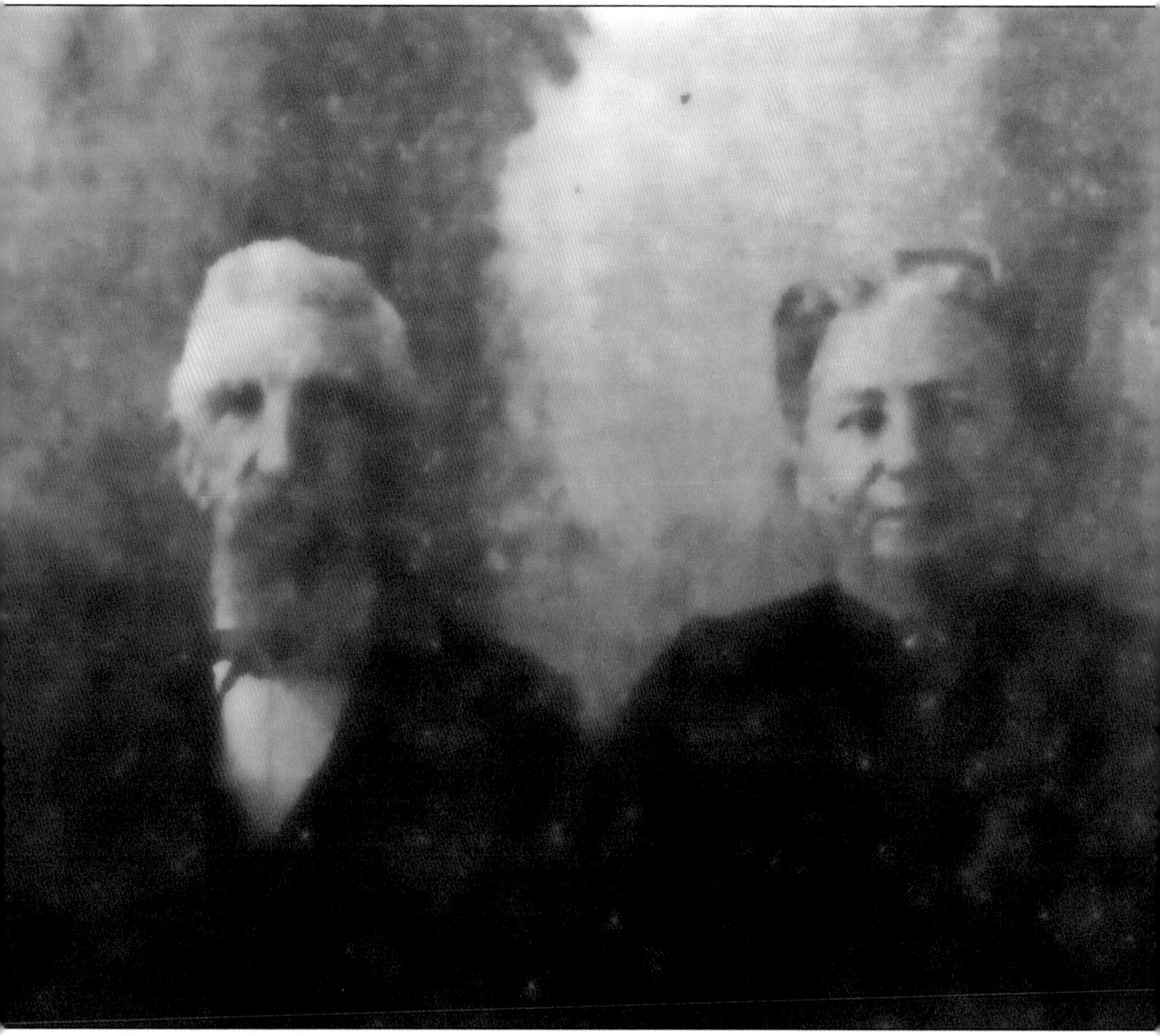

Christian Dorbandt came to America at the age of 16 in 1834. He served with Company K of the 2nd Dragoons and received a Certificate of Merit for his heroism at the Battle of Cerro Gorda during the Mexican War. He was then sent to Fort Croghan, where he served as quartermaster sergeant until the fort was decommissioned in 1853. He settled in the community of South Gabriel and with his wife, Annie, raised a family of 14 children. Dorbandt served as a Texas Ranger with the rank of captain and also served as a captain with the Confederate forces during the Civil War. After the war, he again joined the Texas Rangers, where he served through Reconstruction. Dorbandt's son, also named Christian, was elected sheriff of Burnet County in 1890. (Photograph courtesy of HBFL.)

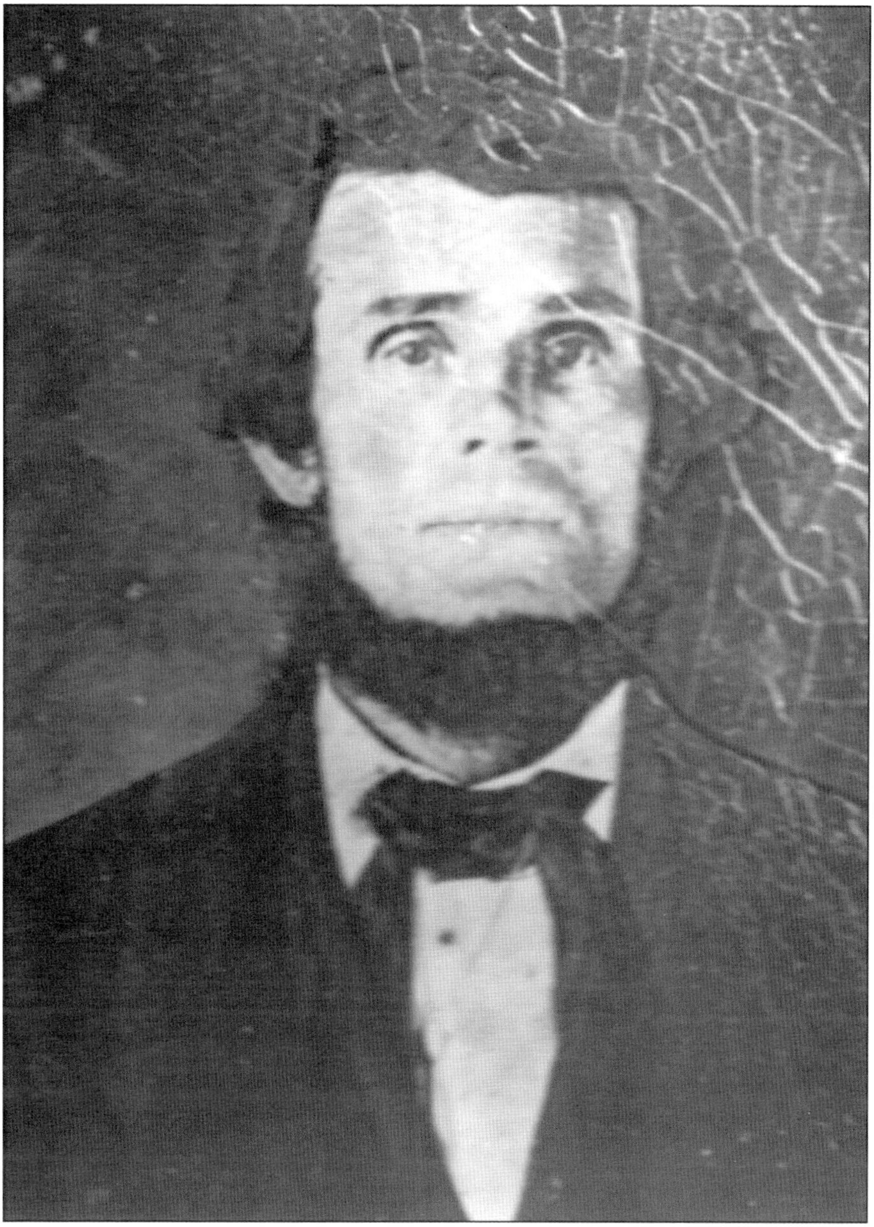

Logan Vandeveer came to Texas when he was 18 years old and settled in Austin's colony at Mina. During the War for Independence, he was wounded at the Battle of San Jacinto. His mule was conscripted and lost at the Battle of the Alamo. For his service, Vandeveer received a land grant that was located at Waterloo, now Austin. He raised cattle there. When the Republic of Texas moved its capital to Waterloo, his land was taken for "public purpose." He joined the Texas Rangers and served until Fort Croghan was established. He then left the Rangers and petitioned the state for a reinstatement of his republic land grant. He received land near Fort Croghan, where he secured a contract to provide beef and commodities to the fort, making him Burnet's first merchant. He was also the first postmaster, built the first commercial rock building and the first schoolhouse, and was one of three men appointed by the state legislature to organize the county of Burnet. Vandeveer died of yellow fever at age 40 while on a cattle drive to New Orleans.

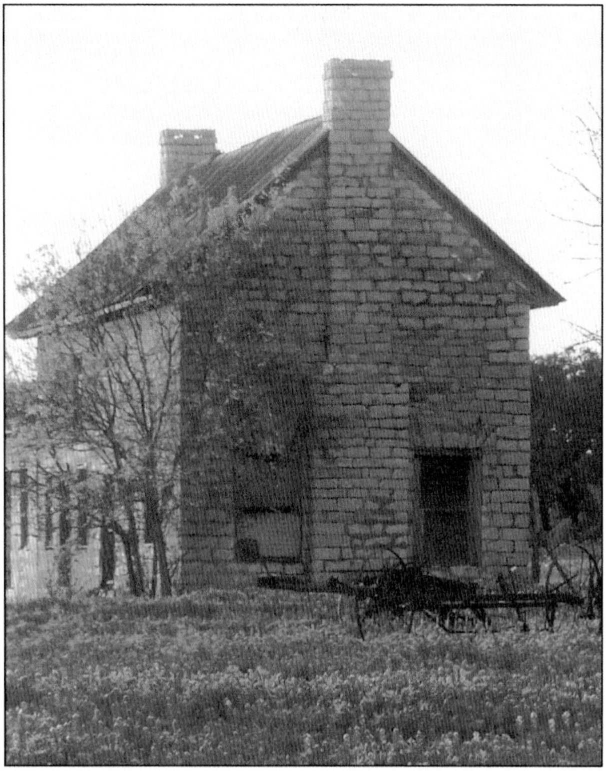

The ruin in the photograph at left once was the home of Logan Vandeveer's daughter, Eliza Hubbard. Her son, Peter Logan Hubbard, is buried there. The house was built by Christian Dorbandt in early 1853. Dorbandt was a dragoon stationed at Fort Croghan but decided to retire and make this area his home. He later sold this land and house and built another one in the South Gabriel community. There he raised his family and lived until his death at age 91. The rock cabin pictured below was Logan Vandeveer's business office. It was located on Hamilton Creek across from the fort, where the Dairy Queen is now. It became the home of his daughter after Vandeveer constructed his store building. Later it was purchased by Dr. Hansford and used as his slave quarters.

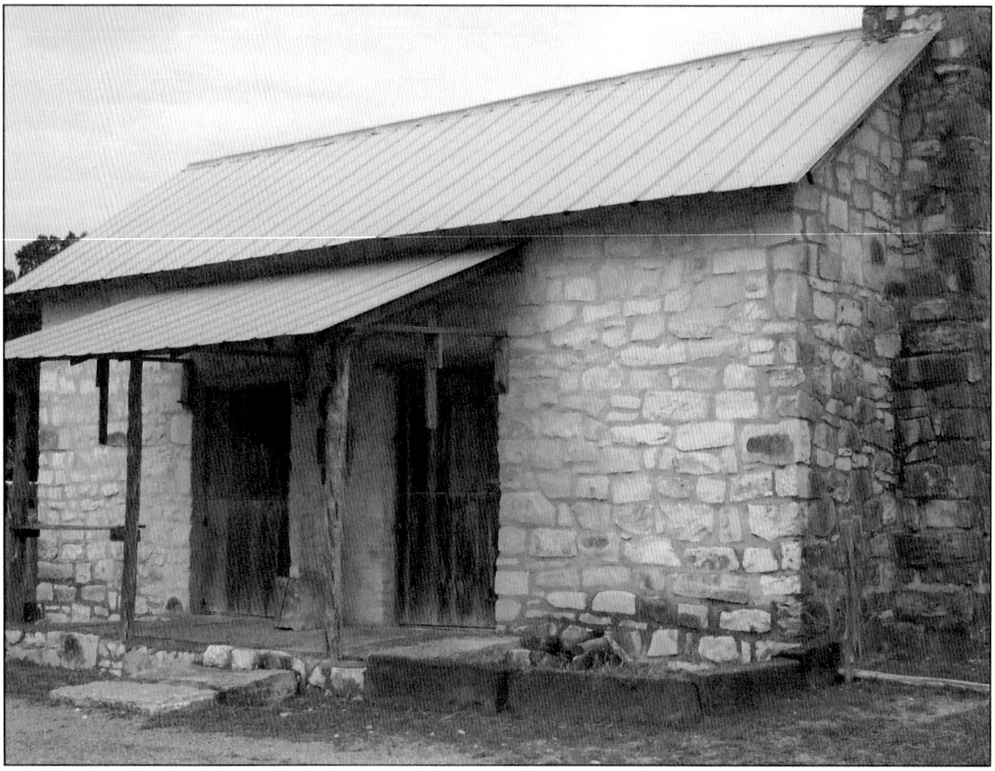

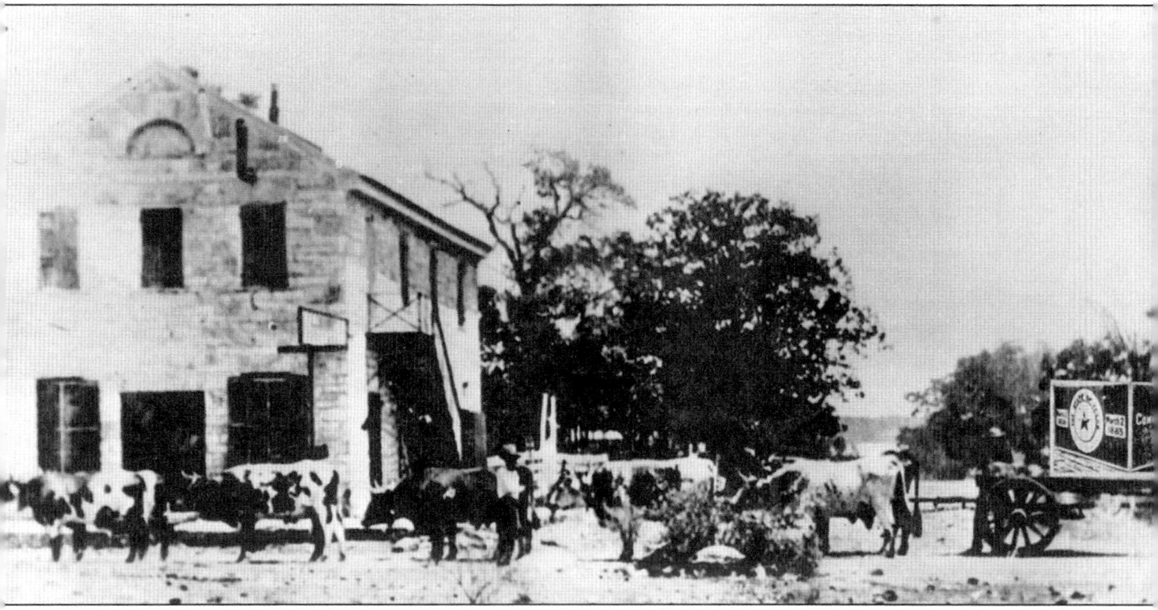

The Texas State Capitol building is constructed of pink granite quarried in Burnet County at Marble Falls. Stone was brought by ox-drawn wagons to a cutting yard in Burnet, where it was cut to order. It was then shipped by rail to Austin. This photograph shows one of those wagons. The wagon is on Main Street in front of Logan Vandeveer's mercantile building. Constructed in 1854, the structure was the first commercial rock building in Burnet. Vandeveer and his partner, a man named Taylor, located their mercantile store on the ground floor. The Masonic Valley Lodge U.D. leased the upper floor. Upon Vandeveer's death in 1855, the Masons purchased the building from his estate and have continuously occupied it since 1854. Well known and respected throughout Texas, Vandeveer is considered a founding father of Burnet.

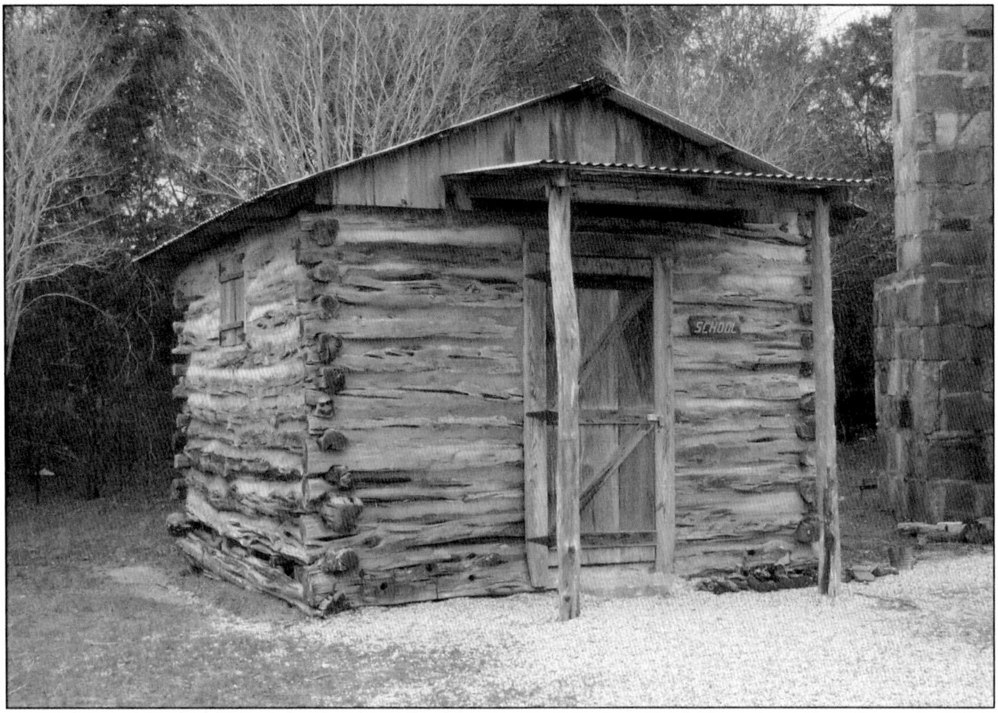

This log building, restored at the fort, depicts an 1800s school. Logan Vandeveer built the first school in Burnet and hired Prof. W. H. Dixon, a Cambridge graduate, to teach there. His log school building was located south of the town. A report card from the school reveals that there were 21 students being taught not only reading, math, and science but Latin, French, philosophy, geography, and public speaking.

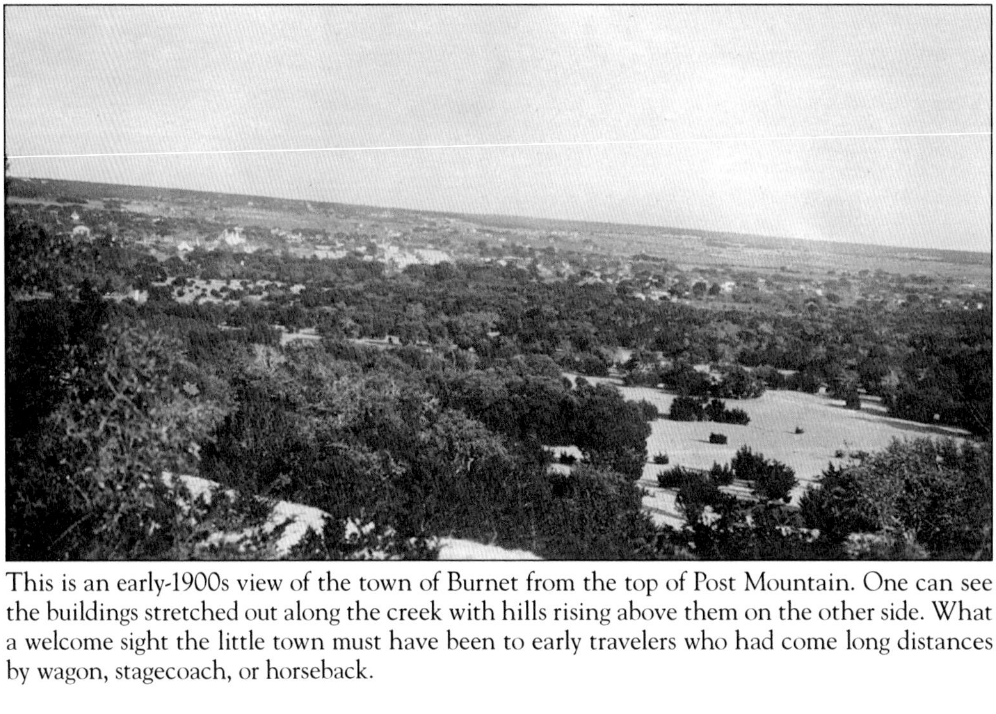

This is an early-1900s view of the town of Burnet from the top of Post Mountain. One can see the buildings stretched out along the creek with hills rising above them on the other side. What a welcome sight the little town must have been to early travelers who had come long distances by wagon, stagecoach, or horseback.

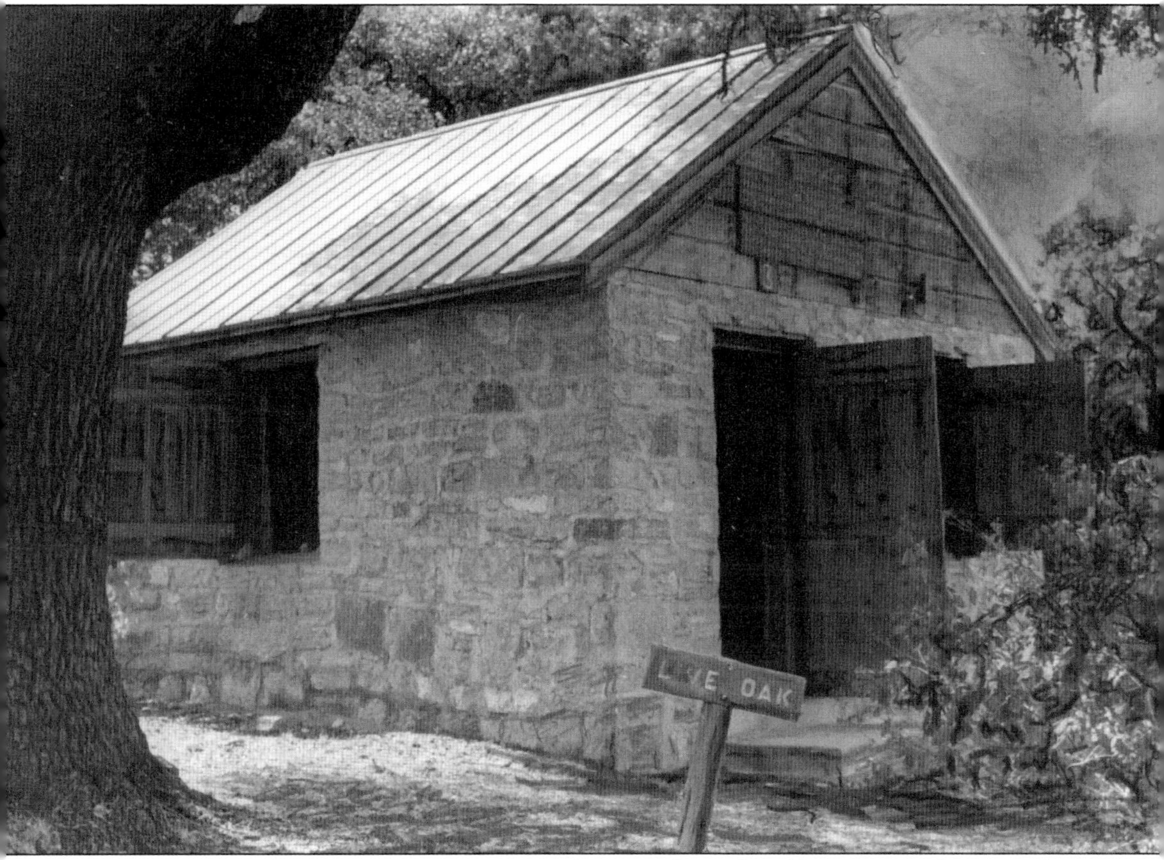

This building was the stagecoach stop at Hamilton Creek on the old Austin to Llano Road. It has been moved to Fort Croghan and restored by the Burnet County Heritage Society. The stagecoach may have afforded a better ride than a wagon, but not much. Some stages had cushioned seats and velvet curtains while others barely offered protection from the rain or sun. All were fair game for Native Americans and outlaws despite having an armed guard. At the way station, travelers could enjoy a hot meal and a cool drink while tired horses were exchanged for fresh ones and repairs were made to the coach or tack. Posted rules for passengers were: "Don't take target practice from the windows, Don't point out places where people have been killed, Don't grease your hair because the ride will be dusty, only spit downwind, and at the driver's request, get out and walk." (Author's collection.)

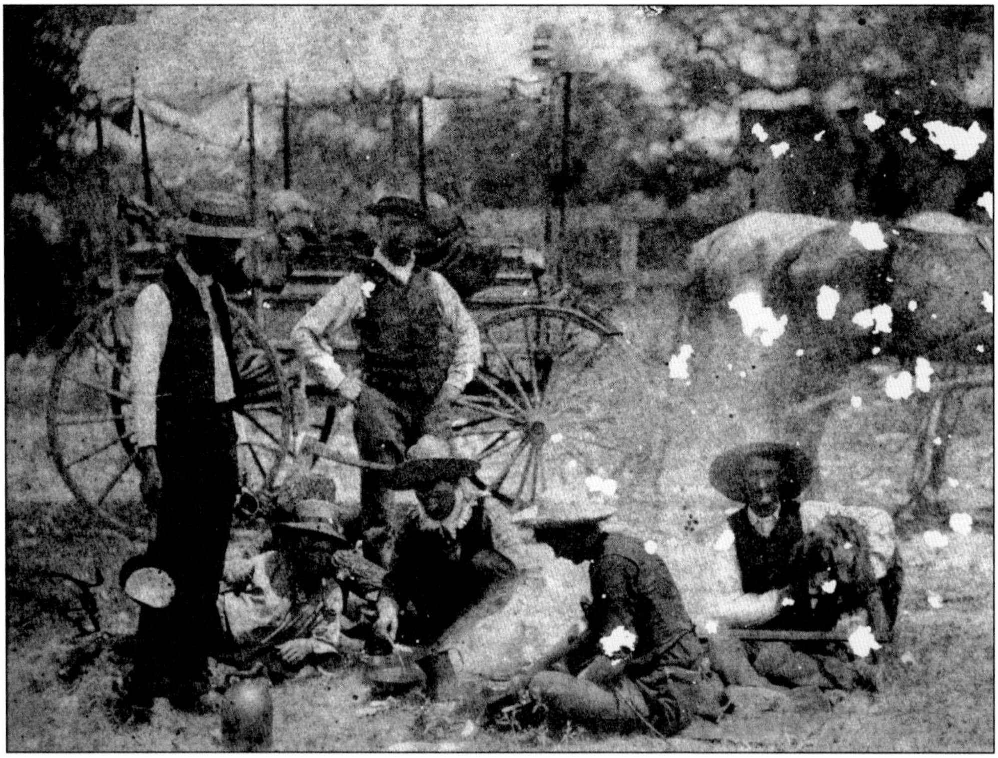

The wagon was the most often used means of local transportation in the 1880s. The more affluent might have buggies as well. This resulted in the opening of "wagon yards." These provided a place to leave the wagon and have the horses attended to while people took care of business. Sometimes cowboys or travelers camped there overnight. This group of unidentified fellows is making themselves a meal at the Burnet "wagon yard." The house below was located on South Main Street and was the home of blacksmith Robert Alexander, the son of Samuel Alexander, who came to Texas in 1848. Robert and his wife, Lucinda, had four children. Pictured are son Frank and, from left to right, daughters Belle, Thurzy, and Annie. Daughter Thurzy was named after Robert's mother, Thurzy Ross. She was a cousin of Texas governor Sul Ross.

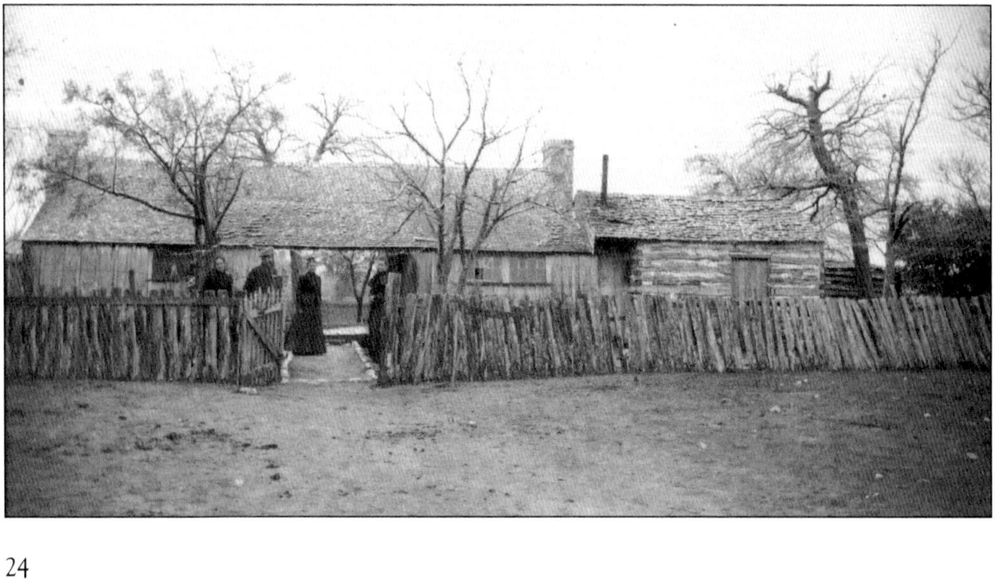

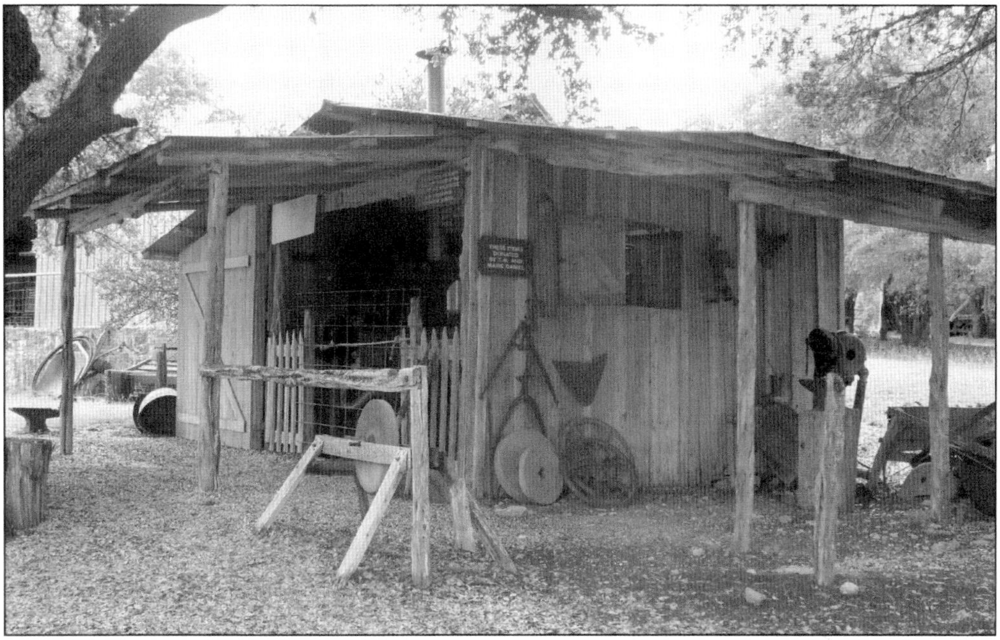

This complete blacksmith shop once belonged to Sam Holland and has been moved to the fort grounds for preservation. The blacksmith was an important person on the frontier. He could make or fix anything, knew where to get a meal or a bath and a bed for the night, and knew where everyone lived. Many blacksmiths also pulled teeth. The cabin below was erected about 1850 by H. C. Allen of hand-hewn logs. Lewis Kincheloe bought it in 1866, and he and his wife, Margaret Bowmer Kincheloe, reared 11 children in it. Originally built near Jennings Creek on the South Gabriel River, it has been moved to Fort Croghan grounds and restored. The rustic furniture inside is handmade from the time period. (Photographs courtesy of Crista Bromley.)

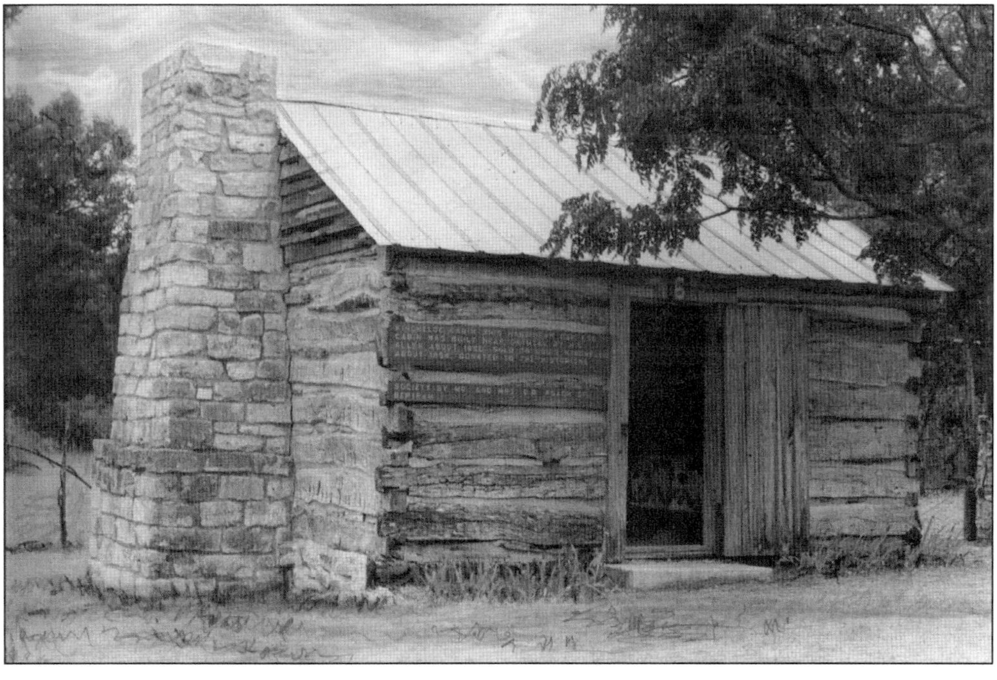

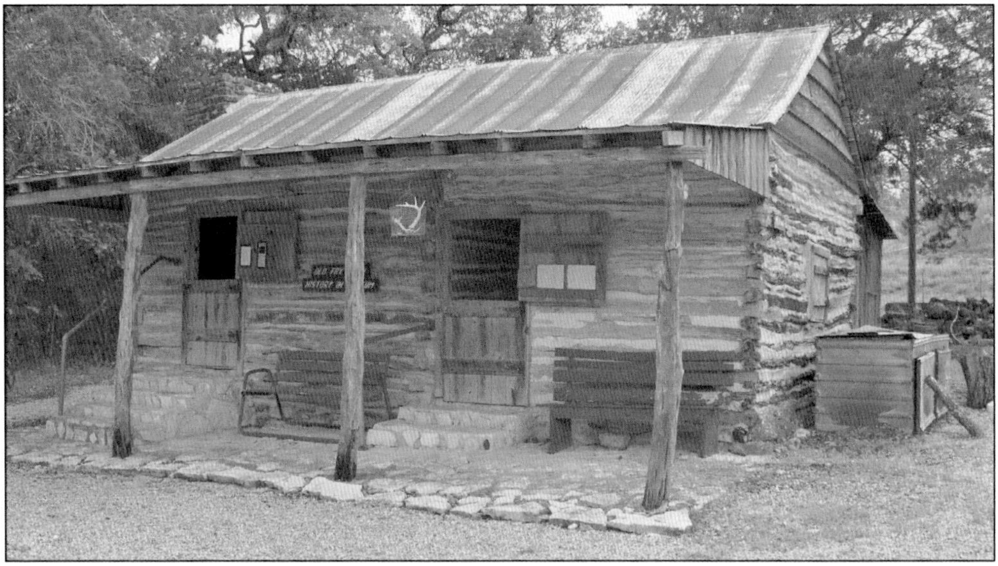

John Waller Fry and his wife, Mary Cariysie Fry, arrived at Fort Croghan on Christmas Day in 1855. They came from Illinois looking for land, which they found on Council Creek. They built this cabin on the land and raised 10 children. One of their sons, Aaron, inherited the cabin and raised his 11 children in it. Aaron's son, Roy Fry, grew up to become the first chairman of the Lower Colorado River Authority. The cabin has been restored at Fort Croghan. The photograph below is of John Waller Fry and several of his grandchildren. Many of the Fry descendants still live in Burnet and the surrounding area.

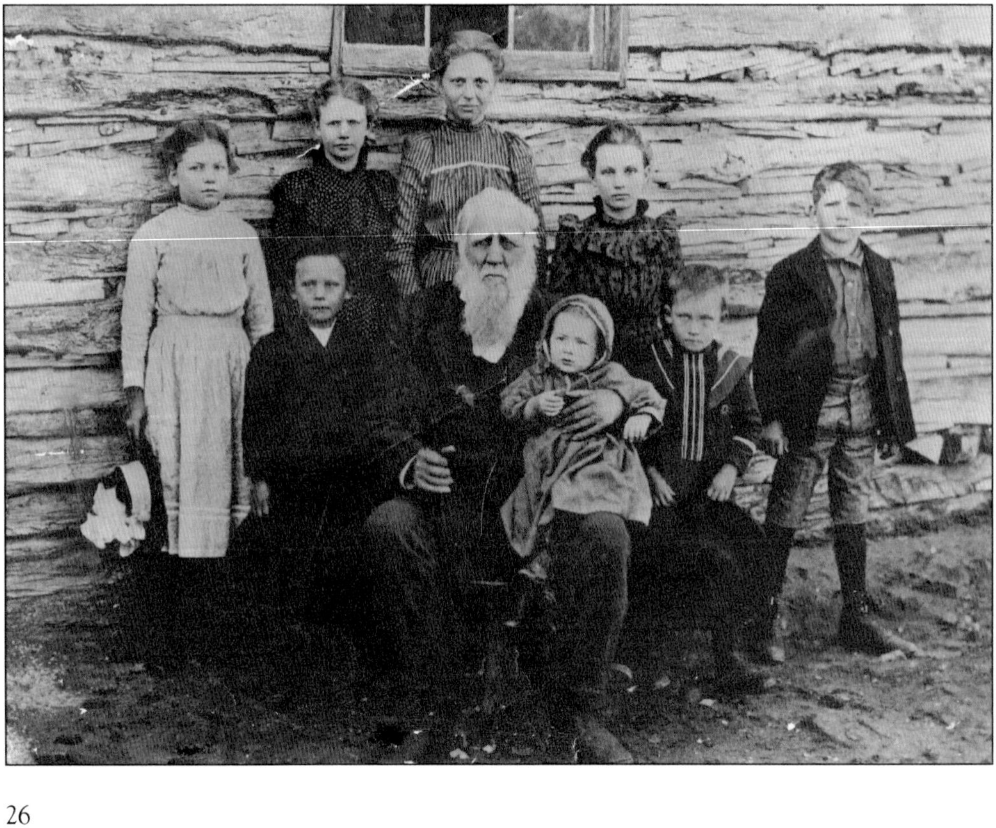

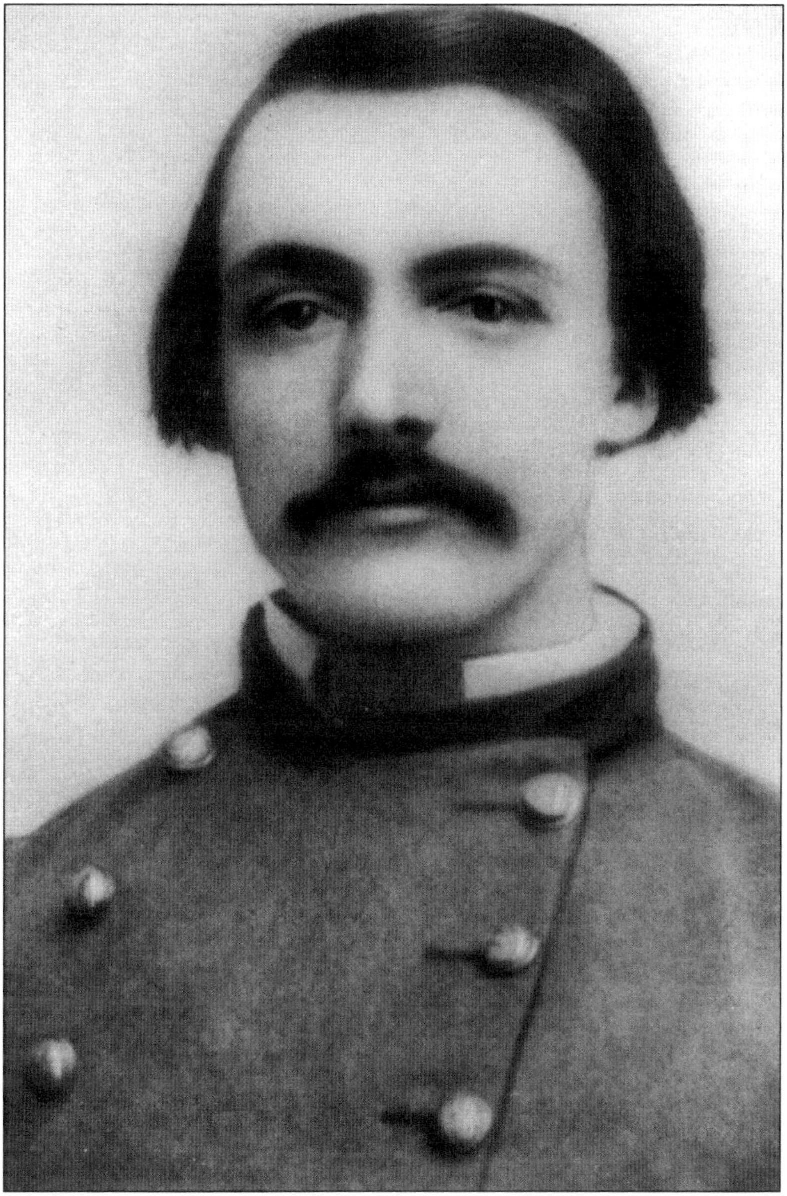

Adam R. Johnson arrived in Texas from Kentucky when he was 20 years old. Hired by a land surveying crew, he learned the country well. An opportunist, he purchased land and became a land merchant as well. He settled in Burnet in 1854 and quickly became a prominent citizen. When the Civil War loomed, he went back to Kentucky and raised a company of men for the Confederate fight. He and his rifle-armed men captured the federal arsenal at Vicksburg, Indiana. Captain Johnson took his supply wagons apart and leaned stove pipes across them. Thinking they were surrounded by cannon, the Union commander surrendered without a shot. This earned Johnson fame and the nickname "Stovepipe Johnson." His subsequent successes earned him the rank of brigadier general. He came back to Texas, blinded by wounds. Although blind, he continued as a land merchant and founded the town of Marble Falls. Later serving as the city manager of Austin, he was active in state and county activities until his death in 1922. He is buried in the Texas State Cemetery at Austin.

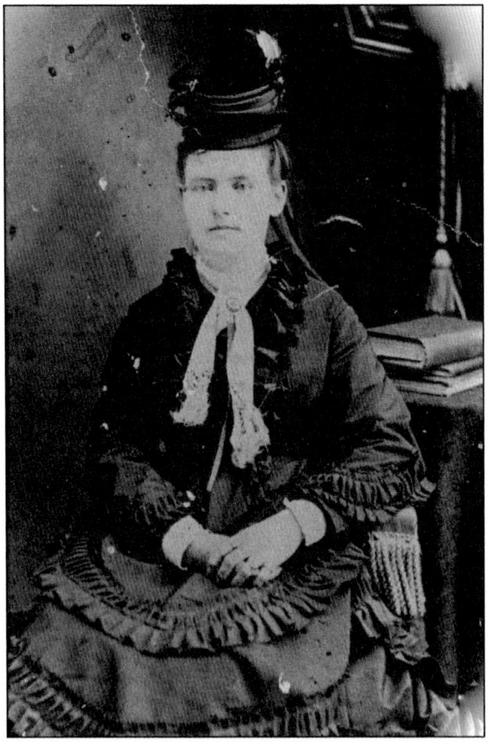

Maria Josephine Eastland Johnson was born in Tennessee. Her family came to Texas when Maria was a baby but soon returned to Tennessee. Maria married Adam R. Johnson in 1861 at Burnet. The Johnsons were the parents of nine children, three of them dying as youngsters. Maria died in 1923 and was buried at the Texas State Cemetery near her husband.

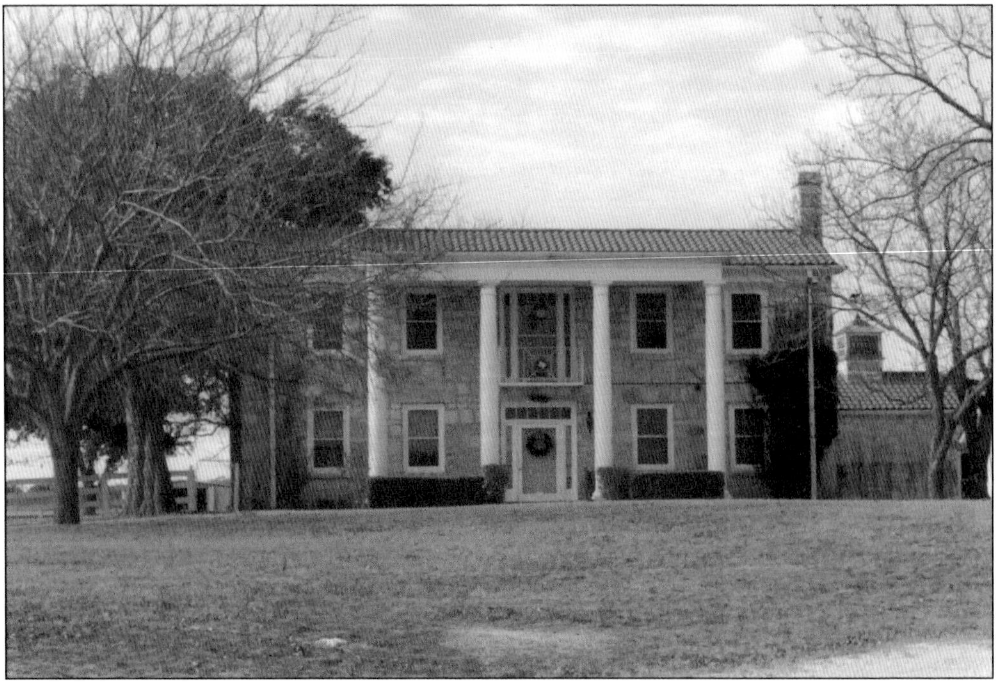

Gen. Adam R. Johnson built Rocky Rest as his first home in Burnet. The house is located beside Hamilton Creek on South Water Street in the heart of the city. The front portico with its tall columns was added later. After the Johnsons built and moved to a second home, Rocky Rest was used briefly as a school and later as the home and medical office of Dr. Joe Shepperd.

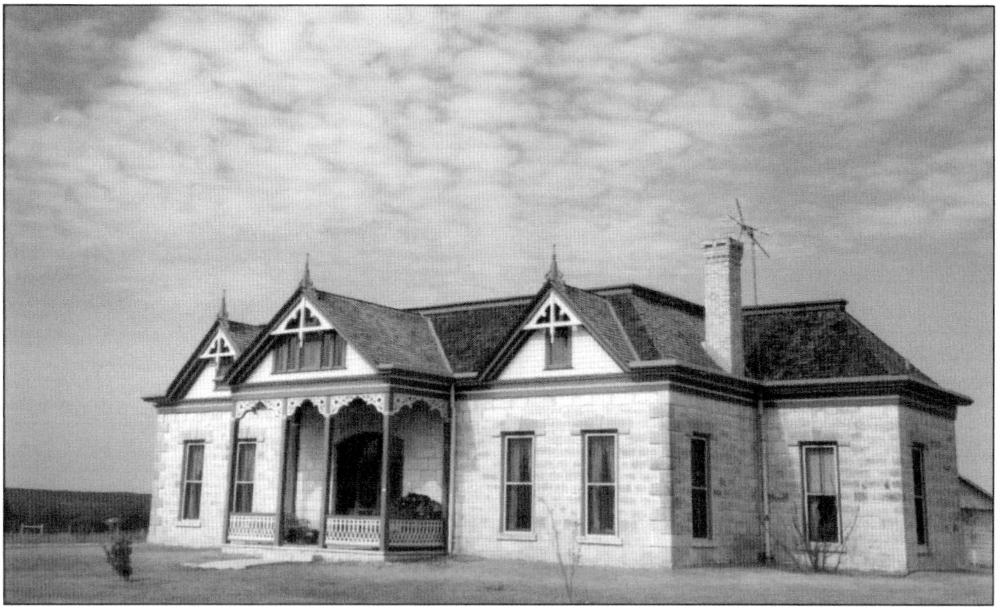

General Johnson was convinced that living near the creek caused his children's frequent illnesses, so in 1884 he built his second house high on a hill overlooking the town. He called this home Airy Mount. This home was built of rock quarried west of the house. The lumber was shipped from Bastrop by oxcart. The construction included a stone barn and cistern. After the death of the Johnsons, the house sat vacant for years until Charles Hayman bought and restored it. Hayman and his wife, Roseann, outfitted the barn as a bed-and-breakfast, which remains a popular haven for visitors. The photograph below is of the Johnson family posing in front of Airy Mount. The man on the upper far left was an employee.

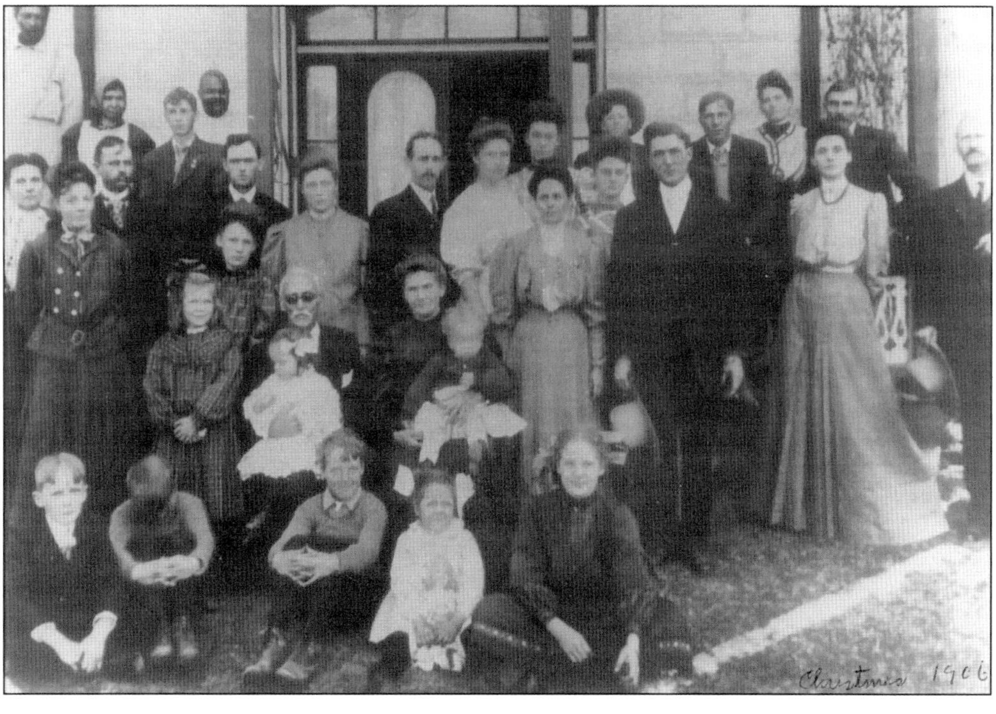

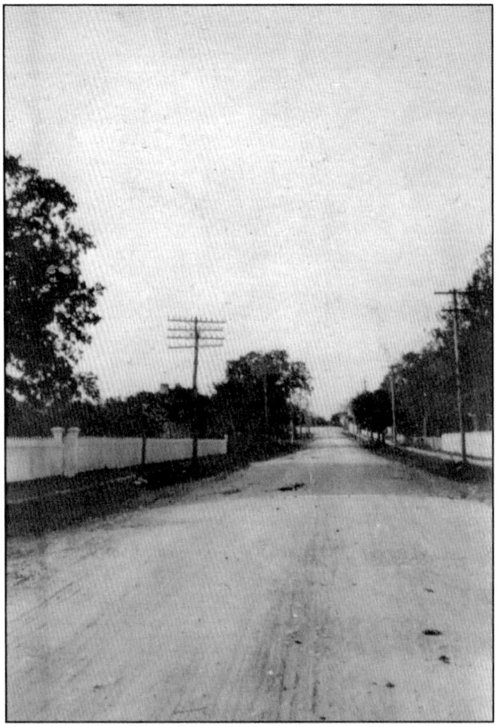

This view of Main Street illustrates the condition of streets in Burnet at the dawn of the 20th century. Of course, these streets had much better surfaces than the rural roads, where horse-drawn conveyances cut ruts that can still be seen in pastures. The game of marbles was not only popular but was serious business at schoolyards in 1909, when this photograph was taken. Note that none of the boys have shoes even though they all have caps and some have coats. The adult standing on the left looks somewhat rumpled. It is unclear whether he is a teacher or a student since anyone wanting to learn could come to school. Considering that children were dressed in their best to go to school, this photograph reflects the economy of the time. (Left, photograph courtesy of Milli Williams; below, photograph courtesy of BCHS.)

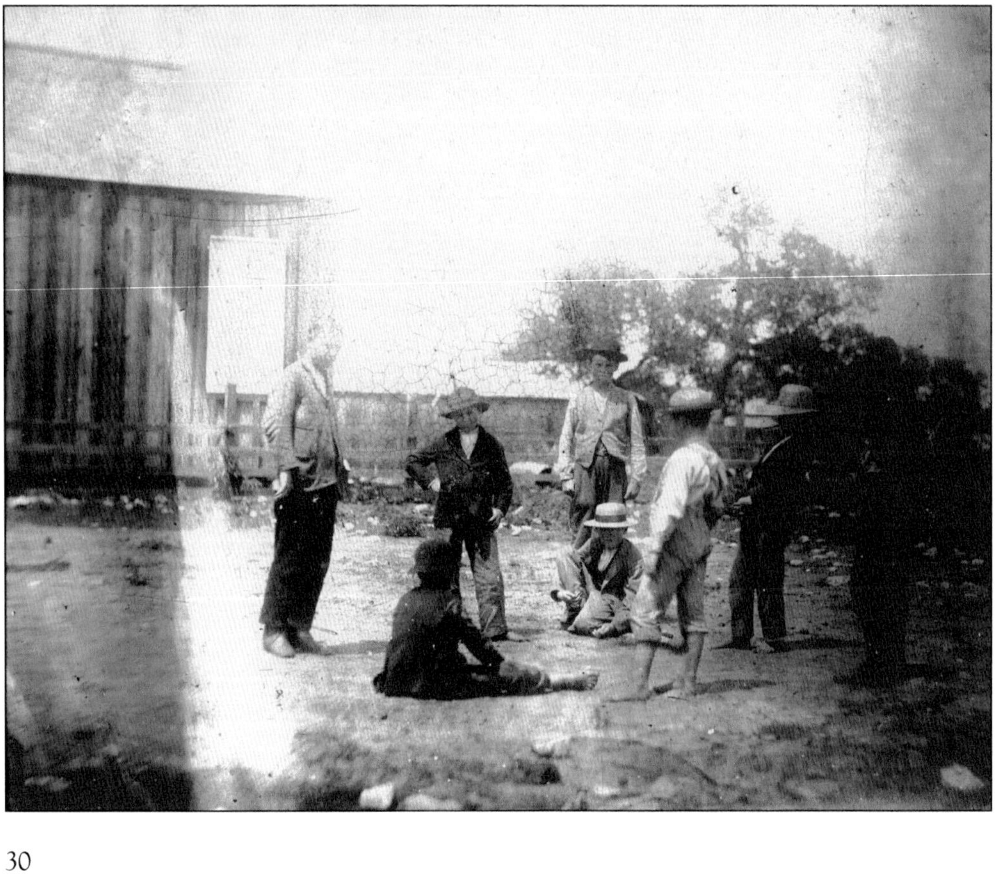

Two

Building a Town

By 1880, the settlement of Burnet had become a small town. Most of the first settlers were merchants or tradesmen expecting to do business with the fort and future settlers. People looking to buy land or those who had secured land grants from the Texas Legislature arrived steadily. Some of them lived in the buildings at the abandoned fort while they found their land and constructed homes. As the population grew, so did the influx of supporting businesses and professional people. Hotels, saloons, doctors, lawyers, preachers, stone masons, merchants, tailors, and barbers, good men and rascals, all arrived to build a future in Hamilton. Lyman Wight, one of the original leaders of the Mormon religion, came to Texas in 1845 with about 150 followers. These families stopped for a time in several places before settling at the waterfalls on Hamilton Creek in 1850. They purchased the land from William Magill, a Hamilton citizen. There they set up a grain mill and a furniture factory, powered by the falls. They were well received by the people of Hamilton, who were happy to use their services and products. Their enclave became known as Mormon Mills.

In 1851, the citizens of Hamilton petitioned the state legislature to create a new county and make Hamilton the county seat. There were 80 petitioners, many of whom were Mormons from Mormon Mills. The legislature then appointed Logan Vandeveer, R. H. Hall, and William Magill to organize the county and hold the first elections. The new county was named Burnet after David G. Burnet, the first provisional president of the Republic of Texas. A legend is that Vandeveer knew and admired Burnet. The county was officially created in 1854 with the county seat at Hamilton. In 1858, the town of Hamilton was changed to Burnet as well. The coming of the railroad was easily the most significant advance for the future of the town. The lives of the citizens of Burnet were broadened and enriched because of it.

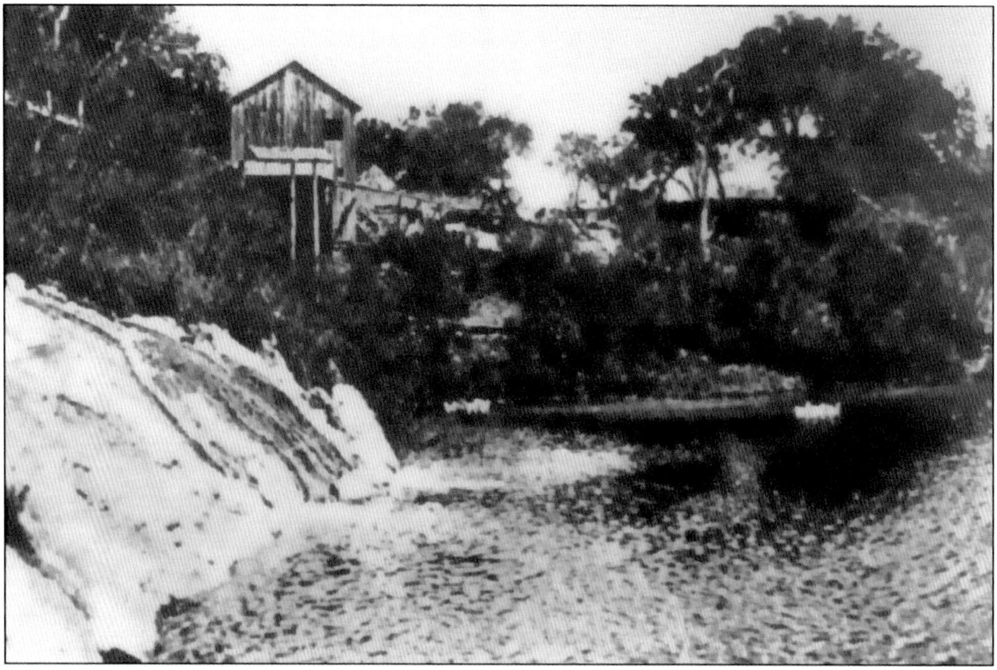

Built by Lyman Wight, later owned by Noah Smithwick and then Samuel Holland, this mill provided for the needs of Hamilton Valley residents and made an adequate living for its owners. The site was a beautiful place with a waterfall cascading into a pond covering some 3 acres at a maximum depth of 60 feet. The mill was operated until 1901, when the owner, Price Kinser, had it demolished and used the lumber to build a barn. The Kinsers allowed public swimming and picnicking, which made the site a favorite spot with Burnet society. The cemetery, shown below, is all that remains of the old Mormon settlement. There is a Texas Historical Marker at the mill site. (Above, courtesy of BCHS; below, photograph courtesy of HBFL.)

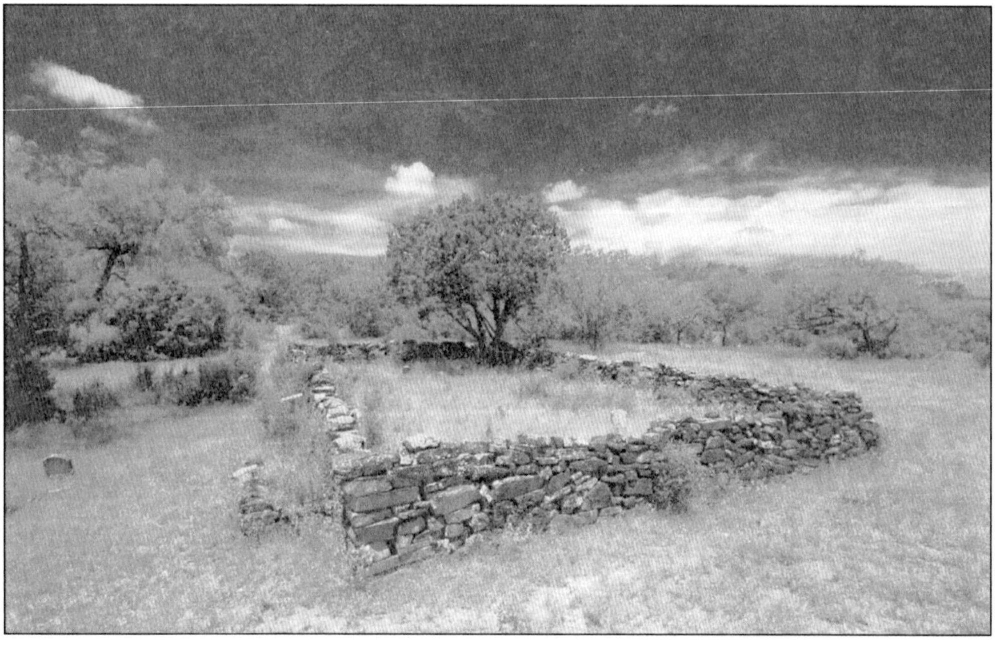

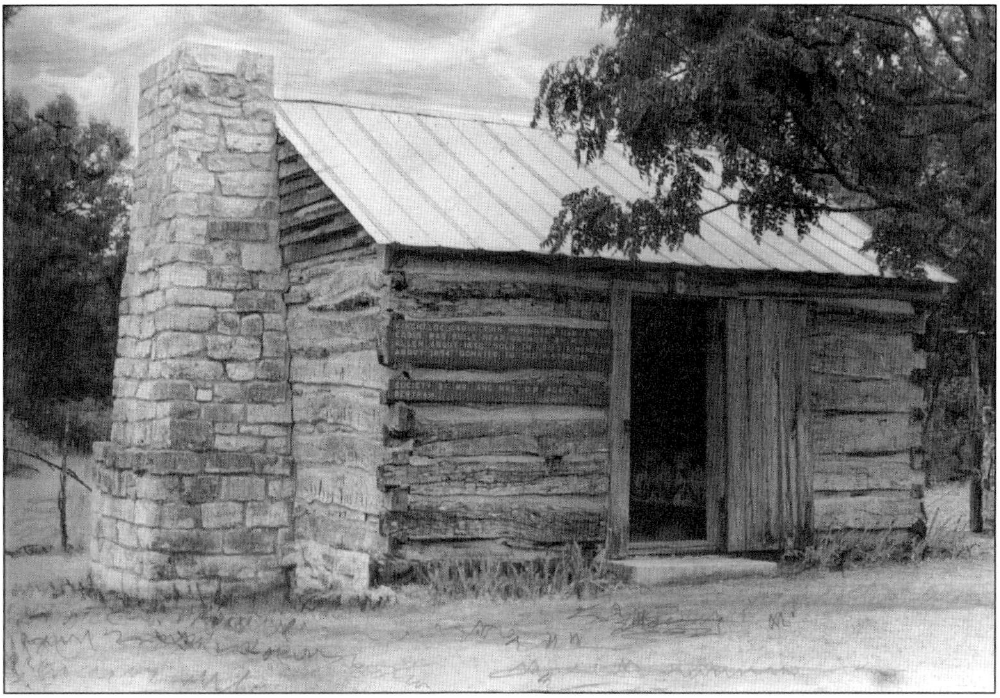

This log cabin is typical of cabins erected in the area of Fort Croghan. This one was built of hand-hewn logs about 1850 by C. H. Allen. Lewis C. Kincheloe bought it in 1866. Arriving on horseback with their firstborn infant, the Kincheloes reared 11 children in this cabin. The Kincheloe descendants became active citizens of Burnet and still remain so. The restored cabin is at Fort Croghan.

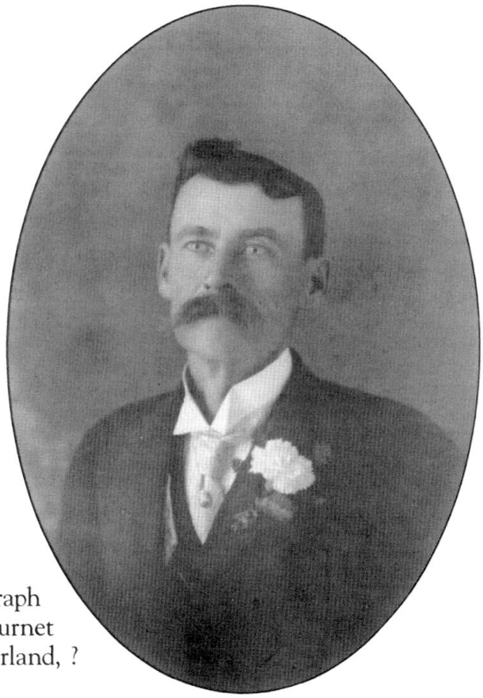

The information given on the back of this photograph says this is Mr. Root and that he was an early Burnet merchant. Some others were Jack Haynie, ? Bourland, ? McKee, and John Ross Alexander.

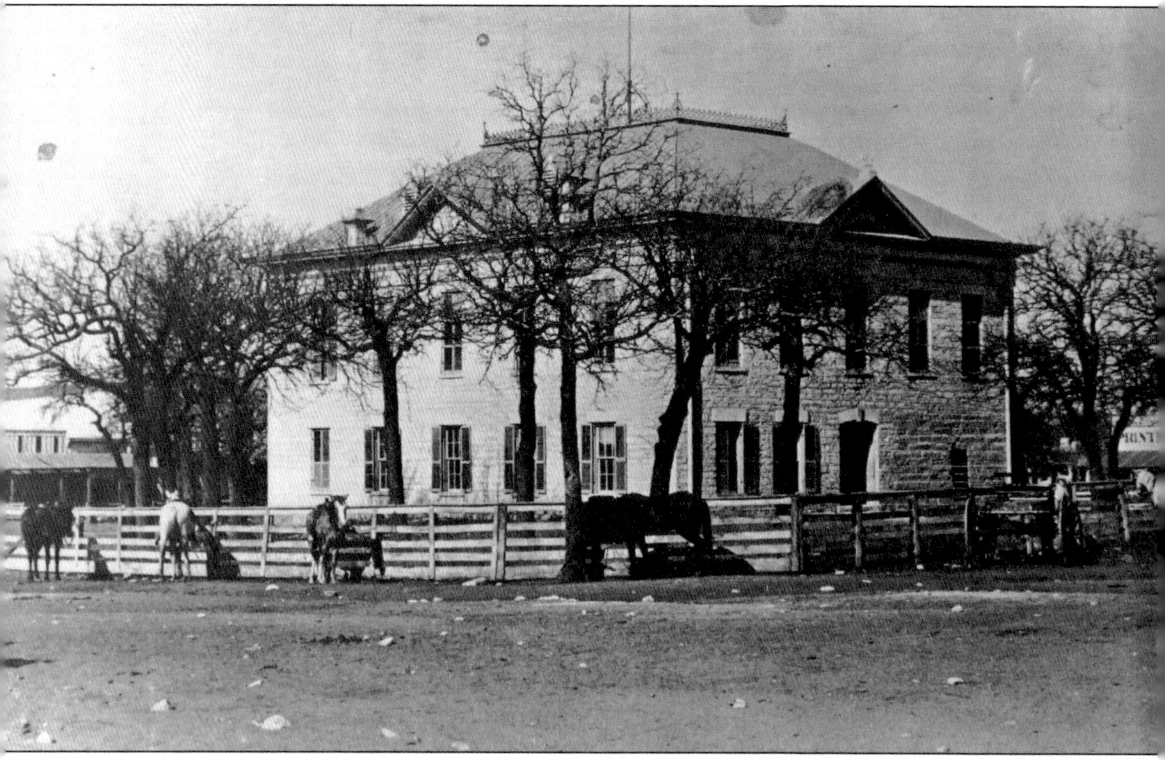

Burnet's second courthouse, pictured here, became the site of a chilling mystery. On March 31, 1889, the bloody body of Burnet mayor U. E. Morgan was found in the attic, an apparent suicide. His straight razor was tightly clutched in his right hand. His hat, coat, and shoes were carefully placed nearby; the hat held his watch and $3 in silver. There was no note. Justice of the Peace P. M. Rogers estimated his death had occurred three days earlier. Morgan had previously mentioned a trip to Lampasas, so he was not readily missed. Morgan had arrived in Burnet alone in 1886 and quickly became popular and trusted enough to be elected mayor. He never talked about his past, but his life in Burnet gave no clue that he was despondent about anything. He was buried in the Odd Fellows Cemetery in eastern Burnet.

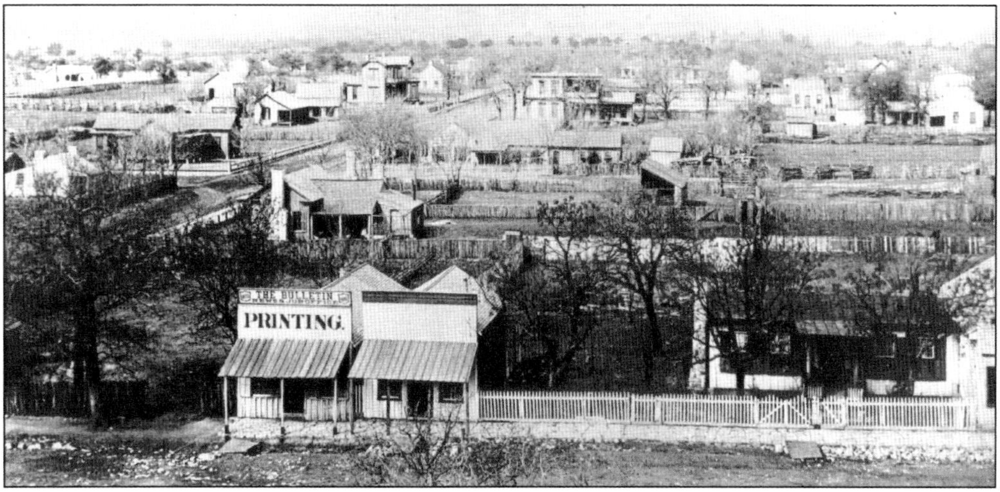

This is a view of the north side of the courthouse square about 1890. The *Burnet Bulletin* newspaper office is on the west corner. The *Burnet Bulletin* was first published in 1873 by George Whitaker and, though there were subsequent owner/publishers, remained located on the courthouse square for more than 125 years. Still being published today, it is owned by Highland Lakes Newspapers. A Burnet office is maintained off the square, but the paper is published in Marble Falls. Appearing at the east end of the sidewalk in the picture below is the Garrett Hotel, and to the left of it is the private residence of the Crawford family. The new two-story rock schoolhouse is visible at the upper left skyline, and the Burnet Presbyterian Church is just above the Crawford house. The First Baptist Church is in the upper right corner.

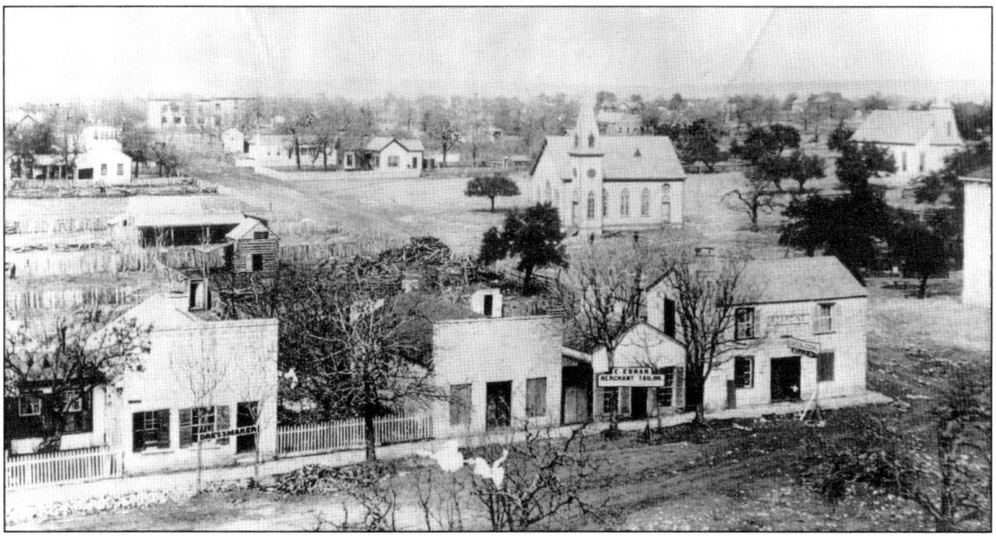

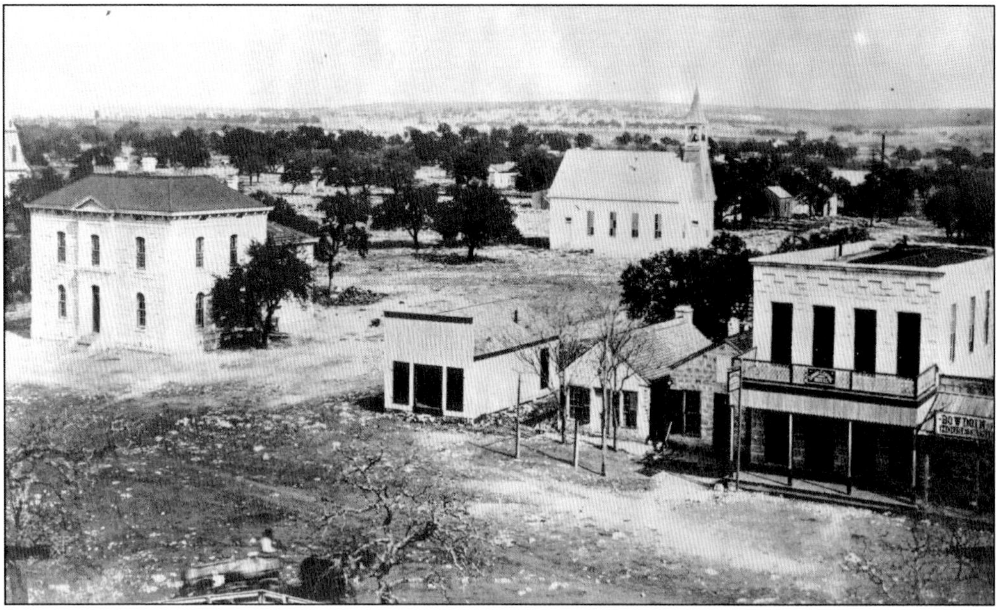

Here is a view of the northeast corner of the square with the 1884 jailhouse on the left and the Grand Central Hotel on the right with the First Baptist Church beyond them. In the photograph below is the southeast corner of the square. At the center of the picture is the Burnet Hotel. It replaced the old Boyd Hotel. Later this hotel was replaced by the David G. Burnet Hotel. The corner building on the right was the second Prince Hotel, built in 1886 by Maurice Kopperl to replace his first Prince Hotel that burned in 1884. Kopperl built the town's first hotel of logs in 1873. The building in this photograph later housed the First State Bank downstairs with, among others, the office of Gen. Adam R. Johnson upstairs.

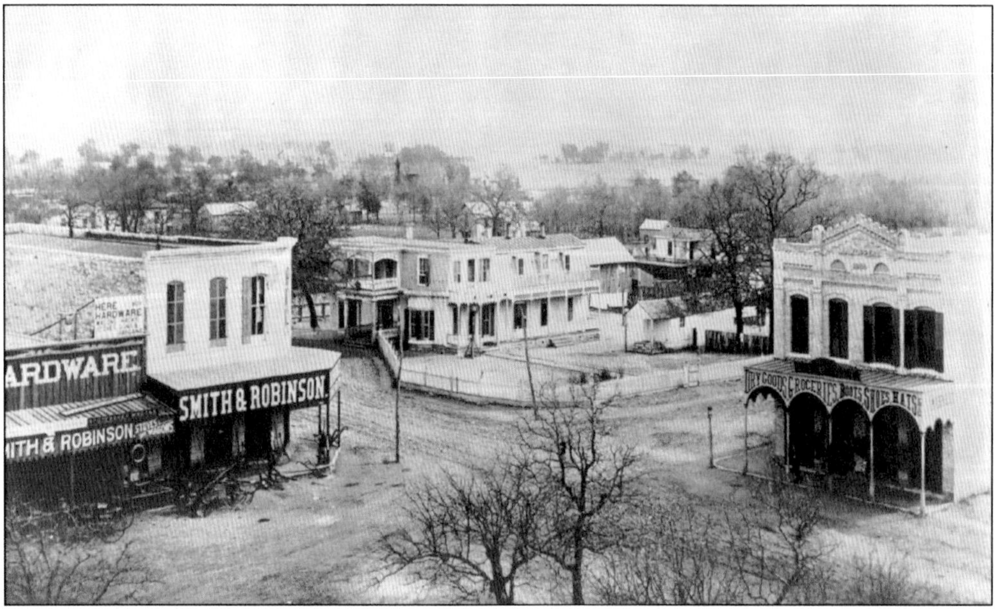

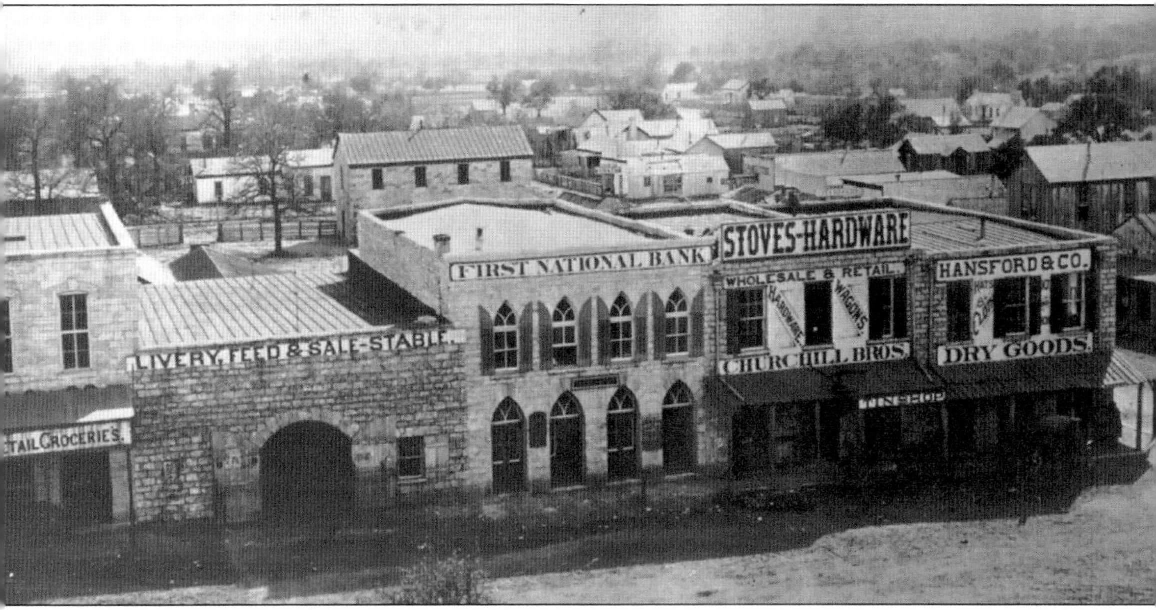

The southwest corner of the square is shown here. At left is Carroll's General Merchandise Grocery store, which later became the Galloway Saloon. The low rock building with the wide arch is the livery stable, a definite necessity in those days. The two-story building with shutter trim is the First National Bank. Just above it, Logan Vandeveer's 1854 mercantile building can be seen. On the corner is Hansford and Company Dry Goods, which later became Stapp Furniture and Funeral Supply. It was commonly rumored that J. H. Stapp took his afternoon naps in one of the coffins. This building later housed the *Burnet Bulletin* newspaper office and printing press.

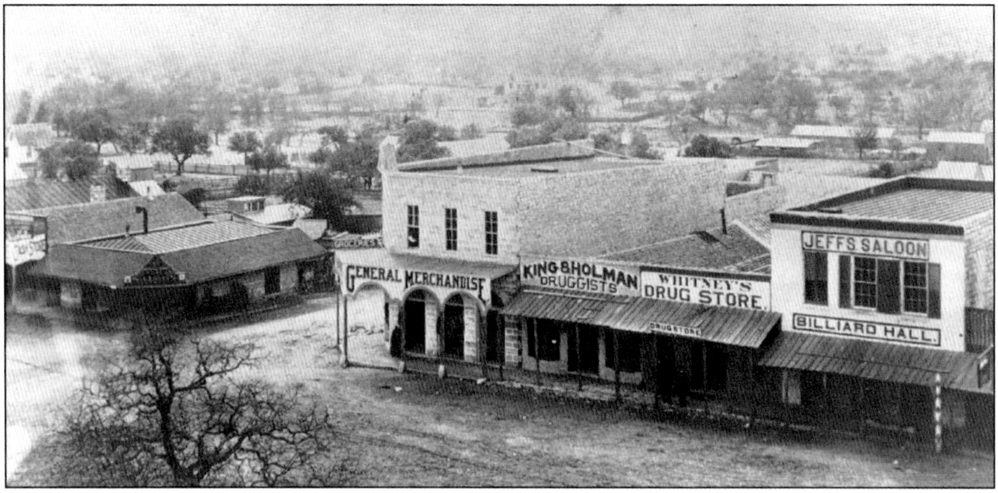

The Brownlee Saloon is at the left of this view of the southwest corner of the square. The corner two-story building was erected in 1883 by A. I. Haber to house his General Merchandise Store. The Southern Mercantile Company and Hudson and Watson were later occupants. A garment factory once occupied the back portion of the building. Heston Whitney opened the first drugstore in Burnet, with King-Holman (the second) setting up right next door. Whitney stayed in business until his death, after which it became Warner's Drugstore. On the right is Jeff's Saloon and Billiard Hall. Saloons were numerous in Burnet at the time, with no shortage of customers. The photograph below is thought to be the interior of the General Merchandise building shown in the picture above. The identity of the business and persons is not known.

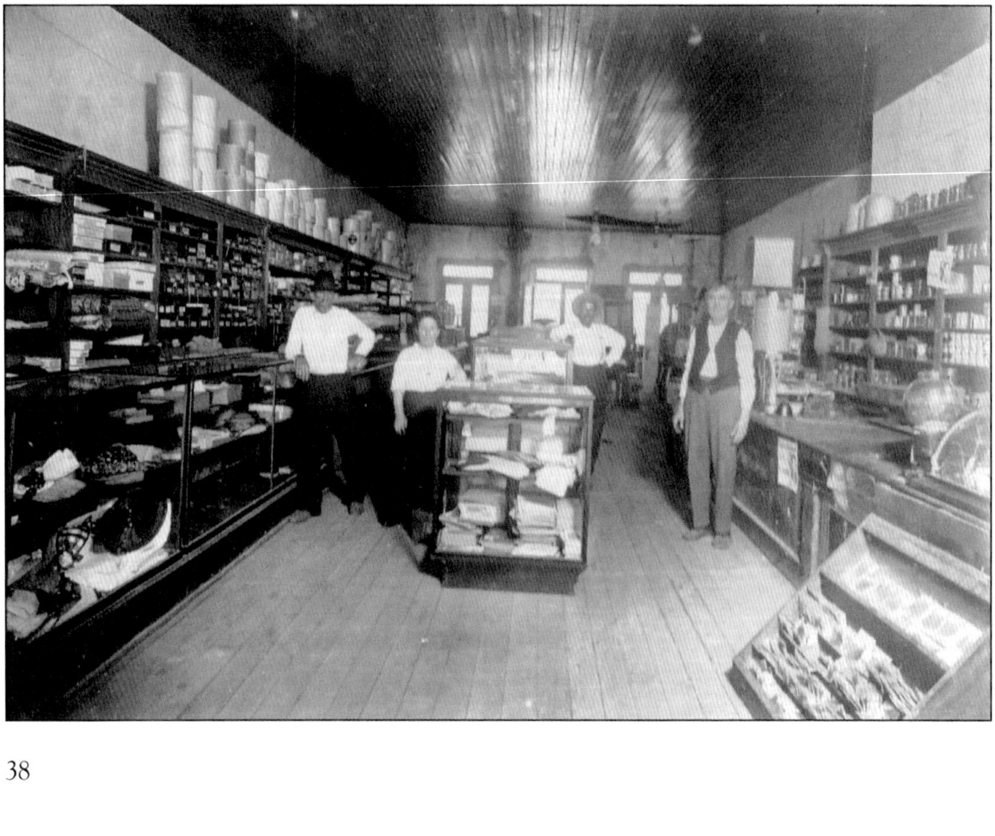

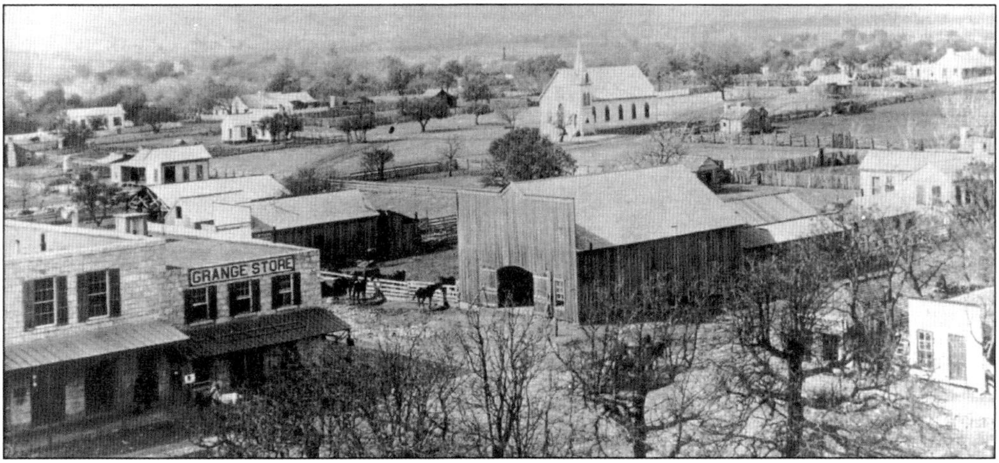

Here the Grange Store stands at the left with a livery stable on the corner. The *Burnet Bulletin* building is in the lower right corner. The old First United Methodist Church is above the livery stable. Behind the tree line at the top of the photograph, Hamilton Creek runs along out of sight.

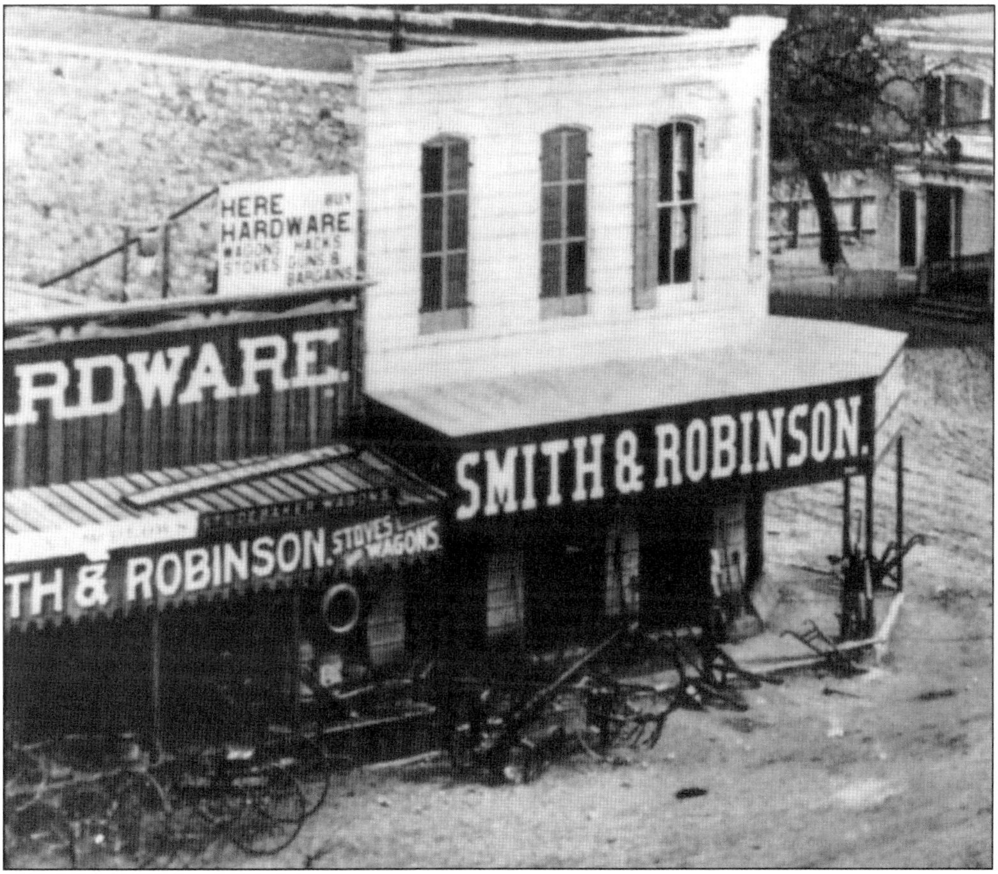

This is the Smith and Robinson building from the photograph on page 36. The Burnet Rural Telephone Company occupied the second floor. In 1901, the Martin Telephone Company was the first to operate in Burnet, followed by the John W. Smart Company. The Burnet Rural Telephone Company either bought or merged with the others to become the only one in town.

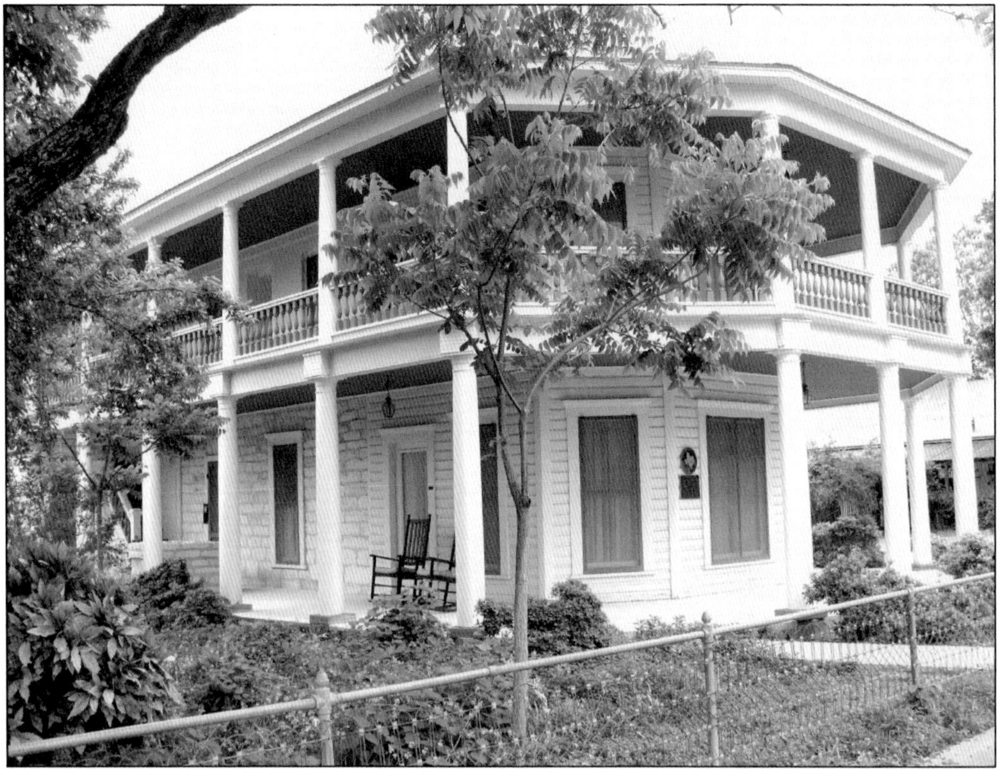

The center rock section of this house was the Calvert Hotel. It was built by H. H. Calvert in the early 1850s and served as a stagecoach stop for Burnet. Later W. C. Galloway purchased the building and added the board portions with the double porches. The family made it their home for two generations. The present owners operate a bed-and-breakfast inn there. (Photograph courtesy of Guy Goble.)

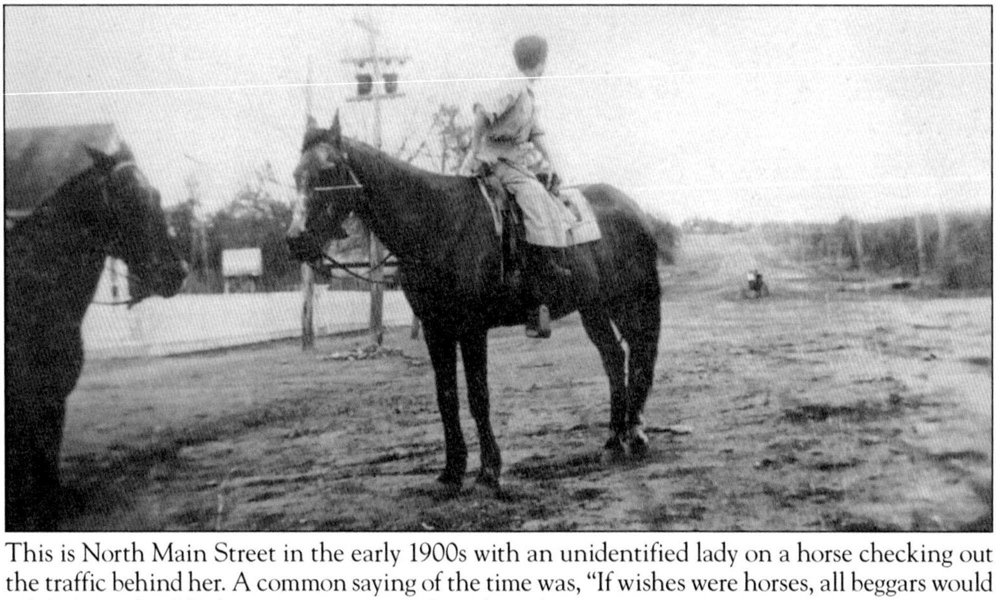

This is North Main Street in the early 1900s with an unidentified lady on a horse checking out the traffic behind her. A common saying of the time was, "If wishes were horses, all beggars would ride." A good saddle horse was a source of much pride.

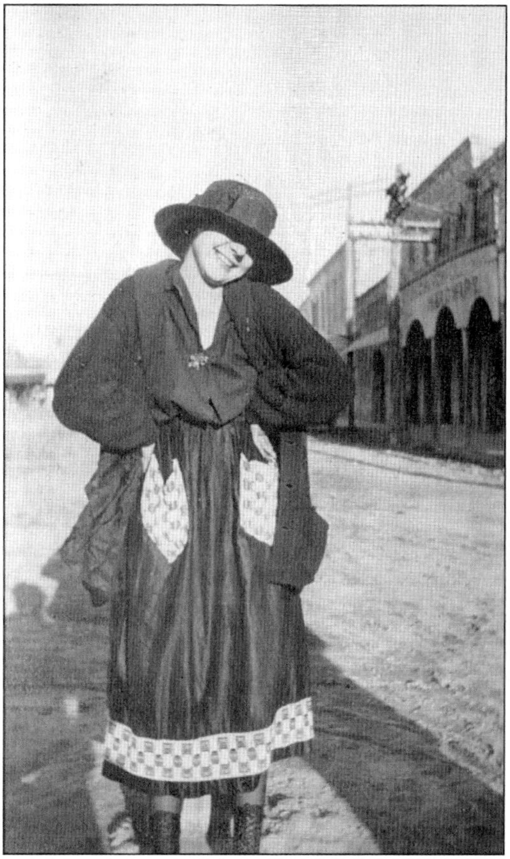

By anyone's standards, at right is a pretty girl in a very fancy dress standing at Main and Jackson Streets on the Courthouse Square. It is too bad no one knows who she is. The photograph below is Clara LaForge on the front step of her family's home at 501 South Main Street. In comparing these photographs, it seems possible that the images are of the same girl.

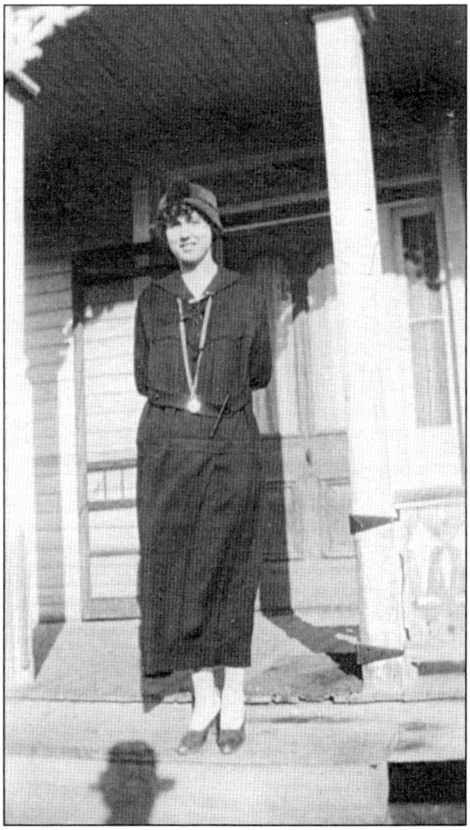

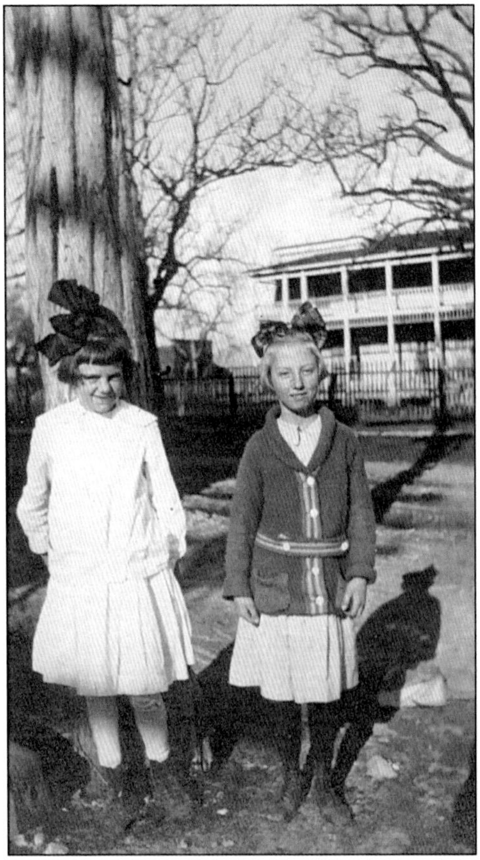

Pictured are Mona ? (left) and Mildred ? (right) standing on South Pierce Street with the W. C. Galloway home behind them. They appear to be dressed for a special occasion. In the photograph below, W. C. Galloway is standing on the porch of his home on Pierce Street. (Photographs courtesy of Milli Williams.)

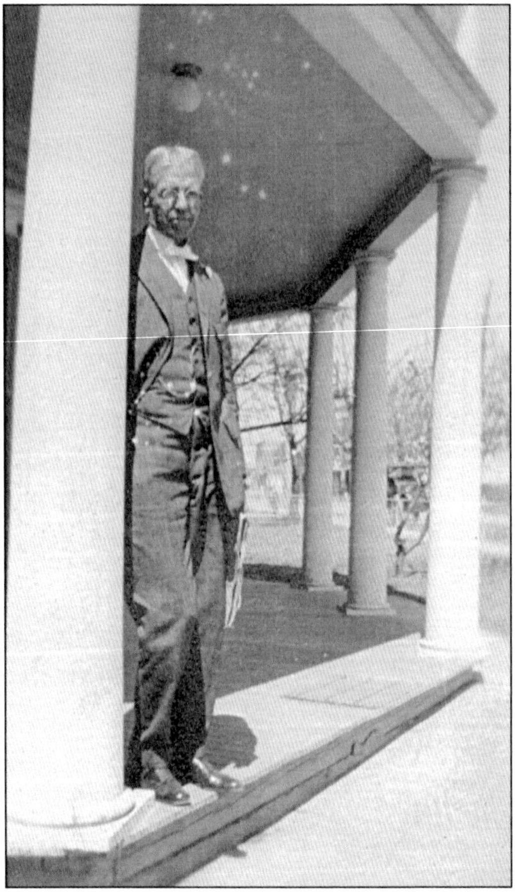

Thomas A. Chamberlain served four times as Burnet County surveyor: 1871–1872, 1881–1890, 1900–1902, and 1913–1926. His brother, John Tate Chamberlain, served as county clerk from 1898 until 1906. John Tate's son, J. H. Chamberlain, took the office in 1906 and served 12 years. The Chamberlain family descendants remained active in civic affairs.

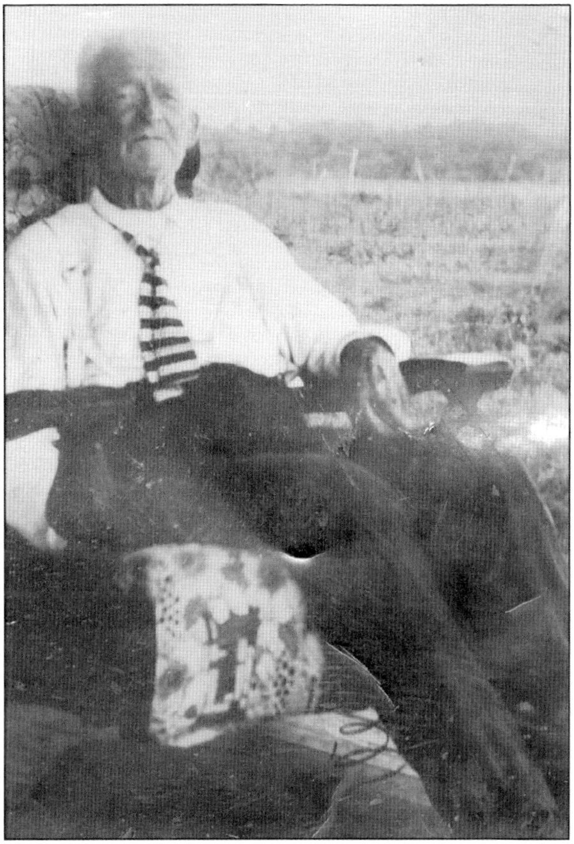

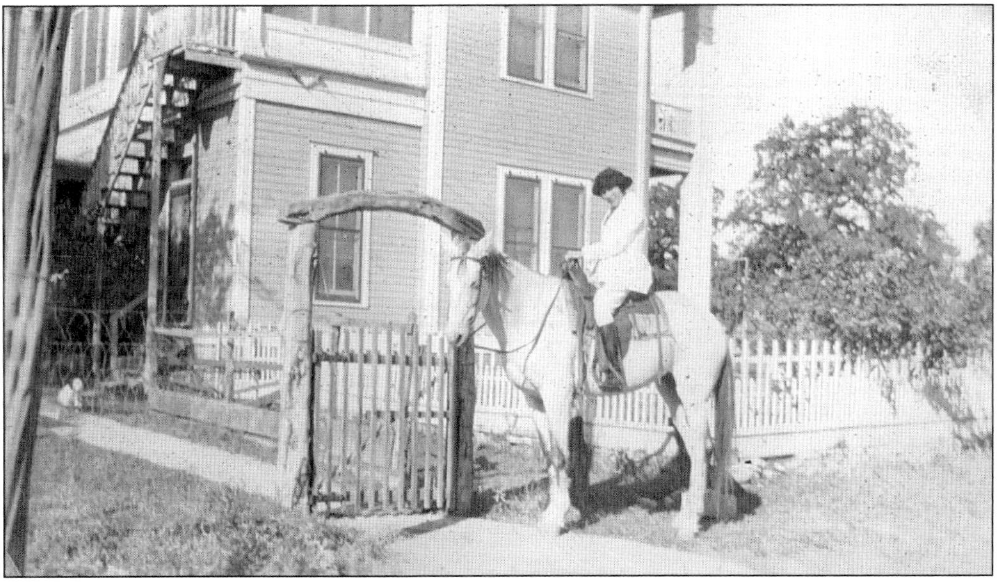

Jamie Lois Duncan sits astride her horse at the back gate of her grandfather Cook's house on North Main Street. James Guin Cook was a lawyer who came to Burnet in 1874 and was elected county judge in 1904. He served until 1916 but was prominent in civic and legal affairs until his death in 1920. Jamie became an important benefactor in the restoration of Fort Croghan.

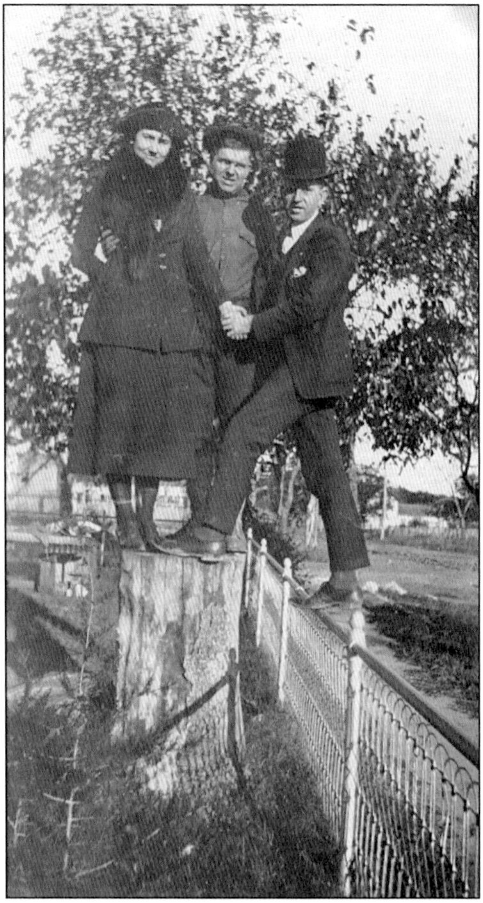

It seems that around this time it was quite popular to make photographs of people standing on top of high perches. There are some in every collection, but this one just stood out. The young lady is quite poised, while her gentlemen friends try to join her on the stump. None of them are identified.

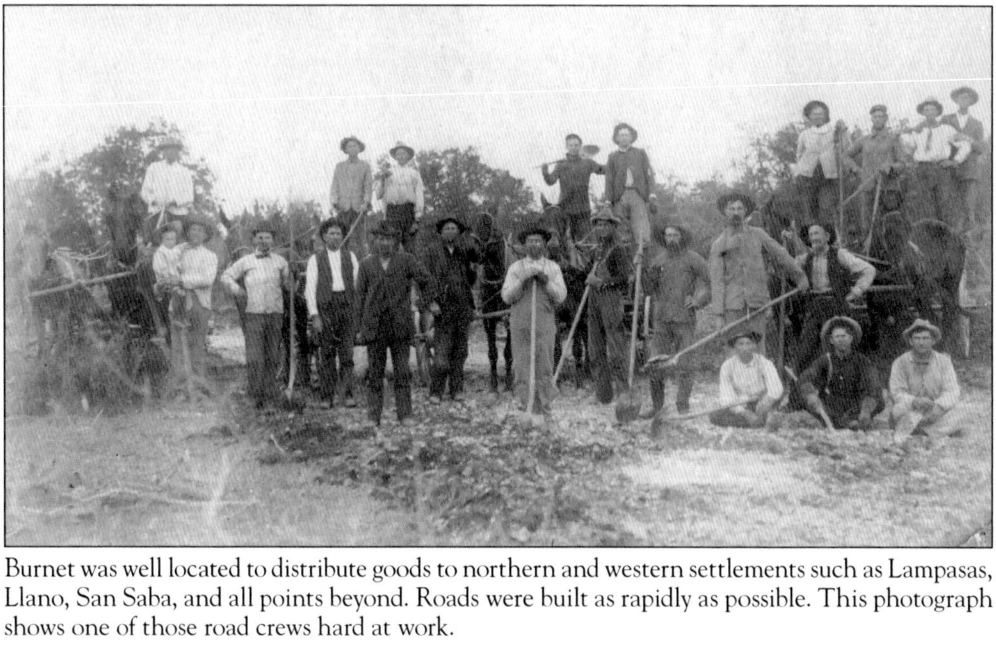

Burnet was well located to distribute goods to northern and western settlements such as Lampasas, Llano, San Saba, and all points beyond. Roads were built as rapidly as possible. This photograph shows one of those road crews hard at work.

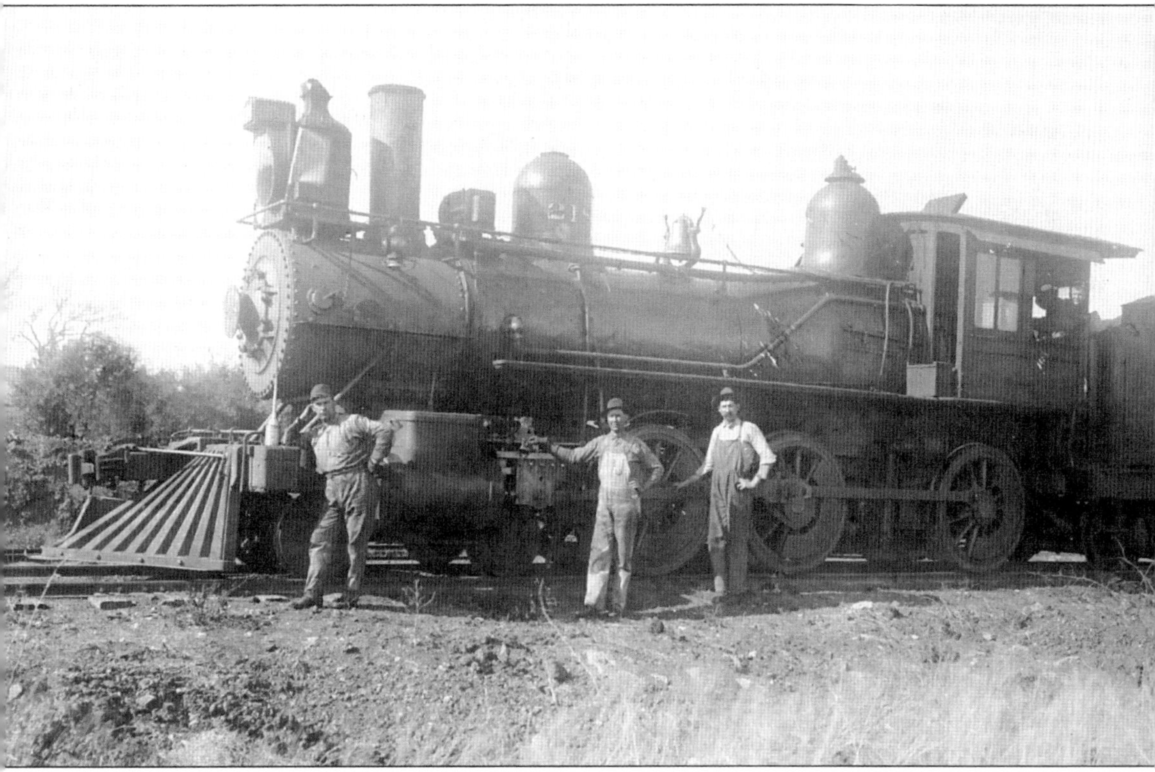

The first train rolled into Burnet on January 1, 1882. The narrow-gauge track was built on a donated right-of-way. It was mostly financed by a group of Austin merchants who were aware of Burnet's success as a trade center. Burnet had 3,000-plus citizens by that time, so the train carried passengers as well as goods. J. A. Rhomberg was appointed superintendent of the road for the Austin and Northwestern Railroad Company, and Rhomberg Street was named after him. Granite for building the state capitol was shipped on this railroad. The men are unidentified.

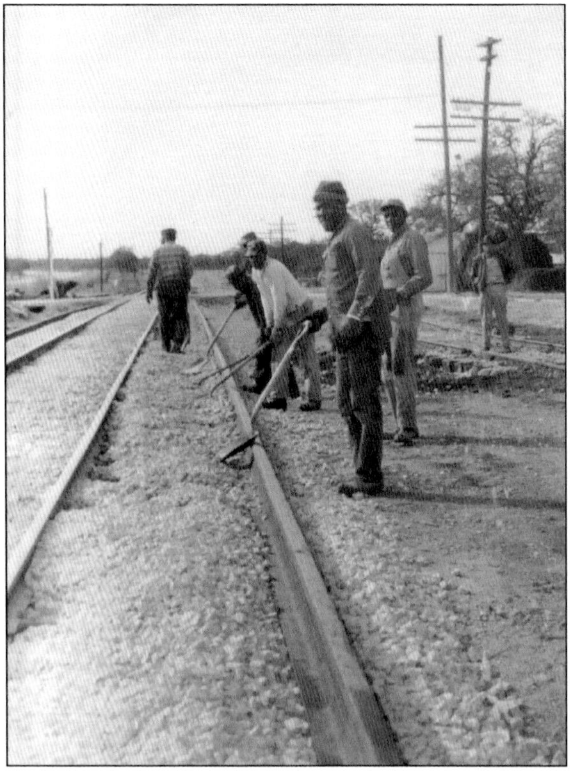

At first, the granite for the state capitol was brought by ox wagon from the quarry to Burnet, where it was cut to specification and loaded on boxcars for the transport to Austin. The rail line was later extended to the quarry site. This crew is working on the track between Burnet and Bertram. The men are not identified.

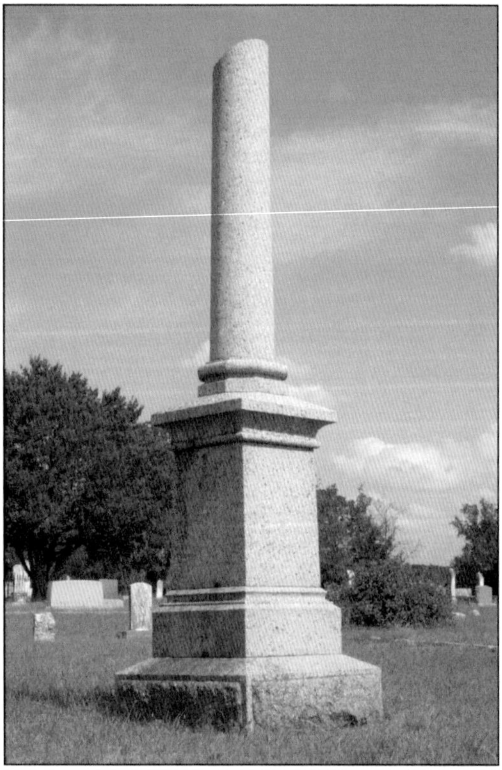

The state legislature voted to use convict labor for building the capitol in order to save money. The American stone builders union boycotted the project. The state then hired and paid for 62 stone masons to come from Scotland to do the job. Fellow workers erected this monument in the Old Burnet Cemetery, honoring those who died here. (Photograph courtesy of Kina Cockroft.)

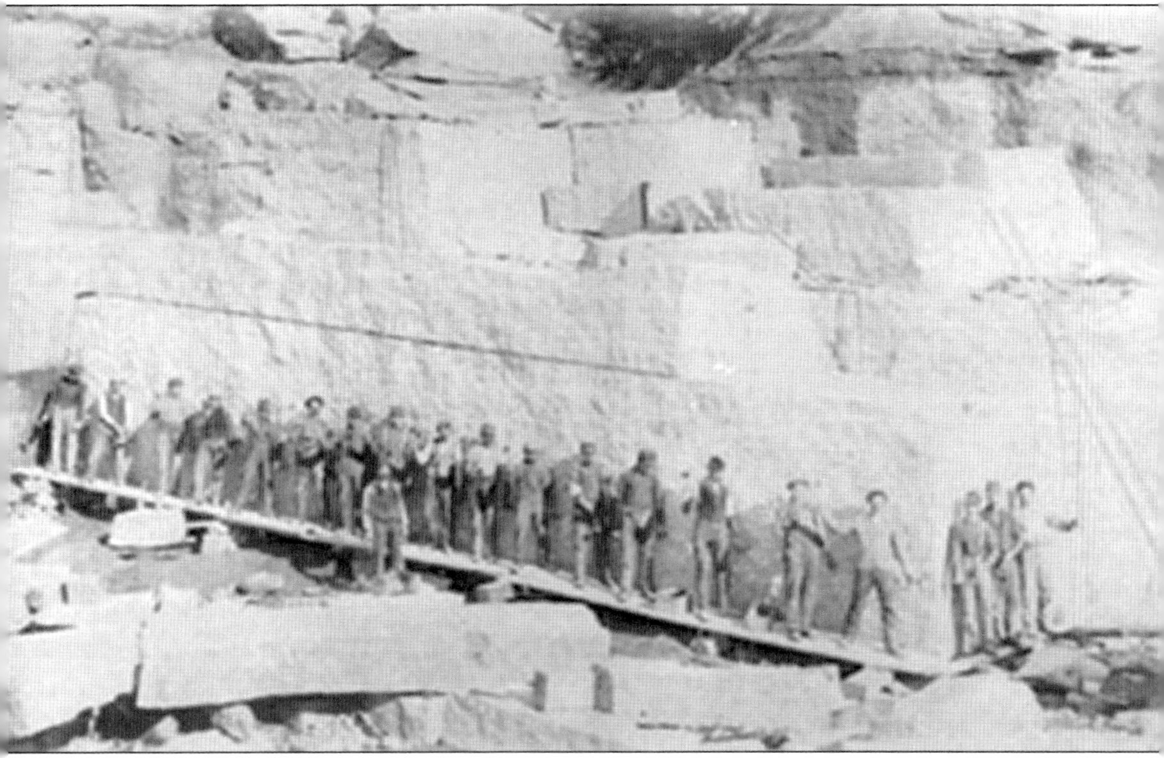

Granite Mountain, shown here during the quarrying of stone for the state capitol, has been an active quarry for more than 100 years. Yet the mountain remains a mountain, and it is said it would take 1,000 years to quarry it level. During the building of the capitol, Burnet enjoyed new prosperity. The cutting yard at Burnet employed hundreds of men to work the stone. The yard, at the railroad south of town, became known as Wilkeville. A saloon, stores, and a hotel were hastily thrown up at the site. The boss of the job was Gus Wilke, who was eventually arrested and stood trial for violating a federal law prohibiting the importation of foreign skilled laborers by contract. He was found guilty but managed to stay out of prison. Meanwhile, the state continued to use convict labor at the quarry and on the capitol building. (Photograph courtesy of HBFL.)

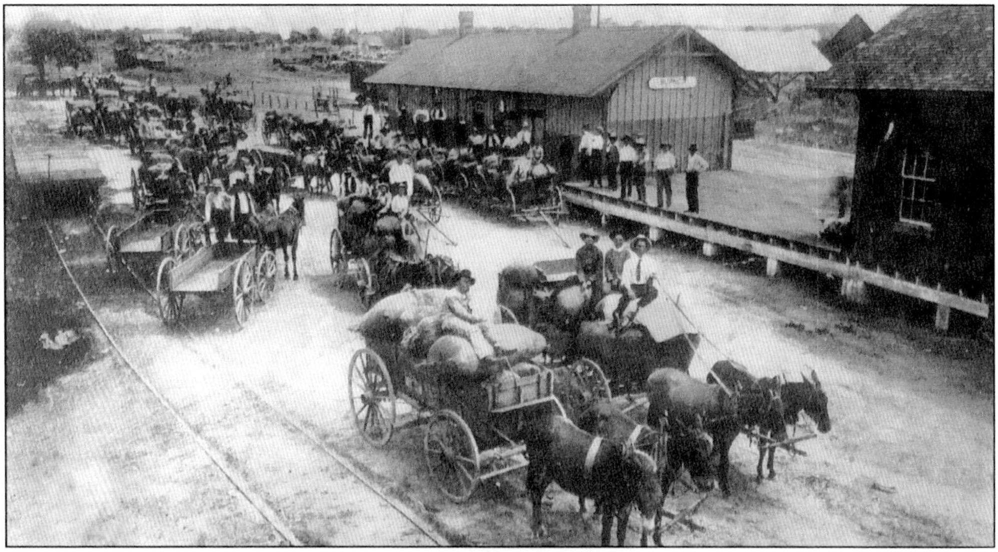

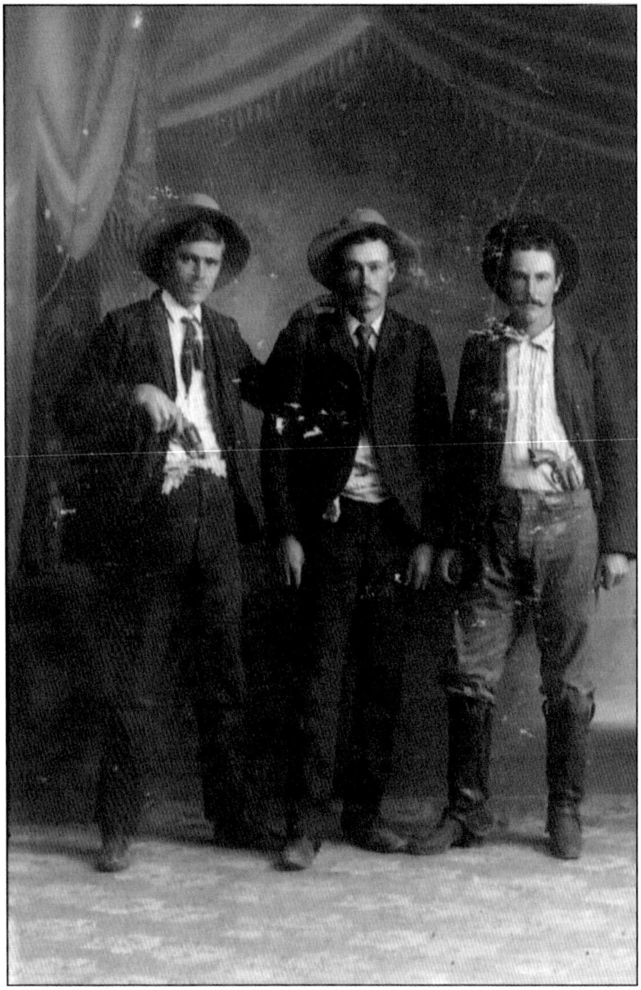

Sheep ranching was a close second to cattle ranching. Sheep were raised for their wool but also provided mutton for food. The wool market was booming, as can be seen in this photograph of a single day's shipment of 225,000 pounds at Burnet. In the picture at left are some unidentified cowboys all dressed up for a photograph. Cowboys often did this after a cattle-drive payday and while on a lark in the city.

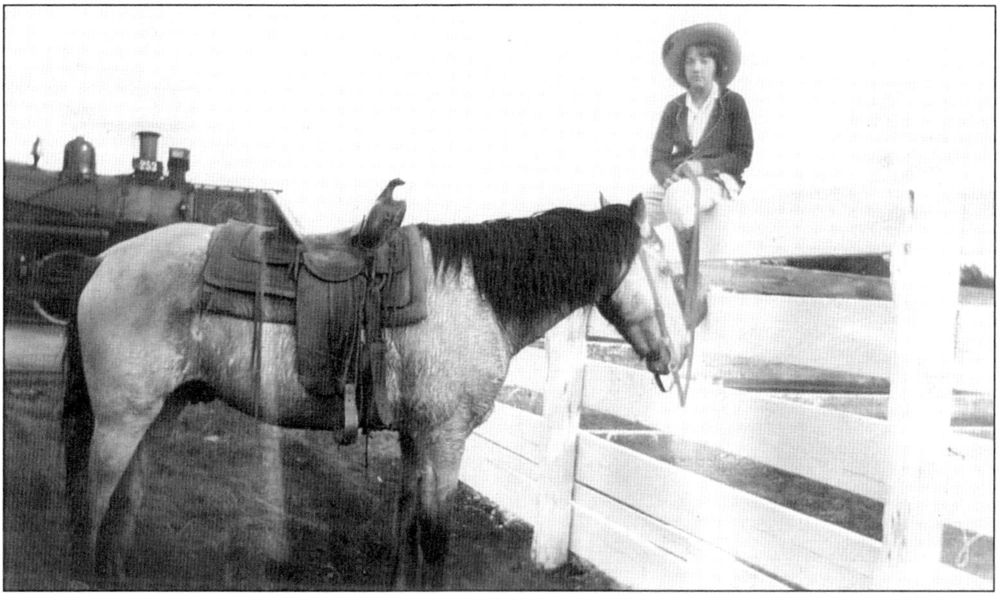

The young lady sitting on the stockyard fence is obviously posing for this picture. There is no name given, but she can be identified by her horse, which is known to belong to "Jimsey" Duncan. In the background is the train. Cattle were held in the pens until they could be loaded for shipment. The Duncans were cattle ranchers, and Jimsey was a capable working cowgirl.

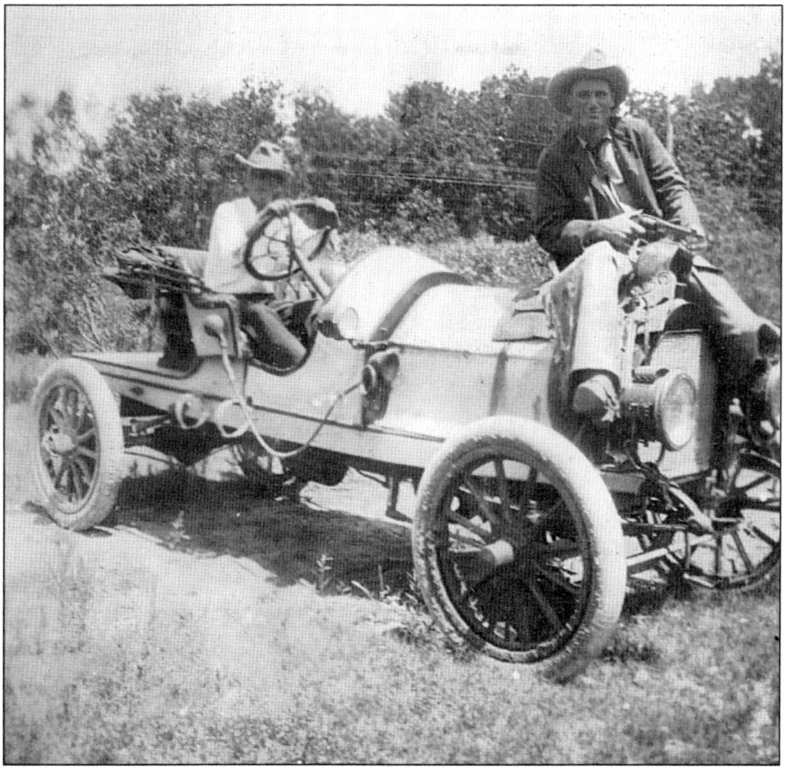

Here is a strange sight—a saddle and armed rider on the hood of a car. Perhaps this was not the case here, but it was the custom, and still is on some ranches, to hunt jackrabbits in this fashion. Now pickups or jeeps are outfitted with tall seats, making the job easier. The men are not identified.

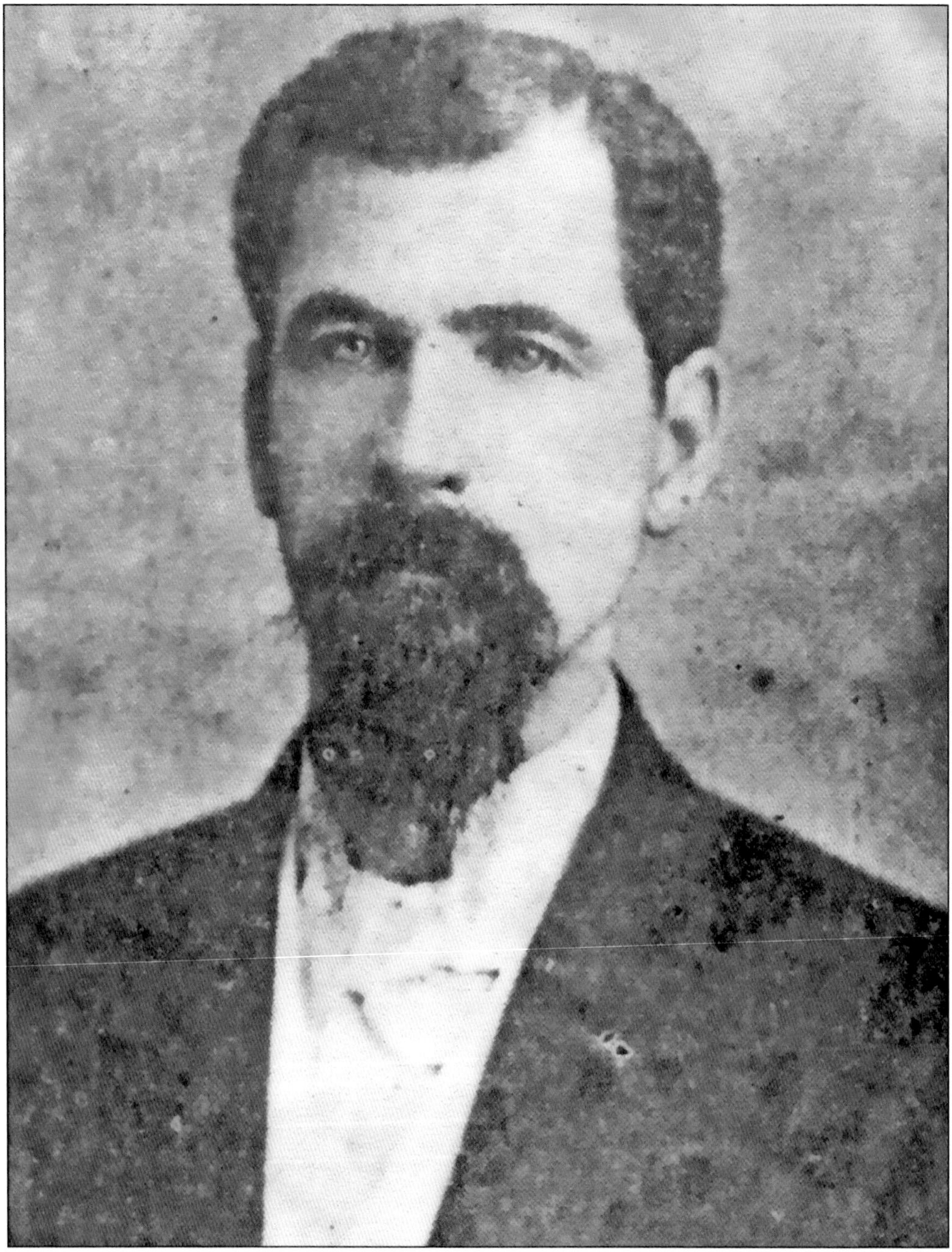

The Burnet Public School District hired Prof. R. J. Richey as superintendent in 1888. The school had been a private one until the Burnet City Council bought the building in 1885. Professor Richey remained as superintendent until 1904, when he left to build his own private school. Richey came to Texas from Virginia, where he had earned bachelor of arts and master of arts degrees from Washington and Lee University. Gen. Robert E. Lee was the president there and one of Richey's mentors. Lee wrote a letter of commendation for Richey. When Lee died, Richey was an honorary pallbearer at his funeral. Because of his admiration for the general, Lee named his school the Robert E. Lee High School. (Photograph courtesy of HBFL.)

Prof. M. B. Brown was hired as superintendent of the Burnet School District in 1905 and served until 1915. In 1887 or 1888, the public school building burned and students met in churches and private homes until a new limestone building was erected. Some of the students began attending Richey's private school. (Photograph courtesy of HBFL.)

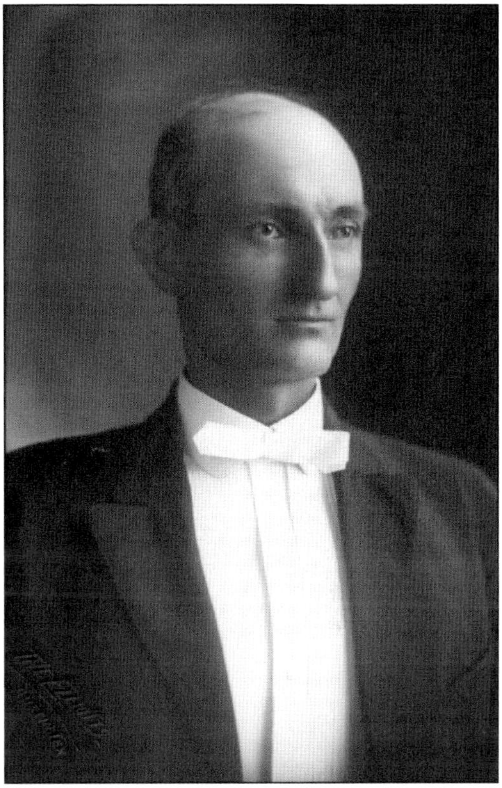

This is Burnet's new school building under construction. It was begun shortly after the first building burned. With classes meeting all over town and the opening of the Richey school, public school enrollment dropped by about a third. The new building was an ambitious one, and people watched the progress with mounting pride.

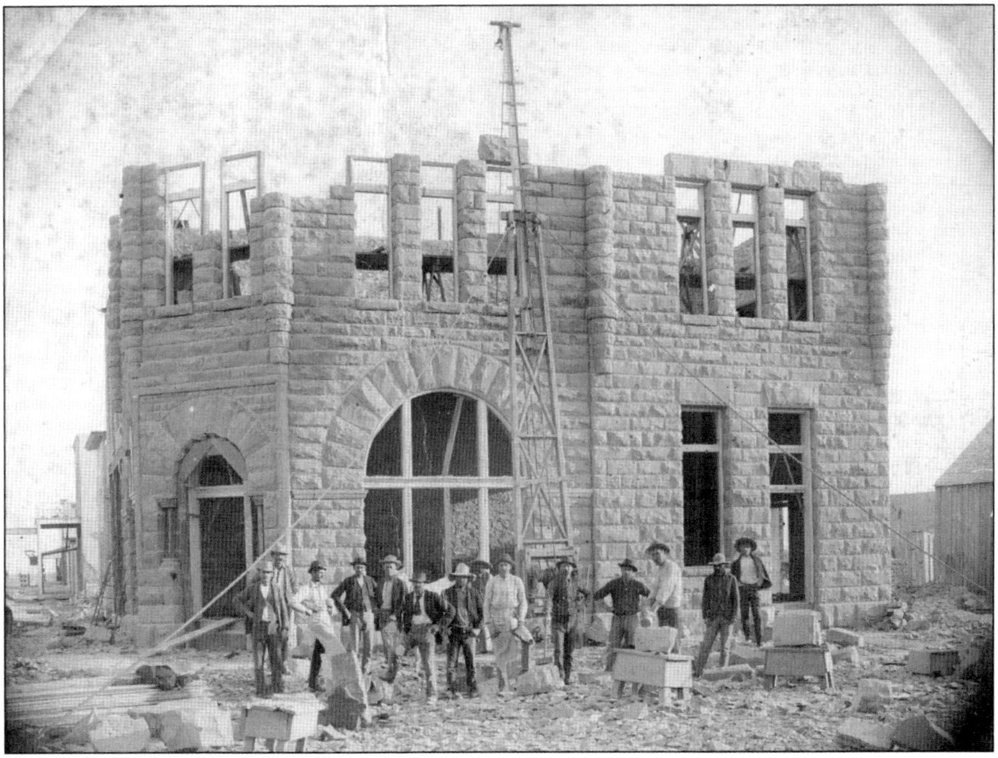

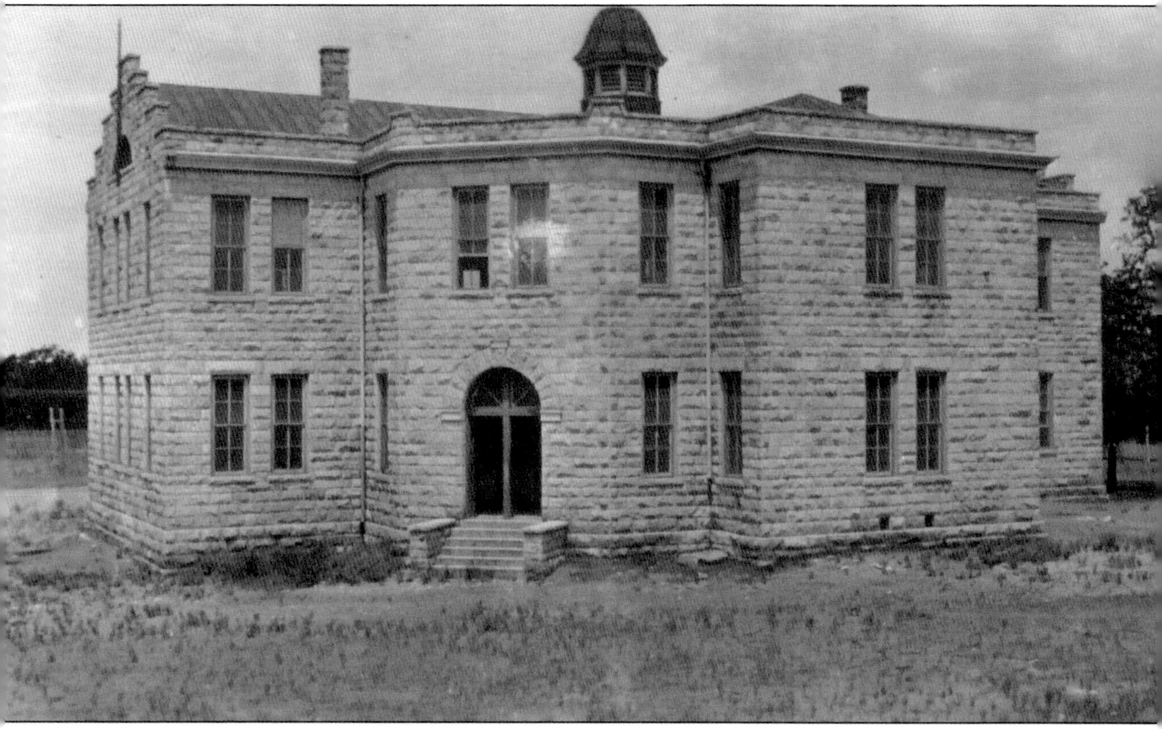

The new Burnet Public School building was completed in the fall of 1889 at a cost of $20,000. According to an unidentified local paper, the building was splendid, built in the shape of a cross with wide halls intersecting to provide great ventilation to the seven classrooms. An auditorium on the second floor could seat 800. The walls were plastered and flues were positioned so that no woodwork could be in danger of catching fire. The upper floors were soundproofed with a layer of plaster, and the foundation under each wall was covered with pitch to prevent wall dampness. The front steps were of blue granite. The stone and granite was quarried within a mile of the town. The architect of this marvelous school was Burt McDonald of Austin, with L. D. Nichols of Fort Worth and A. W. Johns of Burnet listed as builders.

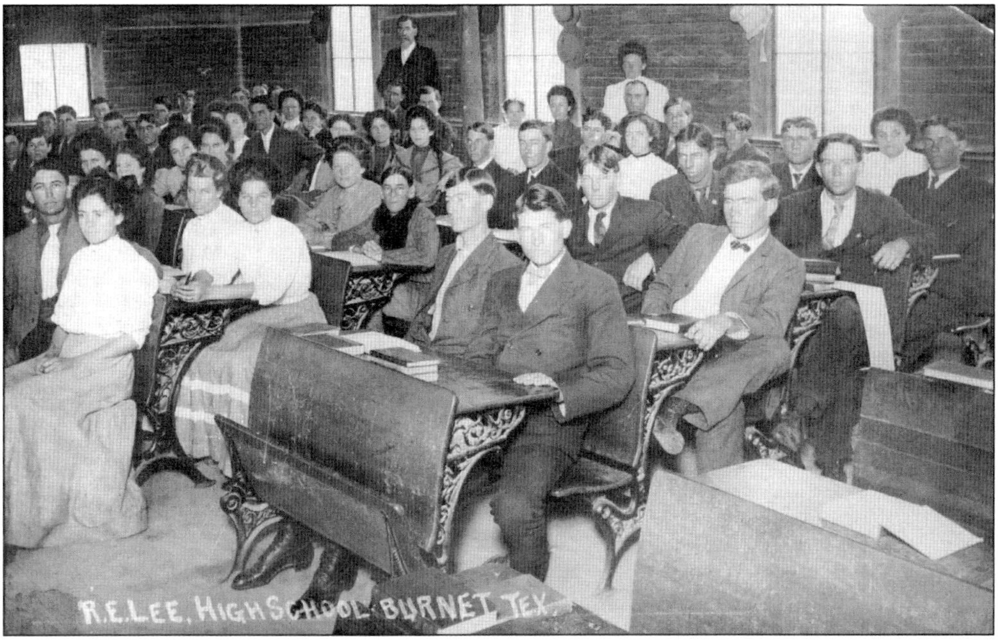

Here is a view of a classroom at Robert E. Lee High School. Students are unidentified. Note the plank walls, hats, and a bonnet hanging on the window facings. Prof. R. J. Richey stands in the back.

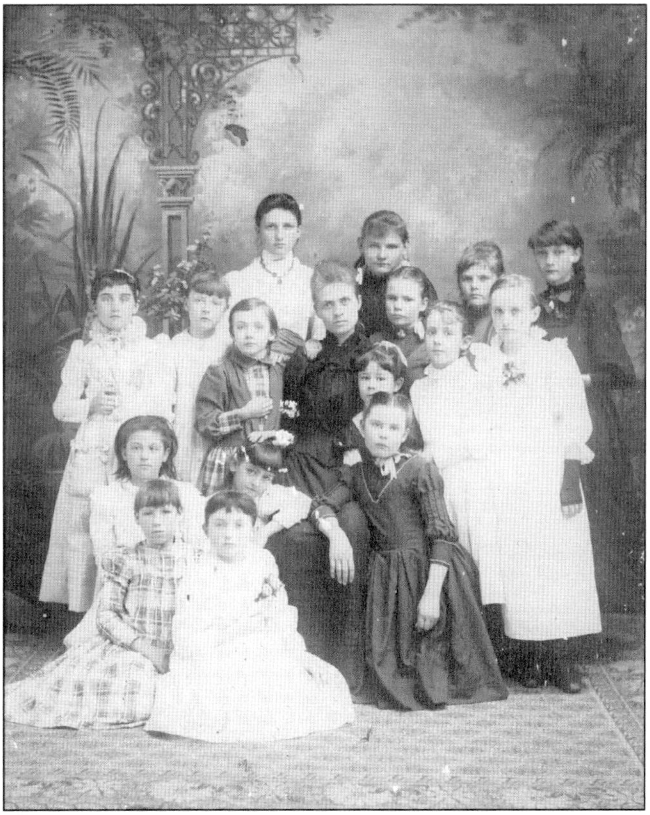

It is noted on the back of this photograph, "Burnet school music class." No names or year are given. It is evidence that early trustees wanted to provide a well-rounded curriculum for students. In 2009, all of Burnet's bands from 7th through 12th grades each garnered number one ratings, sweeping UIL (University Interscholastic League) competitions for the first time in history. (Photograph courtesy of HBFL.)

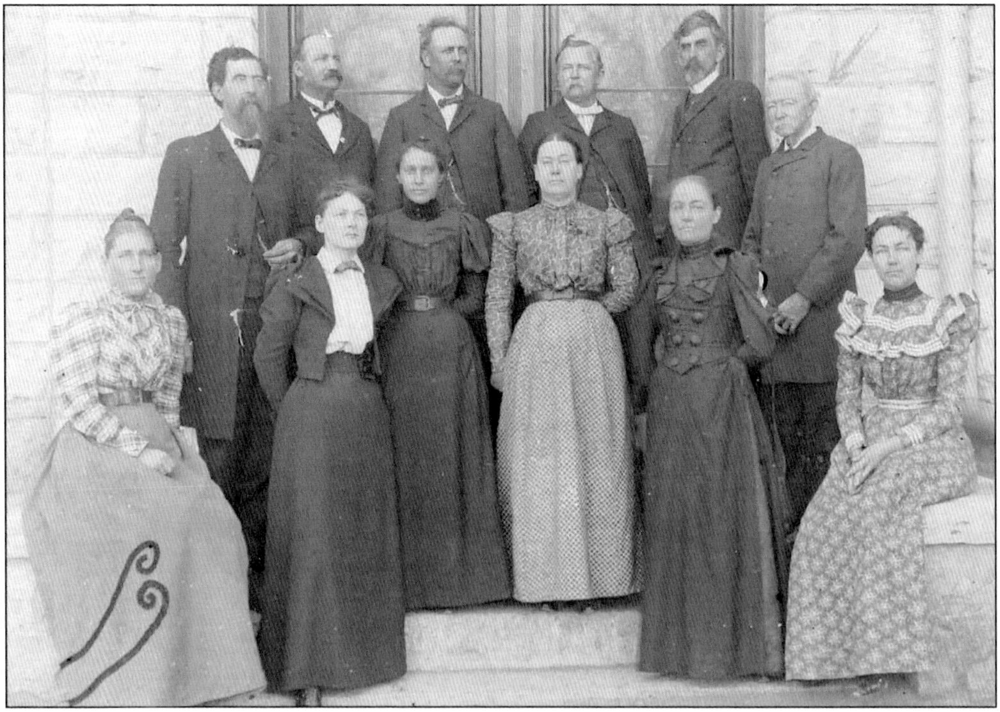

These are the Burnet School trustees and teachers of 1899. They are, from left to right, (first row) Minnie Rawlings, Ruth Gardner, Loula McDonald, Mrs. Tom ("Shorty") Smith, Ruth Garrett, and Villulah Spitler; (second row) Professor Richey, Ealy Moses, John Daugherty, W. M. Ross, Colonel Stevens, and C. C. Cummings. (Photograph courtesy of HBFL.)

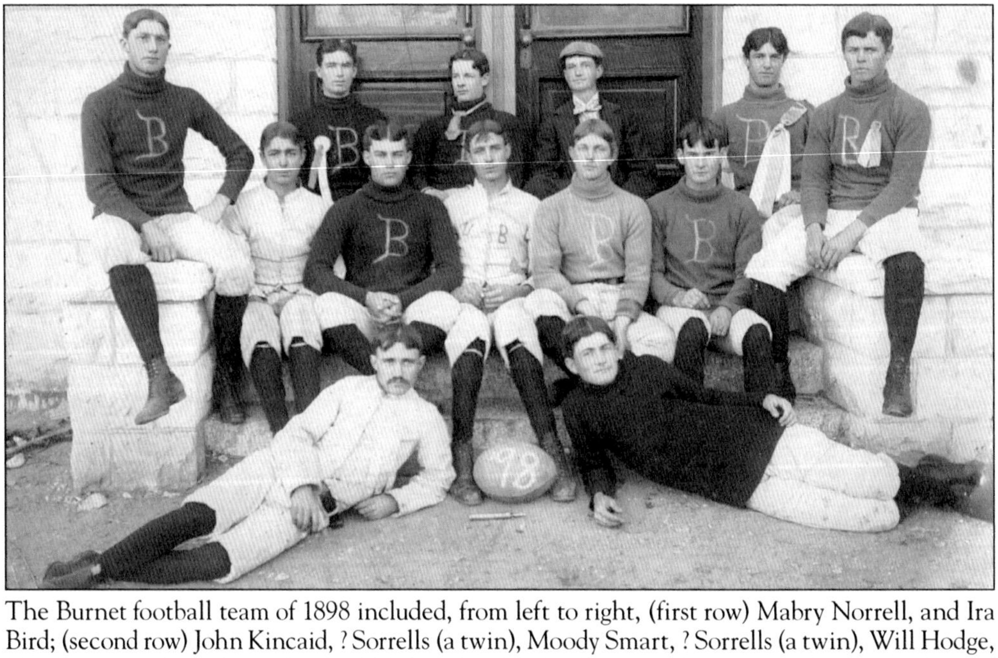

The Burnet football team of 1898 included, from left to right, (first row) Mabry Norrell, and Ira Bird; (second row) John Kincaid, ? Sorrells (a twin), Moody Smart, ? Sorrells (a twin), Will Hodge, Tom Jones, and Toad Daugherty; (third row) Fred Daugherty, Ealy Moses, B. Burns, and G. D. Daugherty. (Photograph courtesy of BCHS.)

Here are the Burnet teachers in 1911. They are, from left to right, (first row) Annie Harrison, Amy Dodson, and Florence Brownlee; (second row) Kate Atkinson, Grace Edman, and Margaret Cotham; (third row) Ed Dodson, M. B. Brown, and Theresa Wilson. (Photograph courtesy of HBFL.)

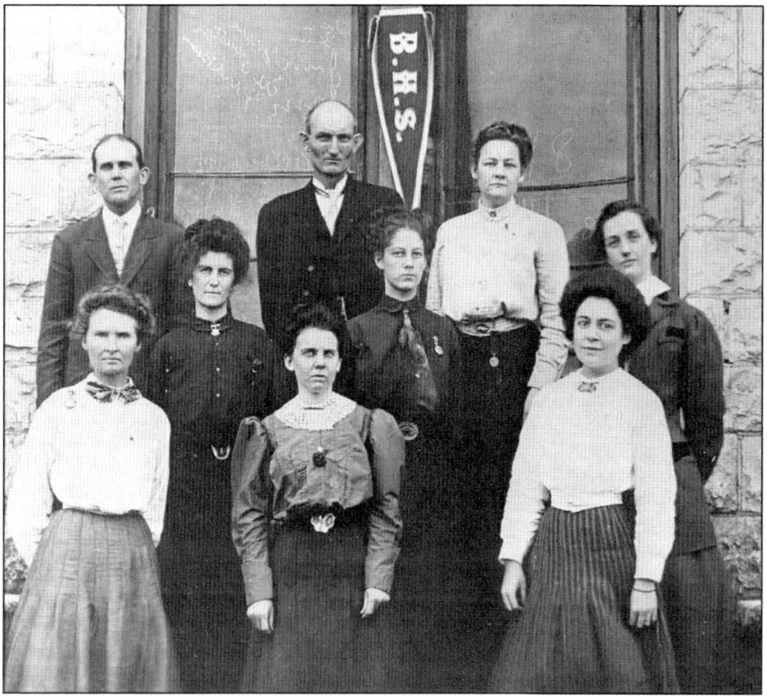

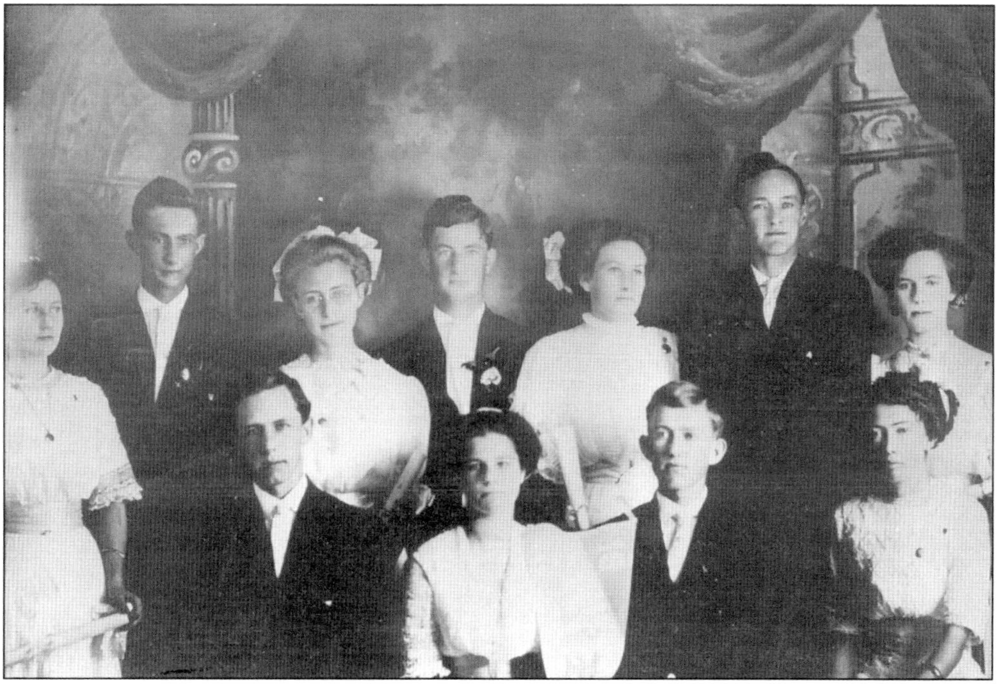

The senior class at Robert E. Lee High School in 1911 is pictured here. They are, from left to right, (first row) Frank Landon, Iva King, James Williams, and Althea Vann; (second row) Jessie Ramsower, Dudley Harrell, Jewel Farquhar, William Holland, Nora Nagiller, Leslie Gordon, and Minnie Landon. (Photograph courtesy of HBFL.)

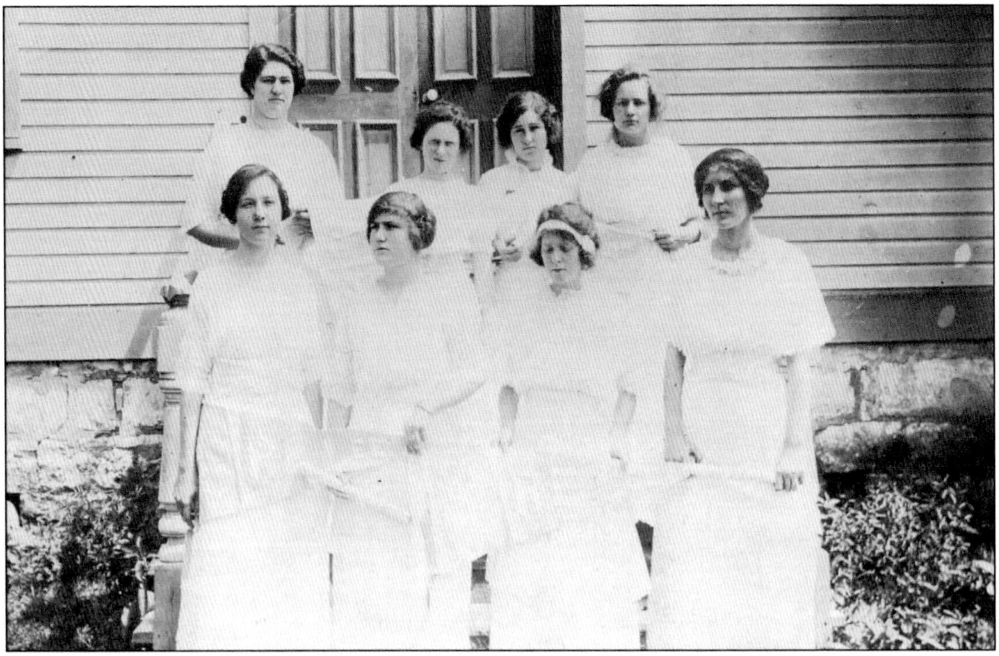

The following are students from the Robert E. Lee High School class of 1914. From left to right are (first row) Ethel Faris, Olivia Lester, Ella Mae Warner, and Florice Eva Cloud; (second row) Ruth Shelburn, Nellie Mar Chamberlain, Myrthe Odell Parker, and Katie Evalena Duncan. There are familiar surnames among these students because all of these families still live in the Burnet area. Many of them live on the land acquired by their pioneer ancestors. (Photograph courtesy of HBFL.)

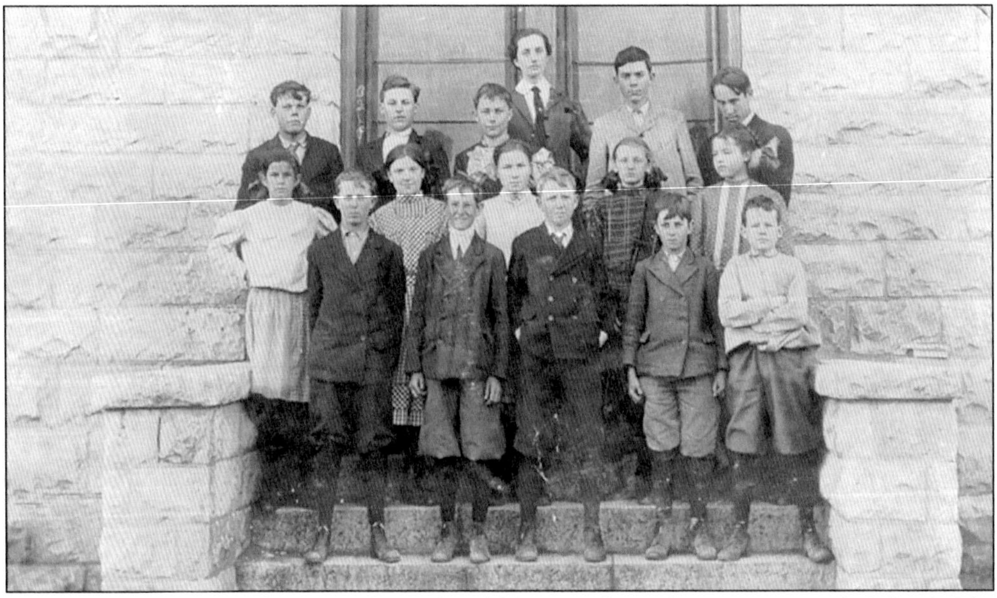

This photograph is dated 1909 and noted as fifth or sixth grade at Burnet High School. The students are (first row) John Landon, Orla Whitney, Hudson Mitchelltree, ? Fisher, and Tad Moses; (second row) Winnie Magill, Webb Lamb, Mabel Nixon, Ruby Stark, and Lettie Mitchelltree; (third row) Rufus McFarland, Ned Boggess, Kyle Holland, George Ramsower, Clayton Boggess, and the teacher, Margaret Cotham. (Photograph courtesy of HBFL.)

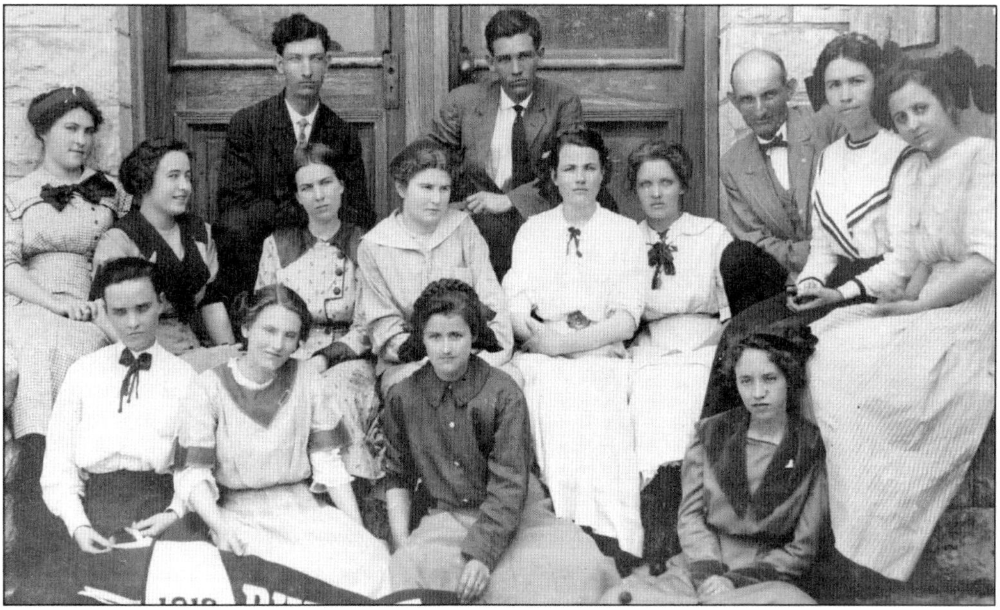

In 1912, this was the senior class at Burnet High School. From left to right are (first row) Florence Kinkead, Ada Moses, Kattie Lewis, and Estella Ramsower; (second row) Marie O'Donnell, Hattie Belle Dennis, Beaula Shipp, Bertha Atkinson. Alma Cotham, Agness Paulson, Supt. M. B. Brown, Ica Cox, and John Eargle; (third row) Principal J. T. Foster and Scott Edman. (Photograph courtesy of HBFL.)

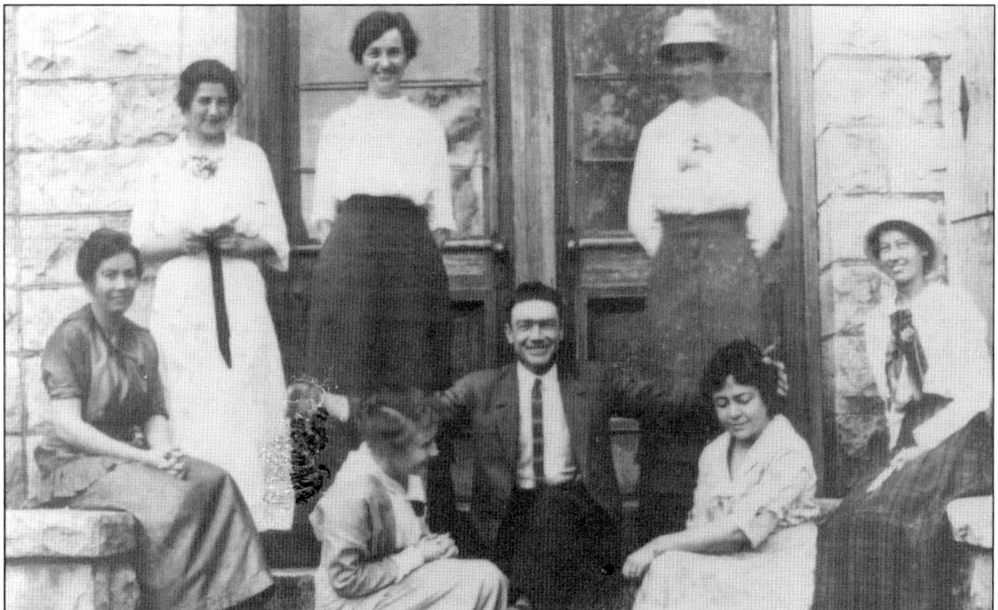

Here the Burnet High School faculty of 1915 seems to be a jovial group. Perhaps it is because all of the ladies are single. From left to right are (first row) Ruth Lamon, Hattiebel Dennis, Supt. J. R. Masterson, Florence Brownlee, and Grace Edman; (second row) Olivia Beal, Margaret Cotham, and Dora Rawling. Olivia Beal later married Dewitt Tankersley, and Hattiebel Dennis became Mrs. Harry Galloway. (Photograph courtesy of HBFL.)

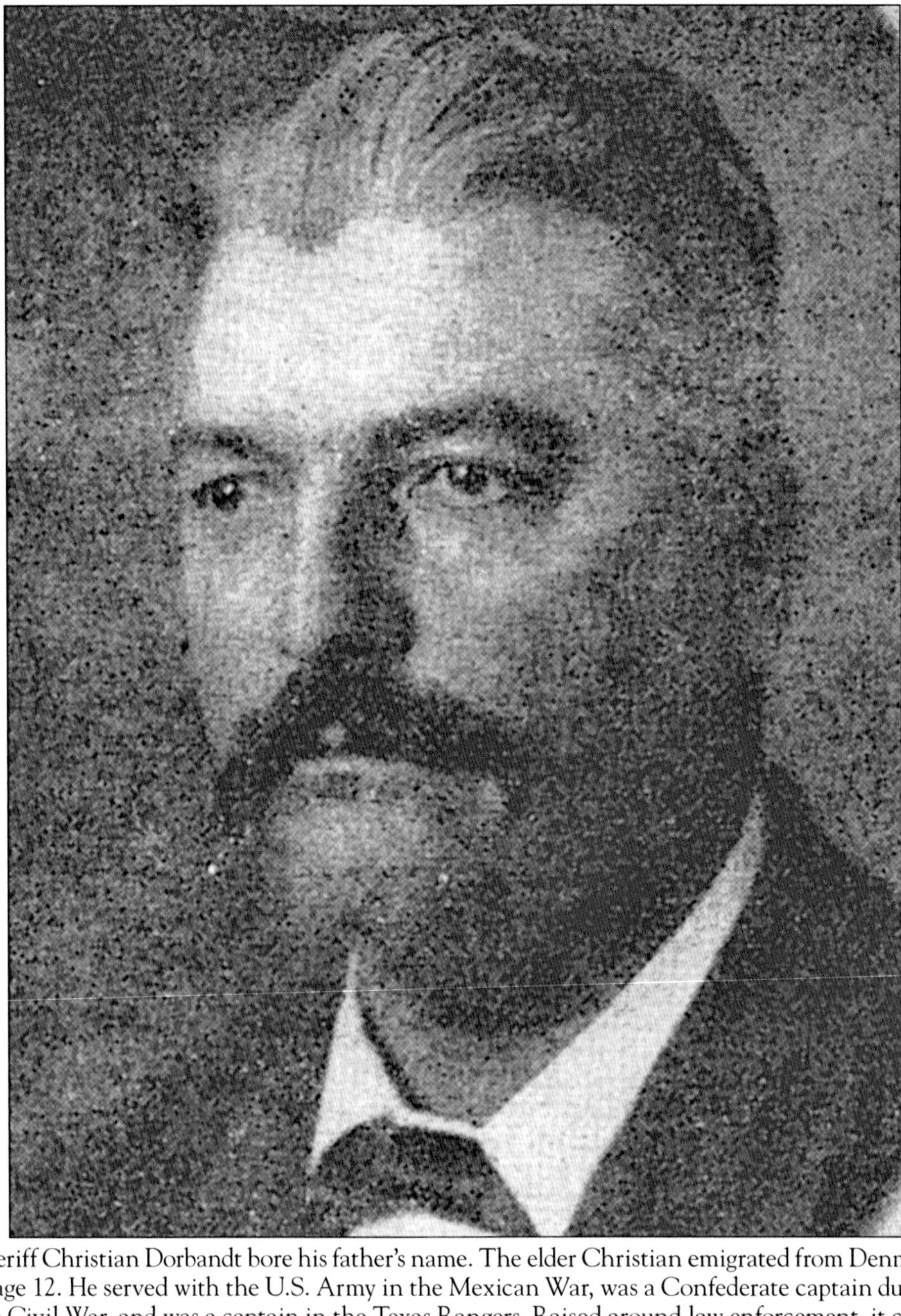

Sheriff Christian Dorbandt bore his father's name. The elder Christian emigrated from Denmark at age 12. He served with the U.S. Army in the Mexican War, was a Confederate captain during the Civil War, and was a captain in the Texas Rangers. Raised around law enforcement, it came naturally to young "Chris," who had 15 siblings. Chris Dorbandt served two years as a Burnet city marshal and 18 months as a county deputy sheriff before he was elected sheriff in 1890. He was known as fearless and faithful to the job and served his county with distinction for 12 years. He married Anna Perkins in 1883, and the couple had 10 children. Dorbandt was also a successful cattle rancher, owning one of the finest ranches in the county that remains in family ownership. He was a Mason and an early member of the Texas Cattle Raisers Association. He was well known as one of the old trail drivers.

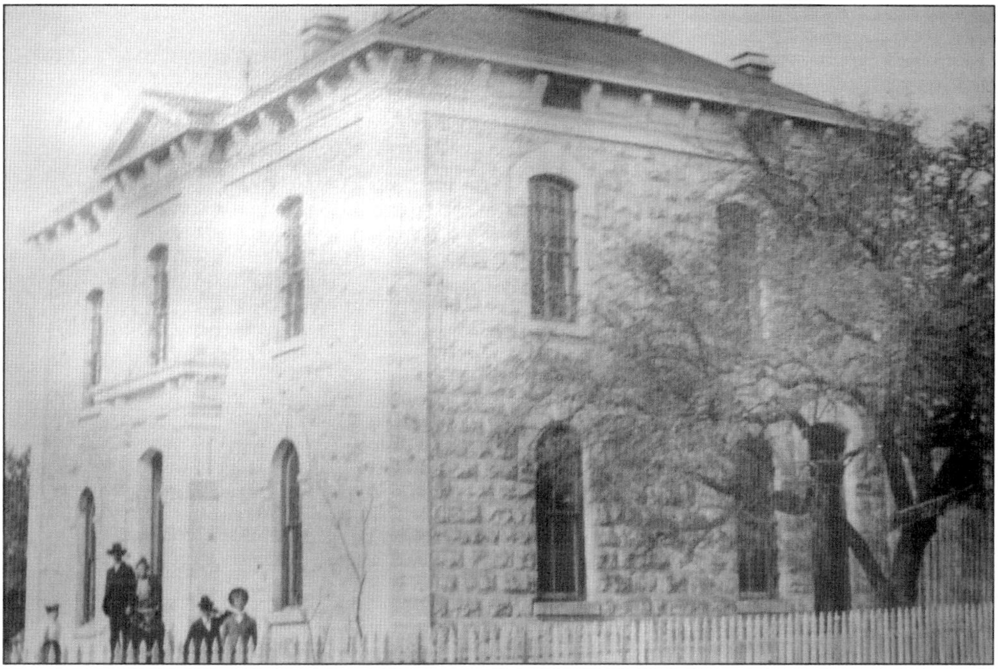

Before the jailhouse was built in 1884, prisoners were held in a cell located in the courthouse. The new jailhouse had offices in front and an apartment in back. The jail cells were upstairs. The sheriff and his family lived in the apartment as part of his salary. Sheriff Chris Dorbandt and his children stand on the steps in this photograph.

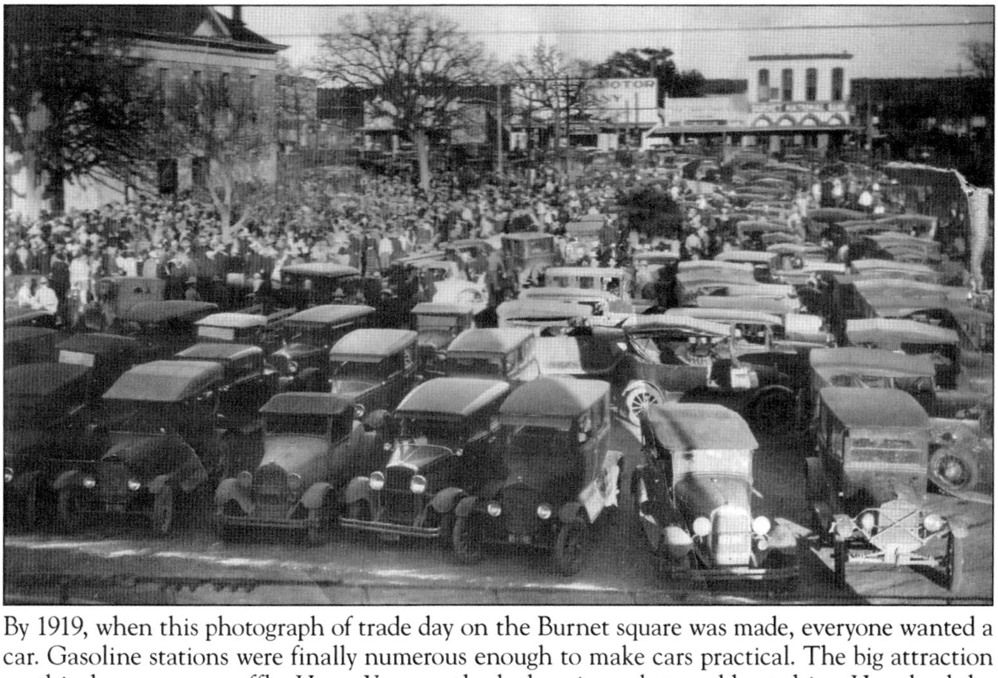

By 1919, when this photograph of trade day on the Burnet square was made, everyone wanted a car. Gasoline stations were finally numerous enough to make cars practical. The big attraction on this day was a car raffle. Harry Yoe was the lucky winner but could not drive. He solved the problem by auctioning off the vehicle. Having won it to begin with, he made a nice pocketful of money.

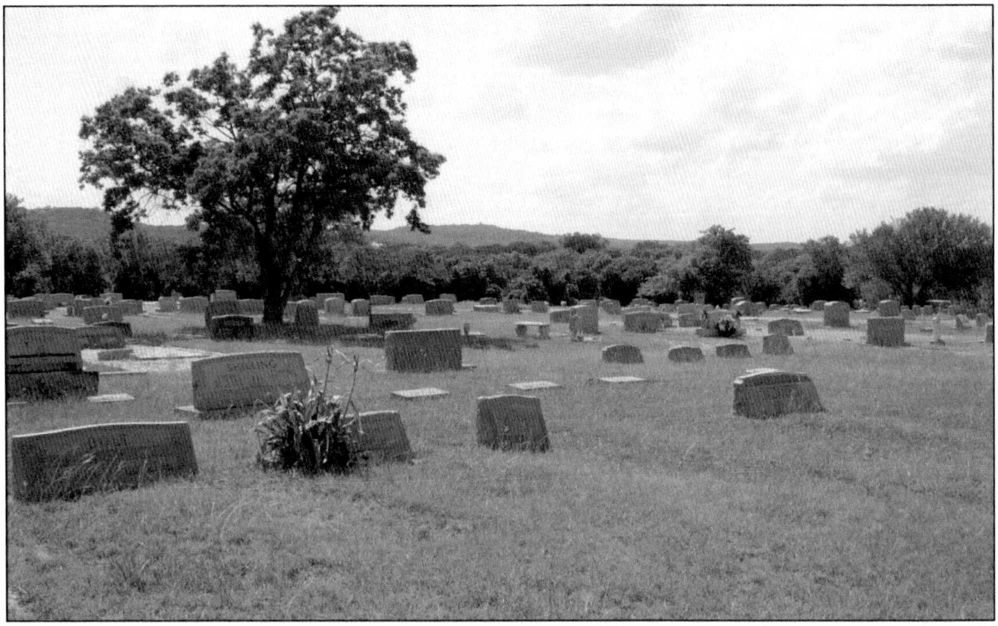

This is a view of the Burnet Cemetery looking west toward the town. It is adjacent to the Old Burnet Cemetery, where many of Burnet's first settlers are interred. One is Peter Kerr, who donated land for the courthouse square. The oldest marked grave is that of Sarah Ann Wills, dated March 14, 1853.

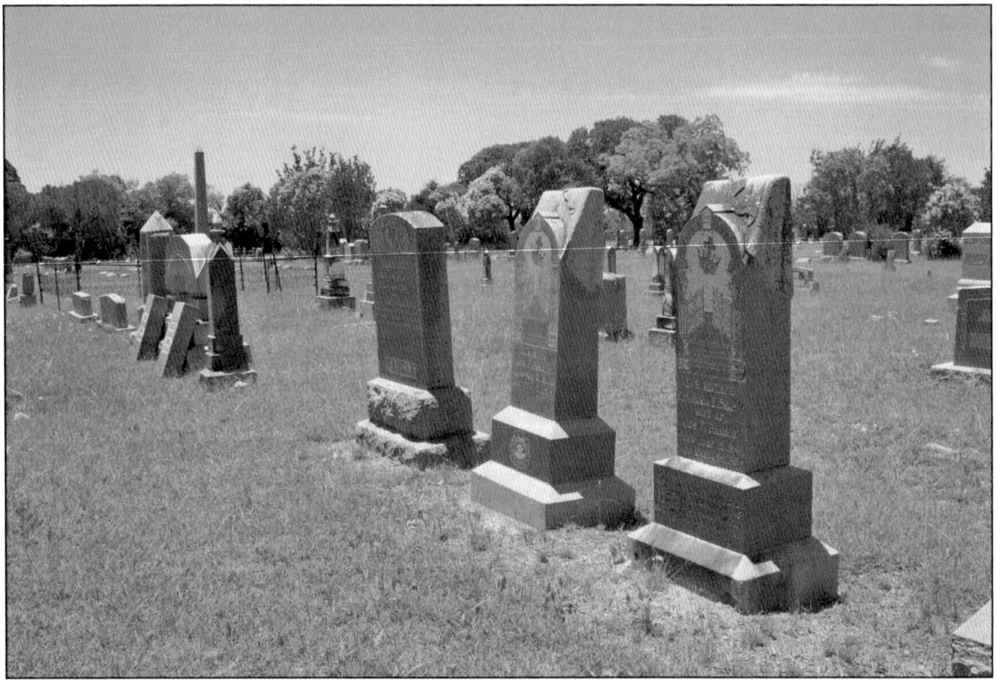

The Odd Fellows Cemetery is adjacent on the east of the Old Burnet Cemetery. The oldest marked grave is that of G. W. Jones, who died in 1874. The Post Mountain Cemetery is located 1 mile west of Burnet near TX 29. The oldest grave there is marked Alice Bell Avery, March 15, 1882. The city manages all four cemeteries.

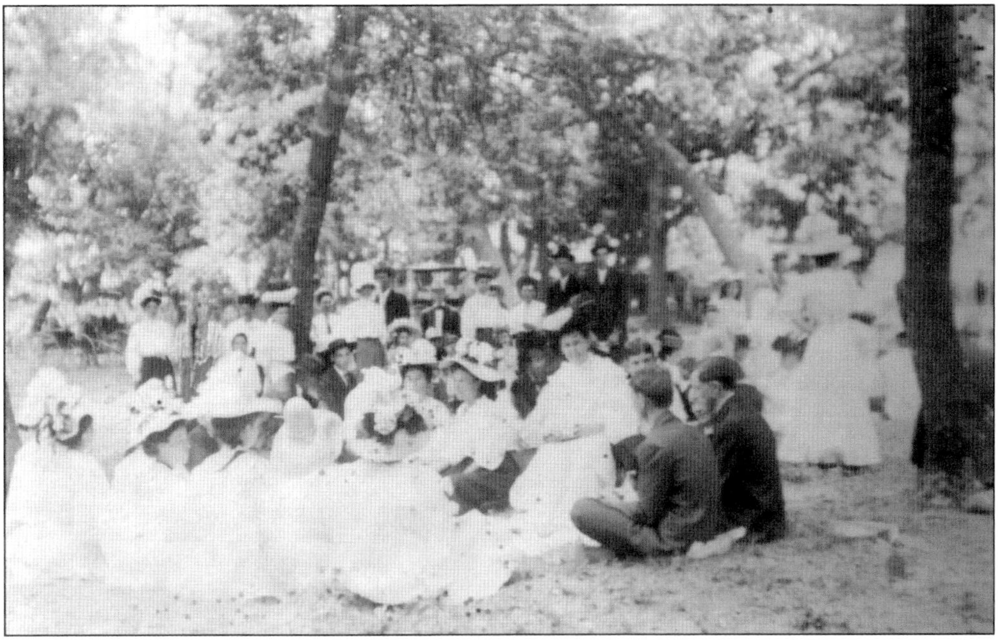

Picnics were the entertainment of earlier times. These picnics were often held on a Sunday after church, when no one was expected to hurry home. There were no names on this photograph, but even though the people are unidentified, it is included here because it is a perfect illustration of what folks most often did for fun. (Photograph courtesy of HBFL.)

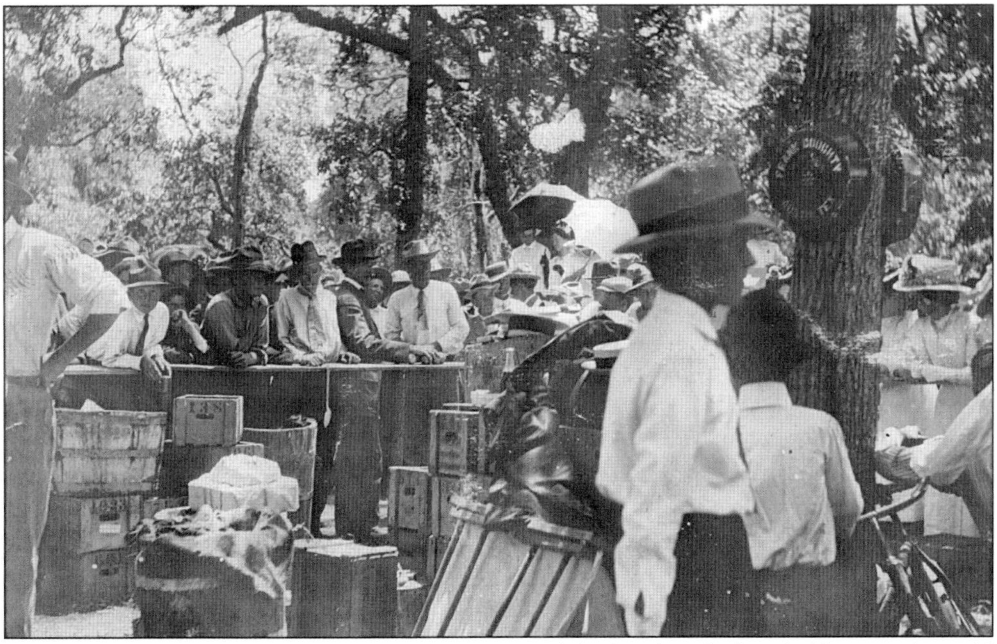

It is thought that this photograph was taken at one of the local trade days, held so people could sell their handmade and homegrown products. In this case, it appears that folks are setting up under shady trees near a creek bank. Aside from making money, this activity provided a much anticipated chance to visit with neighbors and talk over current events. (Photograph courtesy of HBFL.)

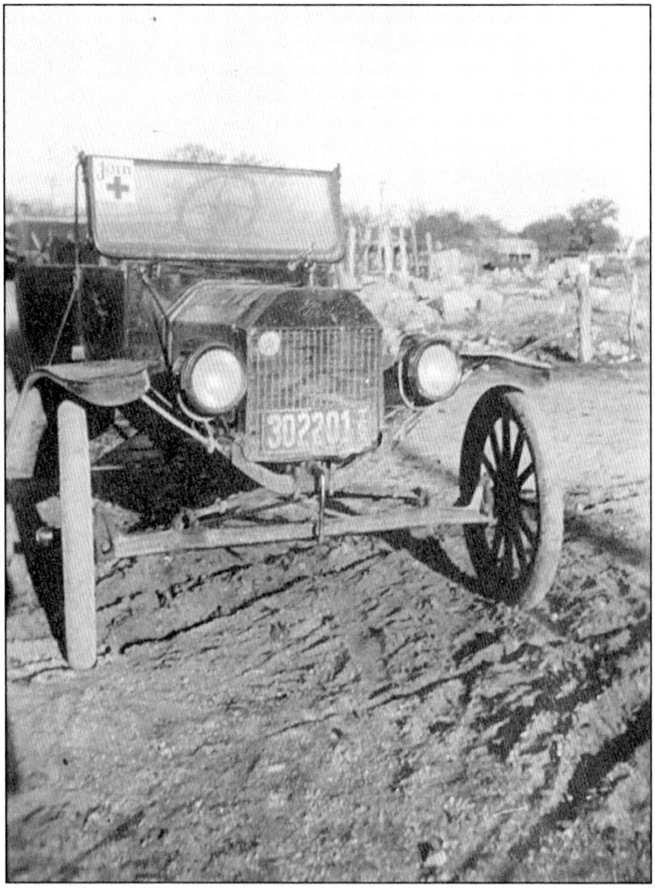

Time has brought the automobile to Burnet, but still the streets are dirt, or in this case mud. Something can be said for the fact that they are amply wide enough to drive around the worst of bogs. In rainy weather, it was common practice to carry along a bundle of cane straw for use as traction material in case one became stuck.

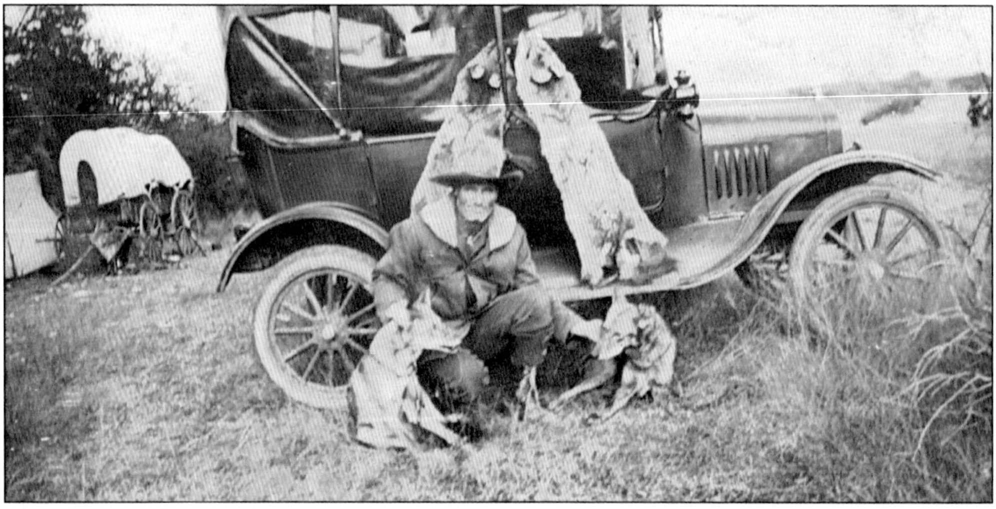

This photograph was taken in January 1910 on the Duncan Ranch. Wolves were hunted because they killed animals that were depended upon to make a living and because a bounty was paid for the pelts. This rancher has had a successful wolf hunt, and these wolves will no longer feast upon his livestock. The car is very much a focus of the picture, but in the background, note that the old reliable covered wagon is still being used.

Three

Becoming a City

The Civil War may not have brought military battles to the streets of Burnet, but it caused much grief and hardship. Vigilantes hanged suspected Northern sympathizers. Native Americans took advantage of men being away and made more raids on homesteads. After the war, citizens who were known Confederate supporters were imprisoned. However, families migrating from the war-torn South brought Burnet new prosperity. During the 1870s, the courthouse square underwent a transformation from mostly frame to limestone buildings. Fine new homes were built. Burnet began to look like a small city. In 1876, the citizens voted to incorporate, but papers were not completed. Another vote in 1883 was acted upon, and the city was officially incorporated. The first mayor was W. A. Cates. Aldermen elected were Robert Alexander, Jeff Breaseale, C. T. Dalton, T. H. Holloway, and M. J. McSween. J. T. Woodward was elected city marshal. When the United States entered the First World War, Burnet County saw 506 of its young men go off to fight. The *Burnet Bulletin* published their names on August 24, 1939.

The railroad to Burnet transported goods from Austin and beyond. Likewise, it was possible to ship anything made or grown in the Burnet area to markets in the Northeast. Burnet benefited as the center for this trade. A telephone company and an electric plant further enhanced everyday life. Slowly horses were replaced by cars and trucks. Mule-drawn farm machinery gave way to tractors and mechanized equipment. New roads were built, so it was easier for farmers and ranchers to get their products to town. Dams were built on the Colorado River, and electricity became available in rural areas. The city steadily progressed even though the Depression saw some businesses and at least one bank close their doors. A volunteer fire department was organized in 1932, and a municipal water works was put into service sometime in 1933. By 1936, Burnet had begun to pave its streets and was clearly on its way into the future.

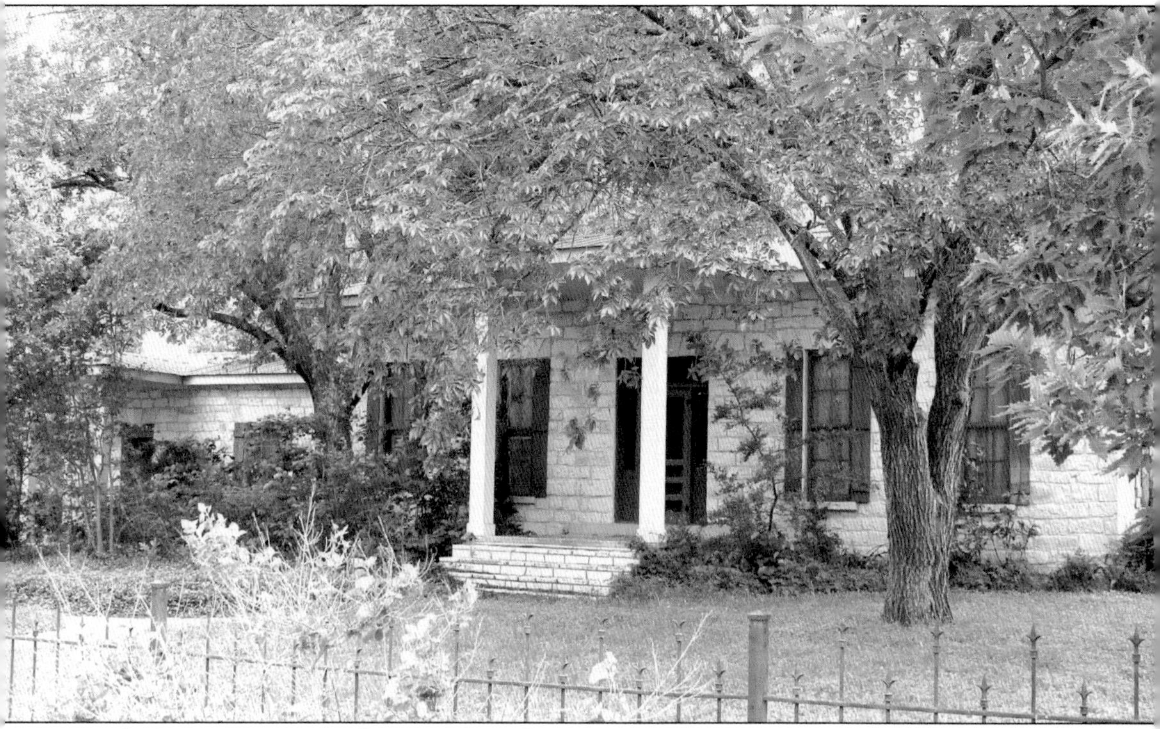

The house at 402 East Johnson Street is known as the Peter Kerr House. Kerr brought the news of Goliad to Sam Houston at Burnam's Crossing and later served as official interpreter between the Texas Army and the Mexicans. Kerr was a cattle and land merchant who came to Burnet about 1851, having purchased the John Hamilton Survey from Hamilton. This house was located within the survey, as was Fort Croghan. The original house is now the back left portion of the building, and Kerr lived there until his death. Kerr's nephew, W. S. Carothers, who settled the affairs of his uncle, sold the house to Marchall C. Oatman on April 3, 1873. Oatman added the front section of the house. Kerr donated 10 acres of land for the courthouse square, thus securing Burnet as the county seat. He left land and an endowment in his will for building a college. His family broke the will, leaving the city only 2 acres for a school site. Kerr is buried in the Old Burnet Cemetery where a Burnet County Historical Commission memorial marks his grave. (Photograph courtesy of Guy Goble.)

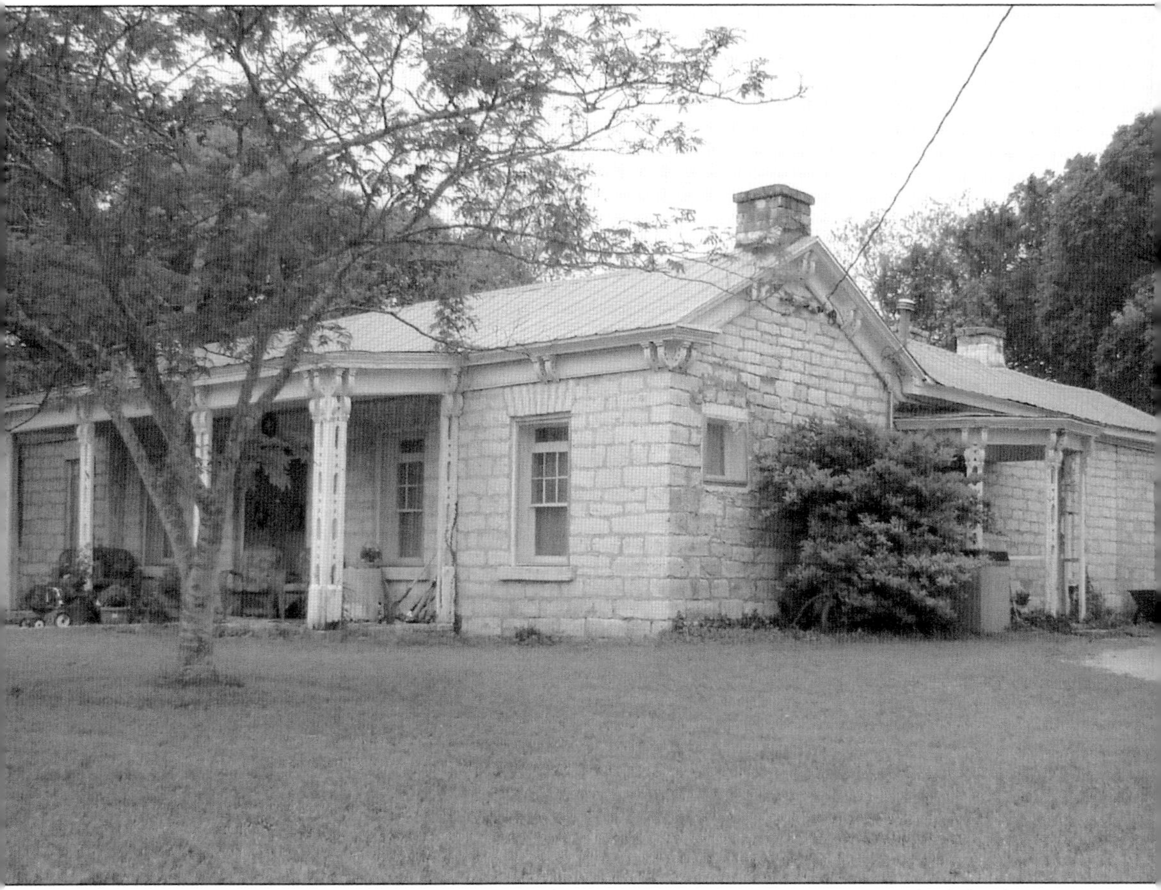

George Whitaker built this house at 804 South Main Street in 1872. It consisted of the front three rooms. Near the back door and on the porch was a cistern for collecting water. The rock was quarried locally and hand cut, as were the large cedar logs for the roof structure. According to a thesis titled "A History of Burnet County Newspapers and Newspapermen" written by Sara Lacy Anderson, Whitaker purchased the *Burnet County Exponent* from T. A. Stone and renamed it the *Burnet Bulletin*. The first *Bulletin* was published on January 26, 1873. Dr. George Scott Allen purchased the property in 1939 and built a two-story addition to the house. Rock from the razed courthouse was used, and care was taken to match the historic architecture of the original home. The cistern was enclosed within the addition. Perry Goble is the present owner of this historic home. (Photograph courtesy of Guy Goble.)

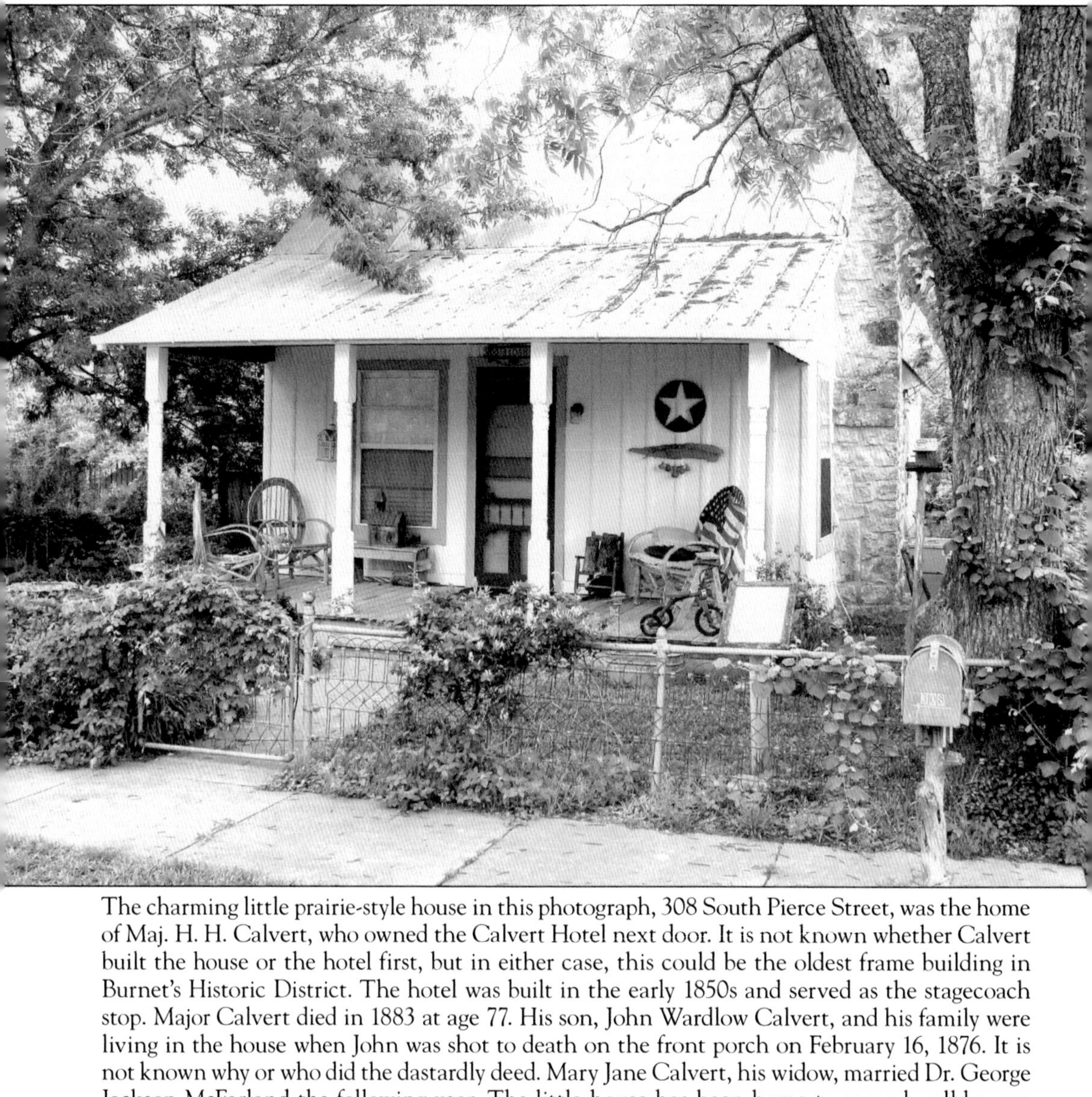

The charming little prairie-style house in this photograph, 308 South Pierce Street, was the home of Maj. H. H. Calvert, who owned the Calvert Hotel next door. It is not known whether Calvert built the house or the hotel first, but in either case, this could be the oldest frame building in Burnet's Historic District. The hotel was built in the early 1850s and served as the stagecoach stop. Major Calvert died in 1883 at age 77. His son, John Wardlow Calvert, and his family were living in the house when John was shot to death on the front porch on February 16, 1876. It is not known why or who did the dastardly deed. Mary Jane Calvert, his widow, married Dr. George Jackson McFarland the following year. The little house has been home to several well-known citizens through the years, including the Foulds and Stanberry families. For a time, it was a popular bed-and-breakfast but is now privately owned. (Photograph courtesy of Guy Goble.)

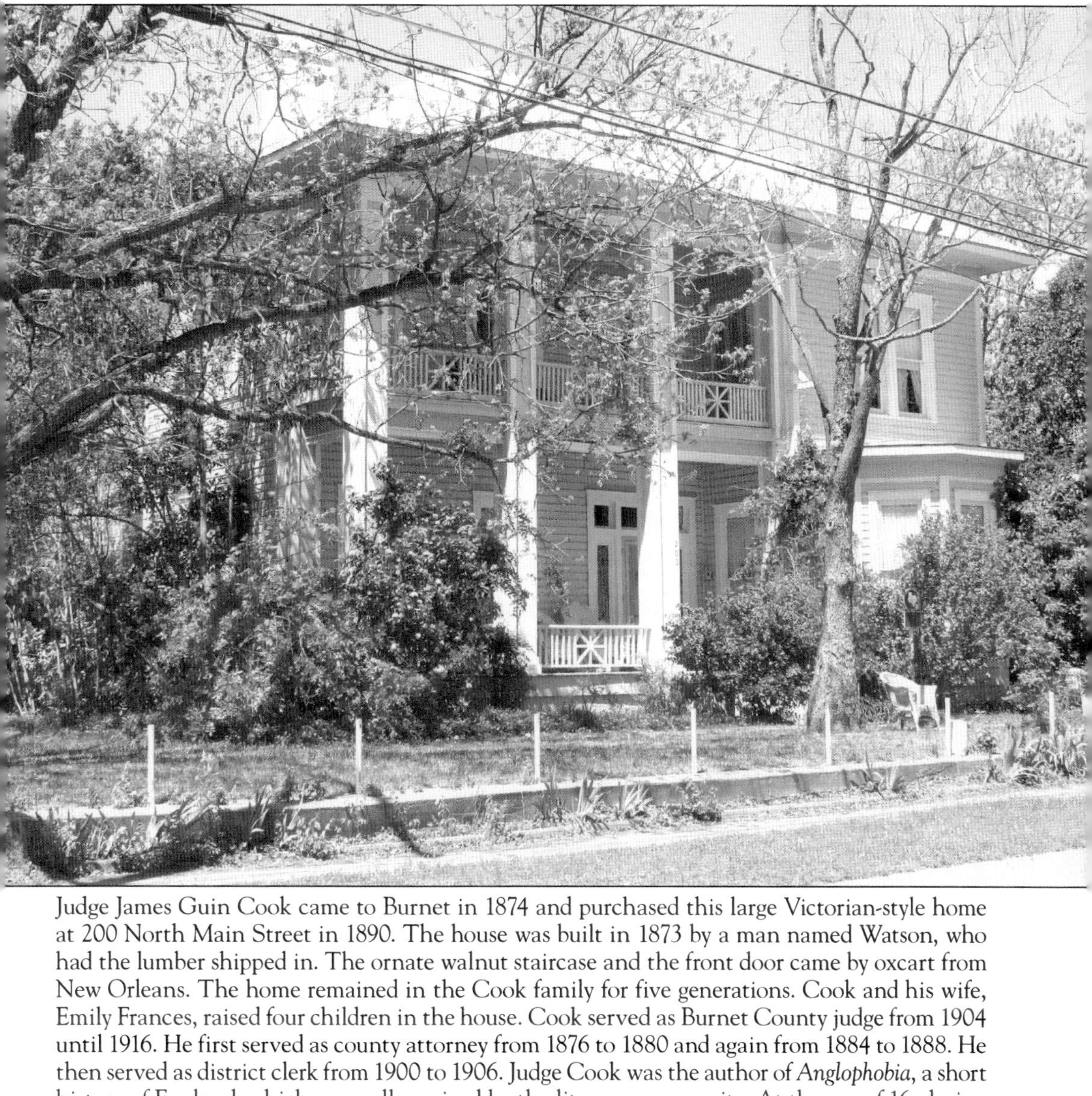

Judge James Guin Cook came to Burnet in 1874 and purchased this large Victorian-style home at 200 North Main Street in 1890. The house was built in 1873 by a man named Watson, who had the lumber shipped in. The ornate walnut staircase and the front door came by oxcart from New Orleans. The home remained in the Cook family for five generations. Cook and his wife, Emily Frances, raised four children in the house. Cook served as Burnet County judge from 1904 until 1916. He first served as county attorney from 1876 to 1880 and again from 1884 to 1888. He then served as district clerk from 1900 to 1906. Judge Cook was the author of *Anglophobia*, a short history of England, which was well received by the literary community. At the age of 16, during the Civil War, Cook served with Company D, 2nd Texas Cavalry. He was a member of the First United Methodist Church and was also active in the Masonic Lodge. Judge Cook passed away on October 21, 1920, at the age of 75. (Photograph courtesy of Guy Goble.)

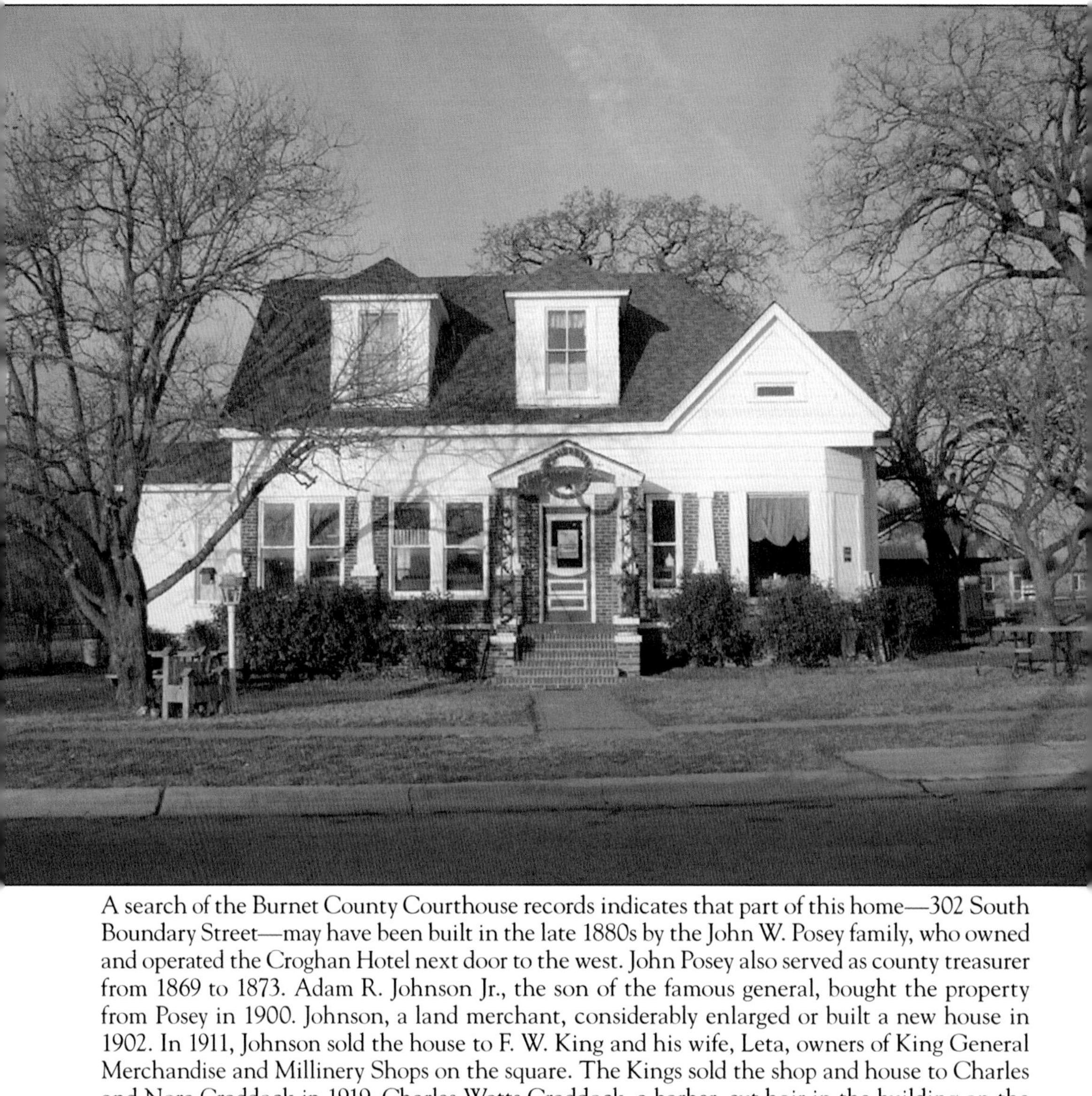

A search of the Burnet County Courthouse records indicates that part of this home—302 South Boundary Street—may have been built in the late 1880s by the John W. Posey family, who owned and operated the Croghan Hotel next door to the west. John Posey also served as county treasurer from 1869 to 1873. Adam R. Johnson Jr., the son of the famous general, bought the property from Posey in 1900. Johnson, a land merchant, considerably enlarged or built a new house in 1902. In 1911, Johnson sold the house to F. W. King and his wife, Leta, owners of King General Merchandise and Millinery Shops on the square. The Kings sold the shop and house to Charles and Nora Craddock in 1919. Charles Watts Craddock, a barber, cut hair in the building on the square while Nora ran the millinery shop. They both attended chiropractor school in Austin and opened their practice in this house, where they also lived. The Craddocks bricked in the front porch and added the brick bay window, working and living in the house the rest of their lives. (Photograph courtesy of Guy Goble.)

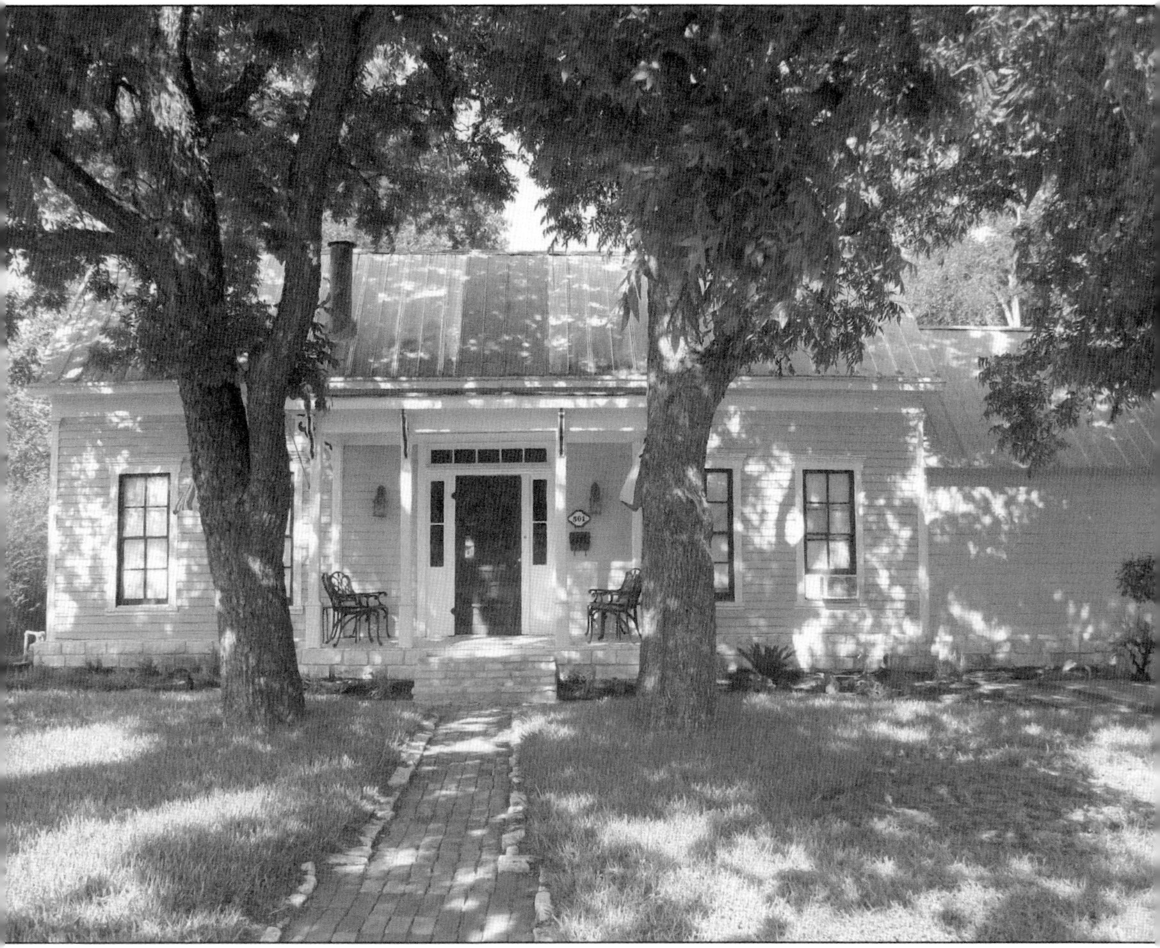

The list of owners of this property at 501 South Main Street reads like a who's who of prominent Burnet citizens. It became known as the LaForge house because William LaForge lived there the longest time. Logan Vandeveer owned the land, selling in 1852 to John Lauraine, who built the first part of the house. Lauraine lost the property in a sheriff's deed in 1854. E. J. Samson bought it in 1855 and sold it in 1877 to Judge James G. Cook. Cook took out a mortgage and built a sizeable addition, possibly bringing the house to its present appearance. Cook sold the house to Dr. Marcus Field in 1902. Dr. Field then sold it in 1903 to his daughter, Mary, and her husband, W. W. Taylor. LaForge bought it in 1926 and lived here for over 45 years. William LaForge owned and operated a hardware store on the square. B. J. Goble bought the house in 1974, and it has been in the Goble family for 35 years. Crista Goble Bromley and her husband, Glenn, currently own and live in the house. (Photograph courtesy of Crista Bromley.)

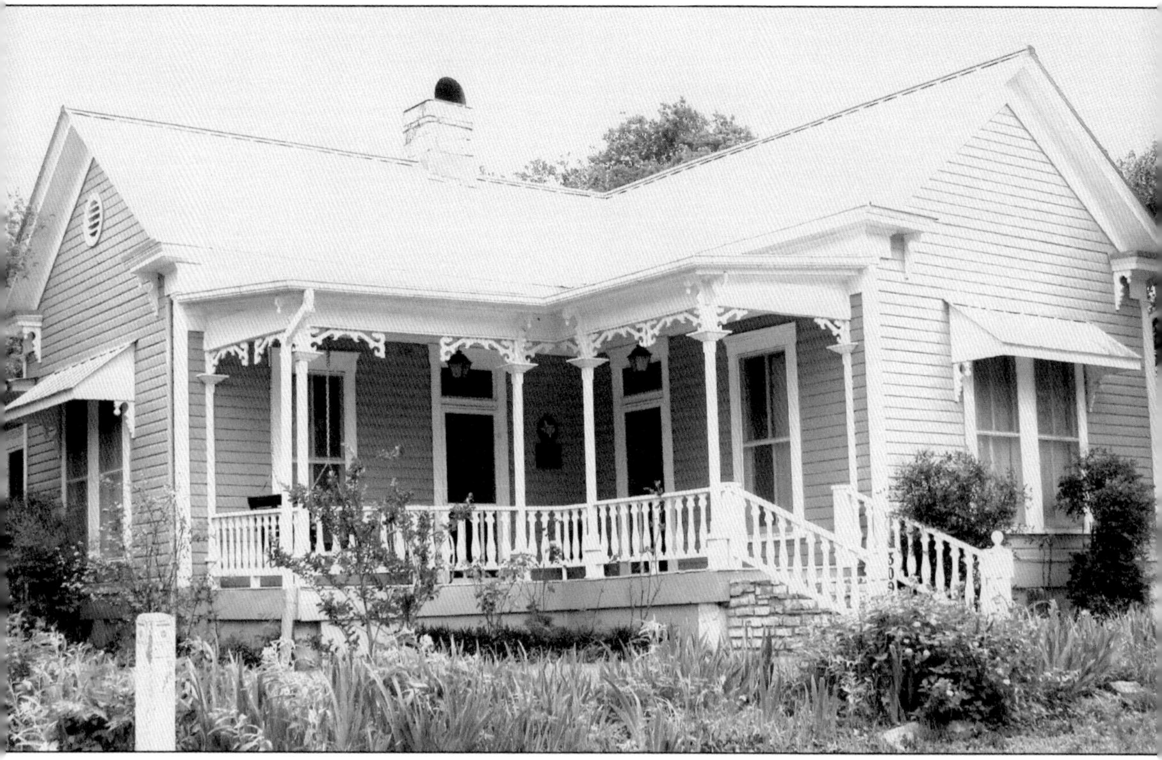

The house in this photograph, 603 North Boundary, is known as the Russell-McFarland Homestead. Prof. William H. Russell and his wife, Mary, built the house in 1883–1884. William, a veteran of the Civil War, was hired in 1882 by the trustees as teacher and superintendent of a private school in Burnet. He held this position until 1887. In 1885, the city council bought the school from the trustees and made it a public school, so Russell became Burnet's first public school principal. Russell sold this house in 1895, and for 27 years the house had tenants. Among them were J. W. Edgar, who became the state commissioner of education, and J. H. Gilbert, one of the first Texas game wardens. Samuel A. McFarland and his wife, Pearl, bought the house in 1922, and it remained in the family for more than 50 years.

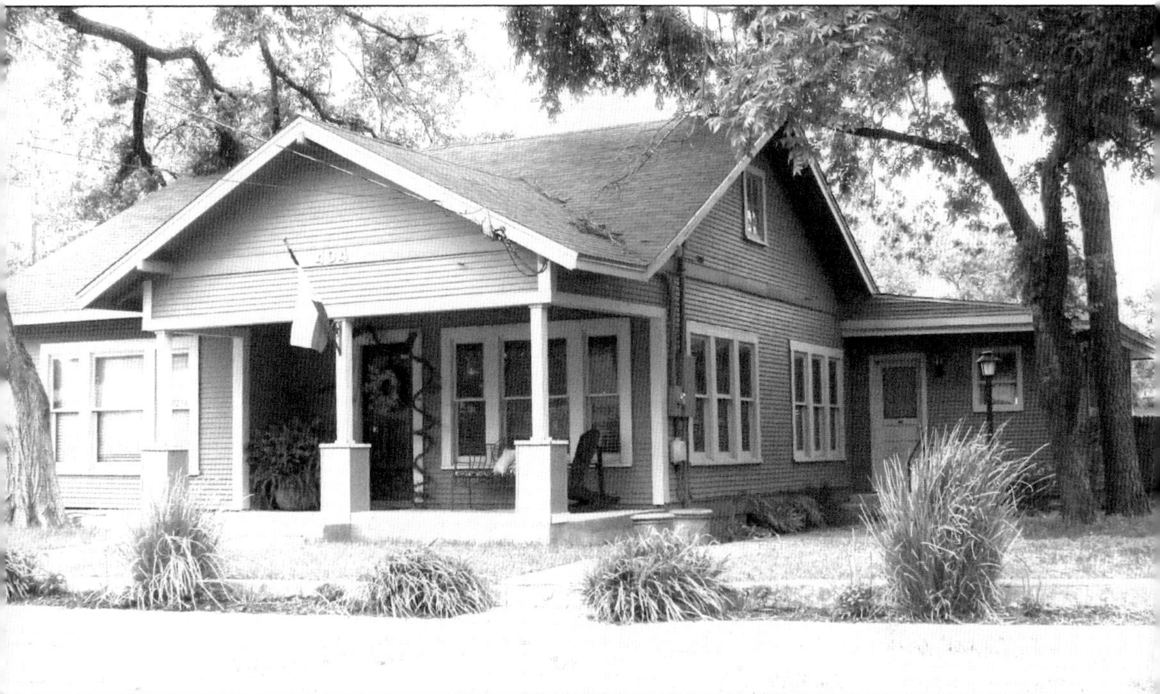

The house in this photograph, 404 South Main Street, was the home of the John Tate Chamberlain family. John T. Chamberlain (1845–1919) was elected Burnet County clerk in 1898 and served until 1906. His son, James Hardee, followed him as county clerk. Another son, Louis Coleman, owned and published the *Burnet Bulletin* newspaper for almost 50 years. John's original house was located behind this one in what became U.S. Highway 281. That house was moved to this site when the highway right-of-way was granted. Unfortunately, the house burned, and the one seen here was erected in its place. John's daughter, Sarah Frances "Fan" Chamberlain (1882–1980), was the last member of the family to live in the house. It was sold after her death. "Miss Fan," as she was affectionately called, worked at Blankenship's Variety Store and had many faithful friends. (Photograph courtesy of Guy Goble.)

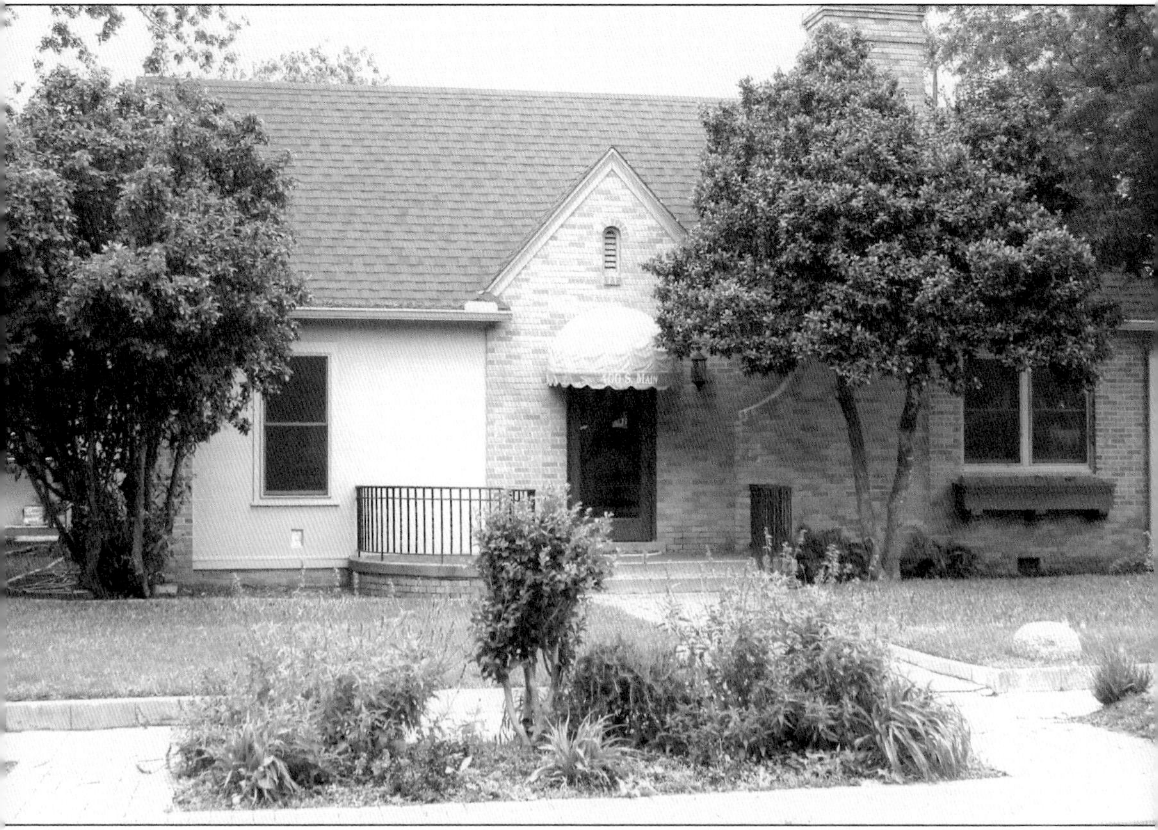

Sheriff Christian Dorbandt (1857–1945) made this 400 South Main Street house his home when he became a Burnet city marshal. He and his wife, Anna, lived here the rest of their lives. The house sat vacant for many years before the law firm of Mock and Brown renovated it for their offices. The Dorbandts also owned a ranch, which was partly flooded by the building of Lake Buchanan, necessitating the moving of their ranch house to higher ground. The ranch ownership remains in the family. The Dorbandt descendants are still active in the many civic activities of Burnet. (Photograph courtesy of Guy Goble.)

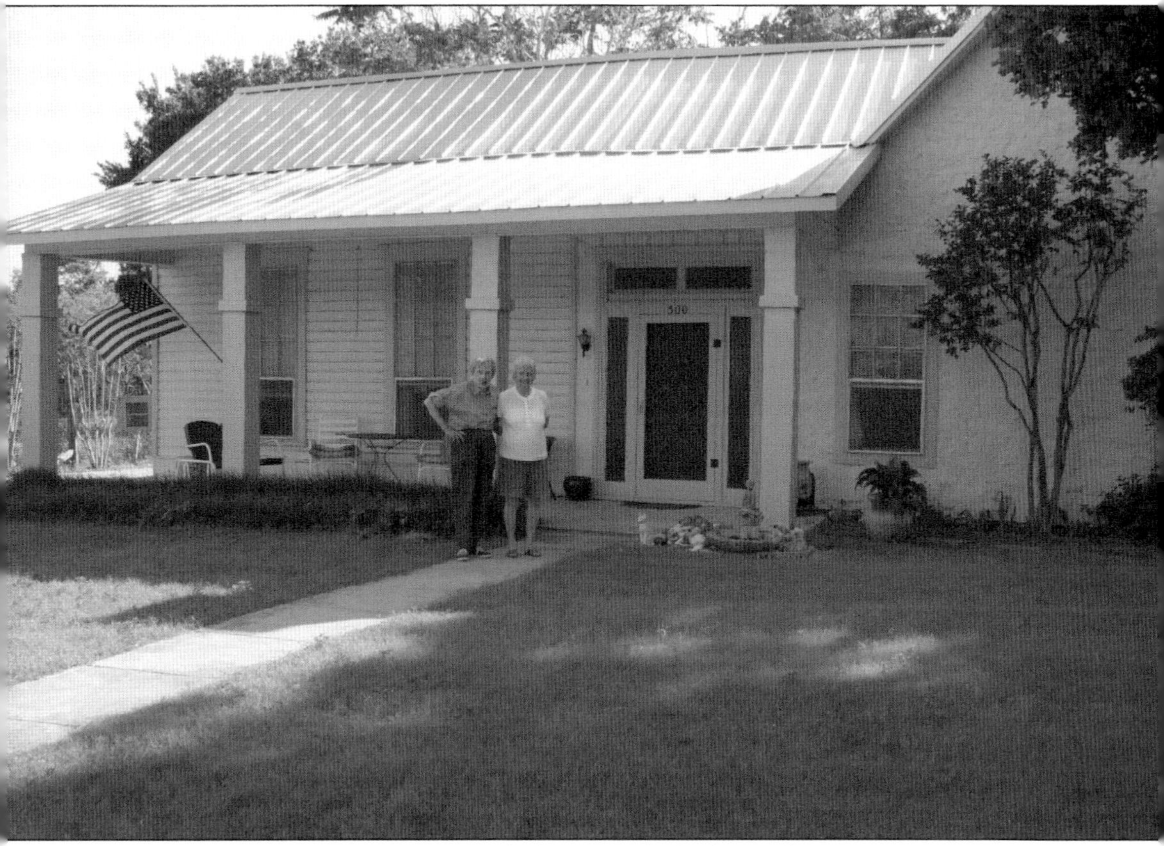

Known as the Blackburn house, this was the homestead of Judge William A. Blackburn at 500 Blackburn Lane. Blackburn (1834–1908) was a lawyer who road horseback from Tennessee to Burnet in 1863. Blackburn taught at a private school the first few months after he arrived. He then opened a law office, eventually forming partnerships with D. C. Barmore, Sidney Posey, and J. G. Cook. Blackburn was elected district court judge in 1876 and held that position until he retired in 1896. Judge Blackburn organized the first courts in many of the 17th District counties that he served. He rode alone on horseback through dangerous territory to carry out his duties. Blackburn and his wife, Sara Adilaide, had four children. Since none of the siblings had children, there are no living descendants. The house is now the home of Jo Foulds and Mary Ann Stubbs. (Photograph courtesy of Kina Cockroft.)

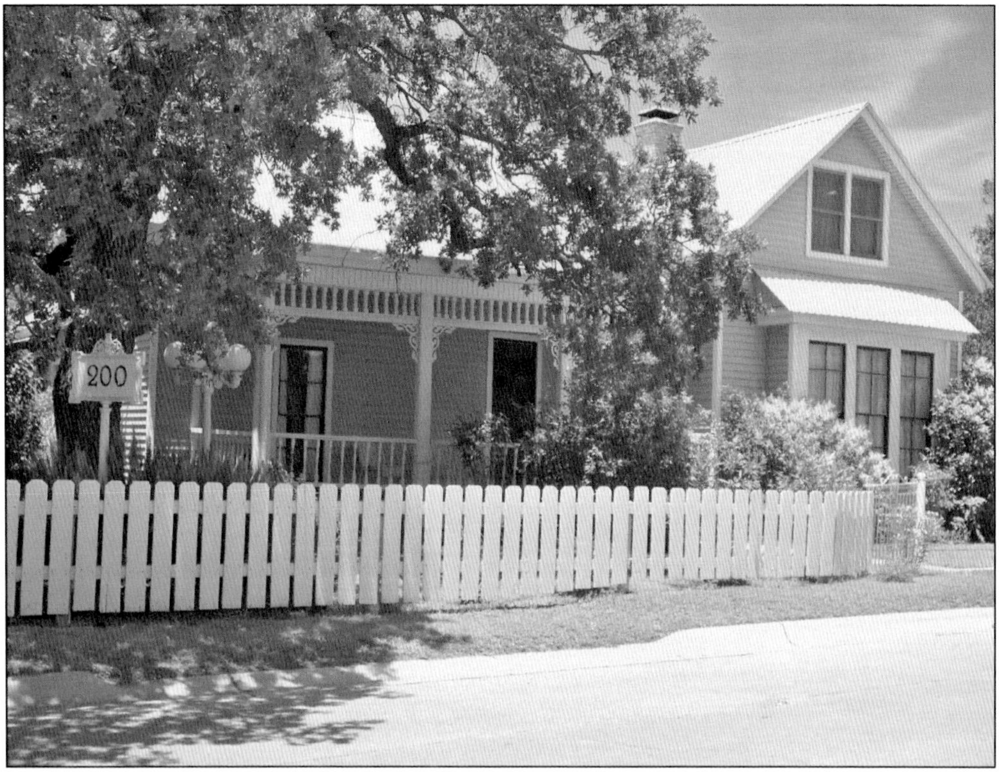

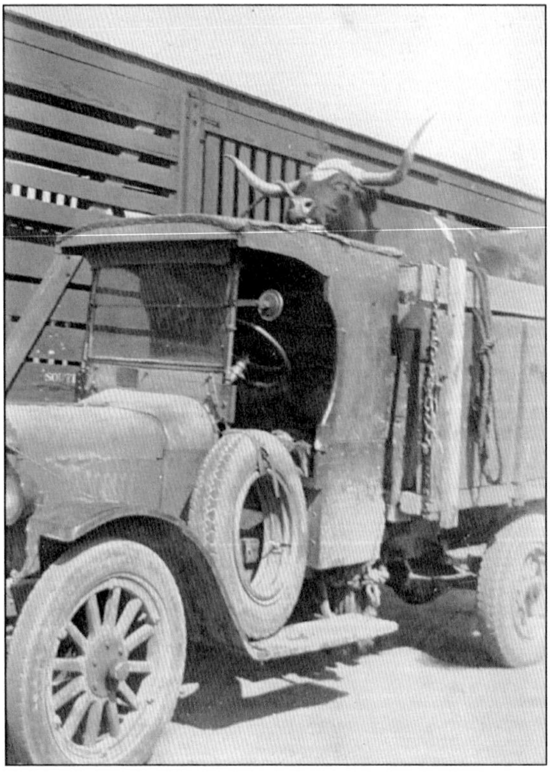

This house, 200 East Johnson Street, first belonged to Scott Edmond but is known as the Dayton Moses house. Moses (1870–1943) was a renowned lawyer who served as Burnet County attorney from 1896 through 1902. He was the attorney for the Texas and Southwestern Cattle Raisers Association for many years. Dr. George McMahan used the house as a hospital in 1935 or 1936. During the 1940s, it was a boardinghouse evolving into an apartment house until Mike and Marilee Albers bought and restored it. It is now the home of the Tiday family. In the photograph at left is one of the reasons the train's arrival was anxiously anticipated. This steer was one of many being shipped to market on the train, Burnet's highway to the world.

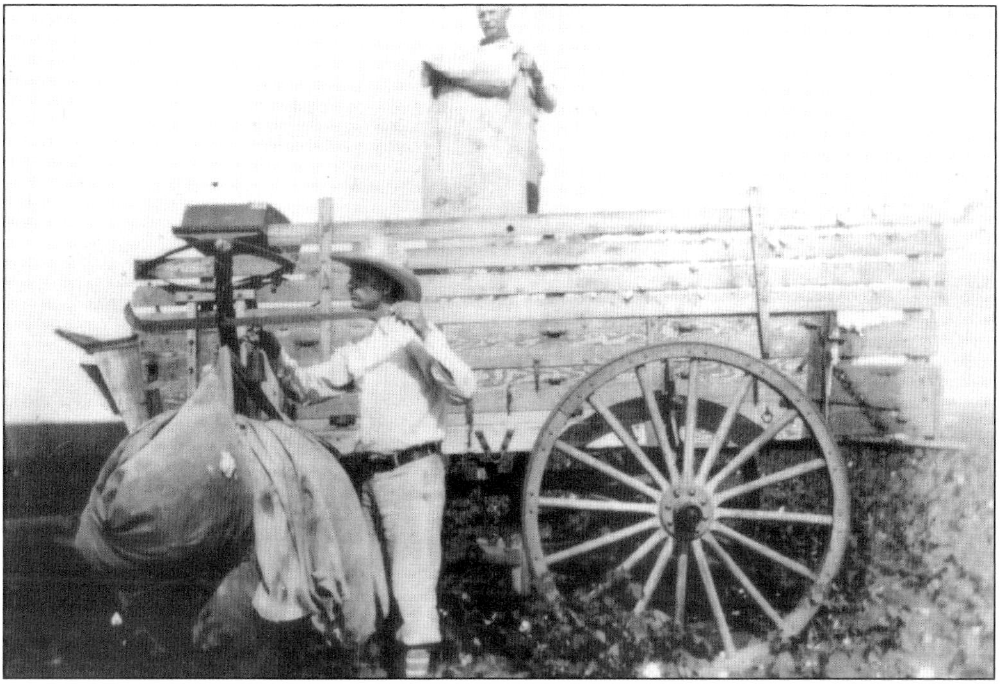

At one time, Burnet had several cotton gins, including the T. W. Gibbs gin on Hamilton Creek. Farmers would line up their wagonloads of cotton to be processed. The real work, however, was in the fields. Here Charles Normann weighs his sack and Ed Harris empties his into the wagon. Wages were paid by the total pounds a worker picked in a day. It was sweaty, hard work.

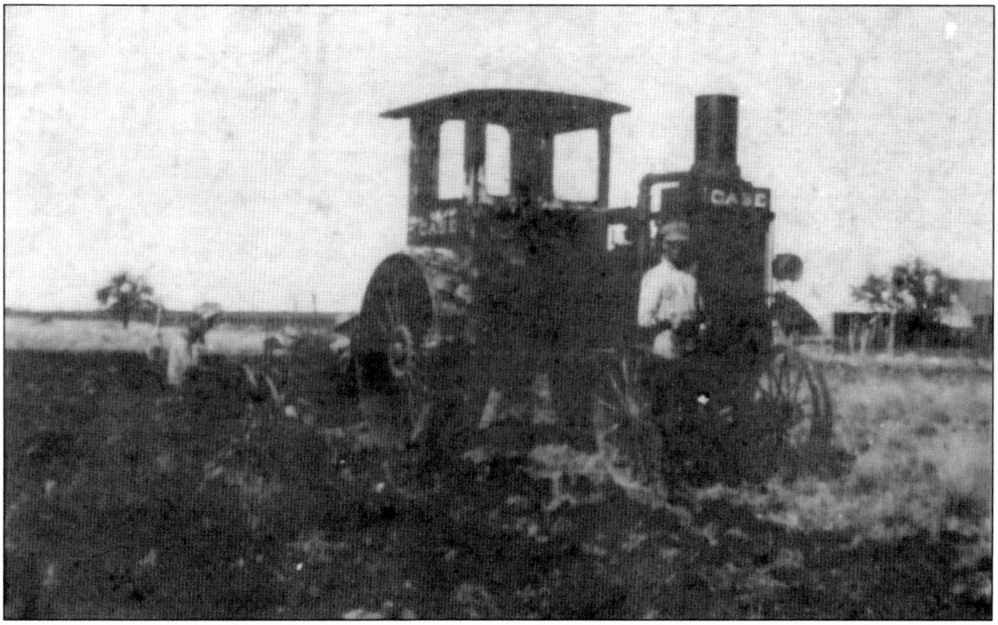

John Ater is shown here in 1907 with his tractor and plow. The man at the plow is Sam Taylor. Farmers upgraded to tractors as soon as they could afford it, but there were not many around Burnet at this time. The fortunate owners often paid for their tractors by charging a fee to work their neighbors' fields. (Photograph courtesy of HBFL.)

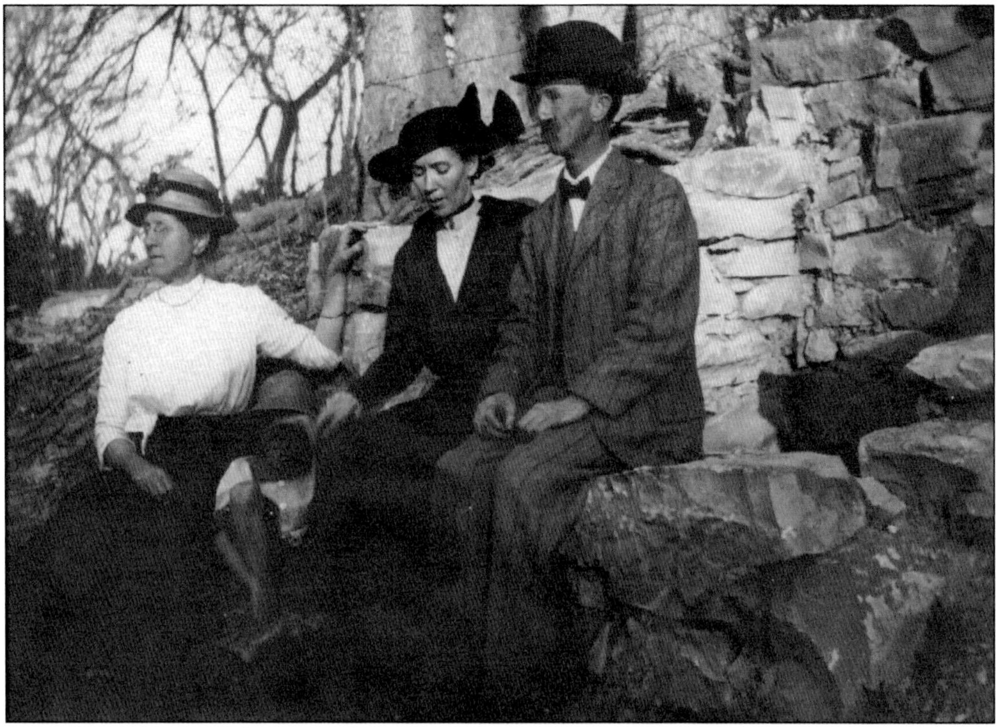

The neatly attired gentleman on the right is Judge William A. Blackburn, whose home is on page 73. The judge was known for his astute knowledge of the law and his ability to convey its meaning in layman's terms to jury members and others involved in his cases. Blackburn practiced law in Burnet until 1901, when his eyesight began to fail. (Photograph courtesy of Bill Foulds.)

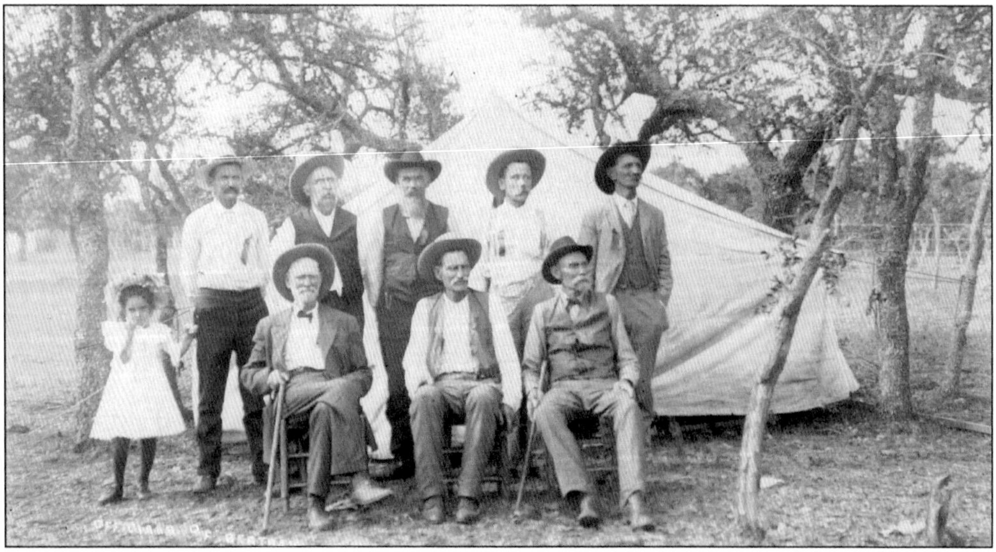

The Burnet County Fair was held at the fairgrounds in Bertram beginning in 1903 annually until the late 1930s. Here are the fair directors on August 16, 1907. From left to right are (first row) J. H. Ellett, Ben H. Stewart, and Hill DeWolf; (second row) John Oliver with his daughter, John Bryson, Terrell Hutto, George White, and Henry Reynolds. (Photograph courtesy of Marcie Masterson.)

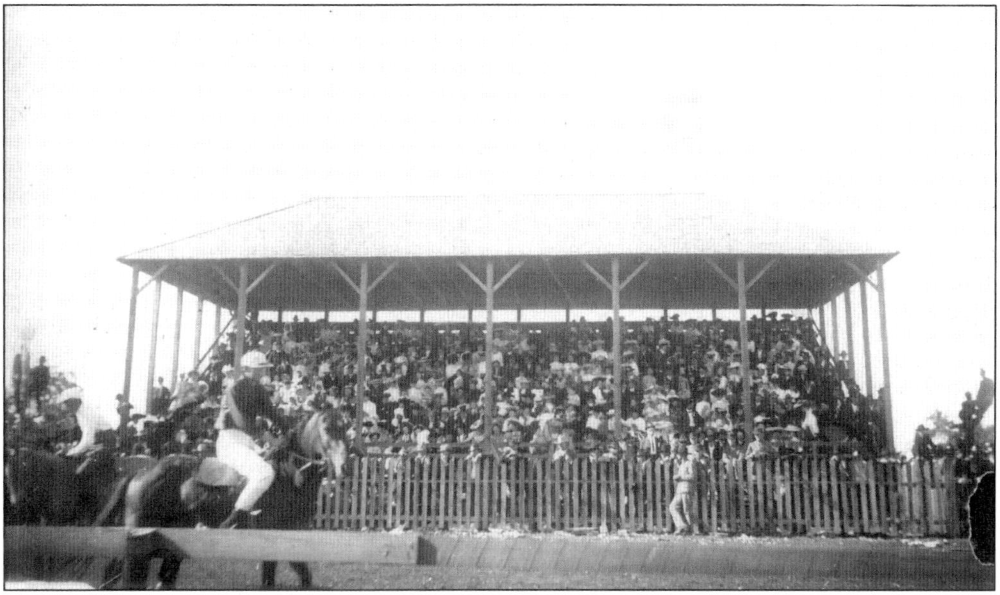

The horse races were the most popular activity at the fair. There were 24 stalls for the main race. There were also cart and trotter races. By 1928, attendance was nearing 7,000 people for the three-day event. This photograph shows the grandstand during a race. The town band supplied music, and a dance was held in the evening. Every exhibit one would expect at a fair was there. (Photograph courtesy of HBFL.)

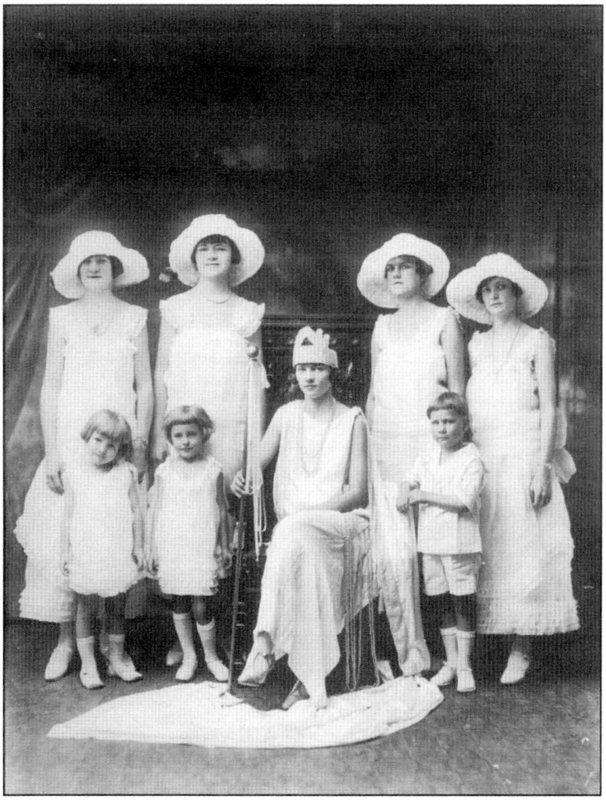

This photograph is labeled "Burnet County Fair Queen's Court, 1925." No names were listed but Dayton Reed Taylor, who was the boy on the right in the first row, was able to identify two of the lovely ladies. The queen was Katherine Bryson (seated), and Cleo Jennings is the young lady in a hat standing on the left. All dressed in white finery, they are an impressive group. (Photograph courtesy of Marilynn Goode and Marcie Masterson.)

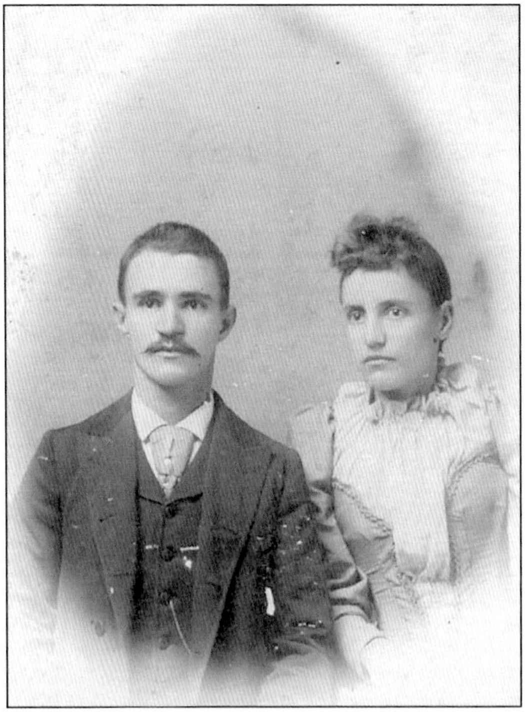

This attractive young couple was photographed on their wedding day. John A. Kinkead and Amanda "Mattie" Nichols were married on June 27, 1892. The Kinkeads became the parents of eight children, all born in Burnet. One was Mattie Ada, who married Earl Foulds. The youngest was Grace, who became the City of Burnet secretary. (Photograph courtesy of Bill Foulds.)

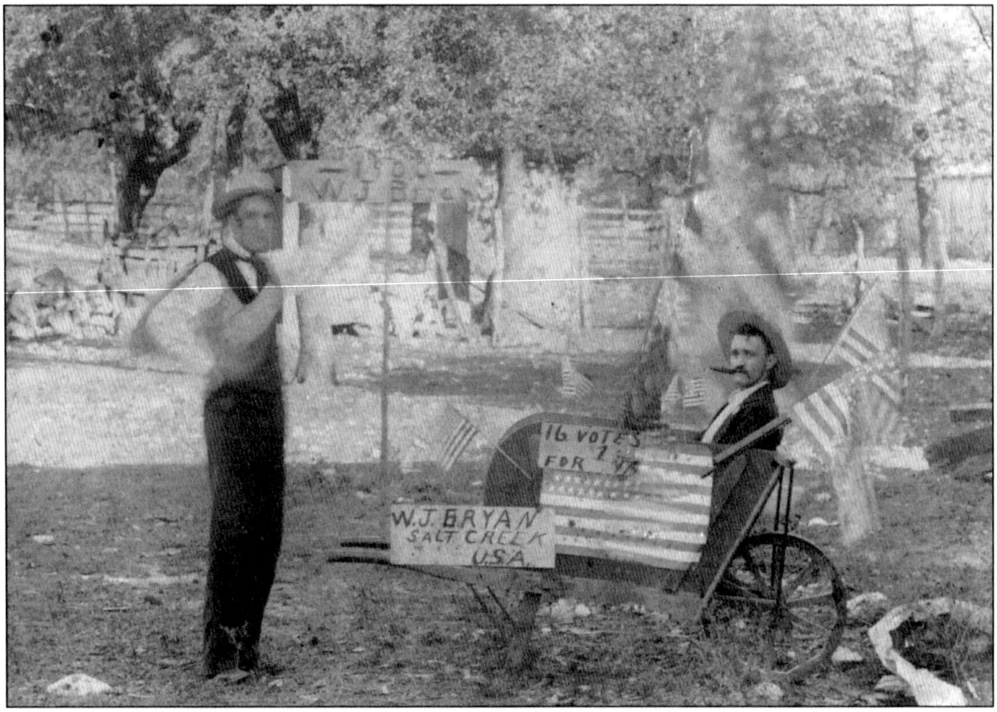

These two gentlemen are keeping a bet they made on the 1909 presidential election. The loser had to push the winner around the courthouse square in a wheelbarrow. William Howard Taft won the election, and John A. Kinkead won the bet. He is seated in the said conveyance waiting for the loser (left, unidentified) to make good on his word. (Photograph courtesy of Jo Foulds.)

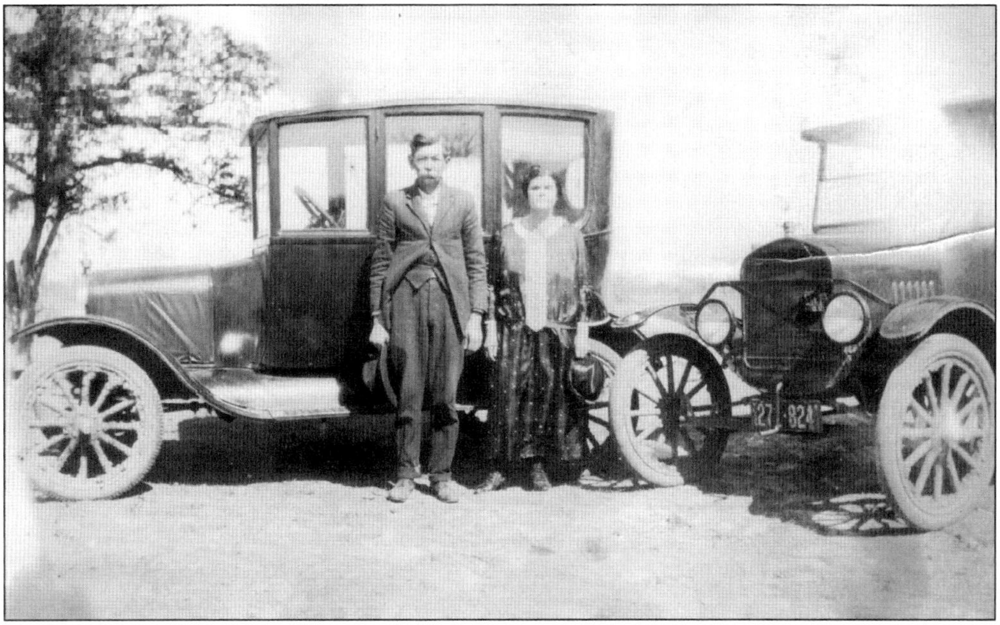

Dave and Lula Sivley are photographed with their new car. It was probably the most costly purchase they had ever made, and they were very proud.

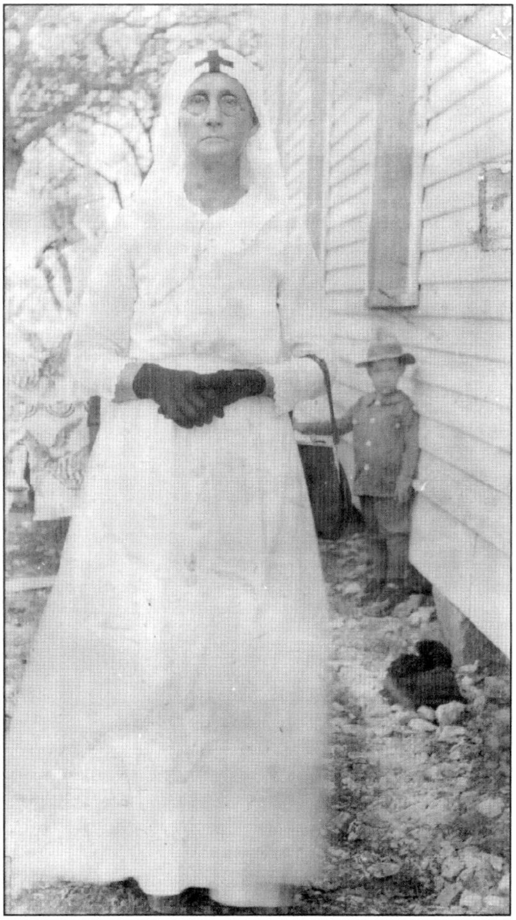

During the First World War, women all over the United States volunteered as Red Cross workers. They knitted socks, boiled cotton cloth and rolled it for bandages, and did anything else to help the war effort. This is Frances Hutto in her uniform. Note the young boy behind her, also in uniform.

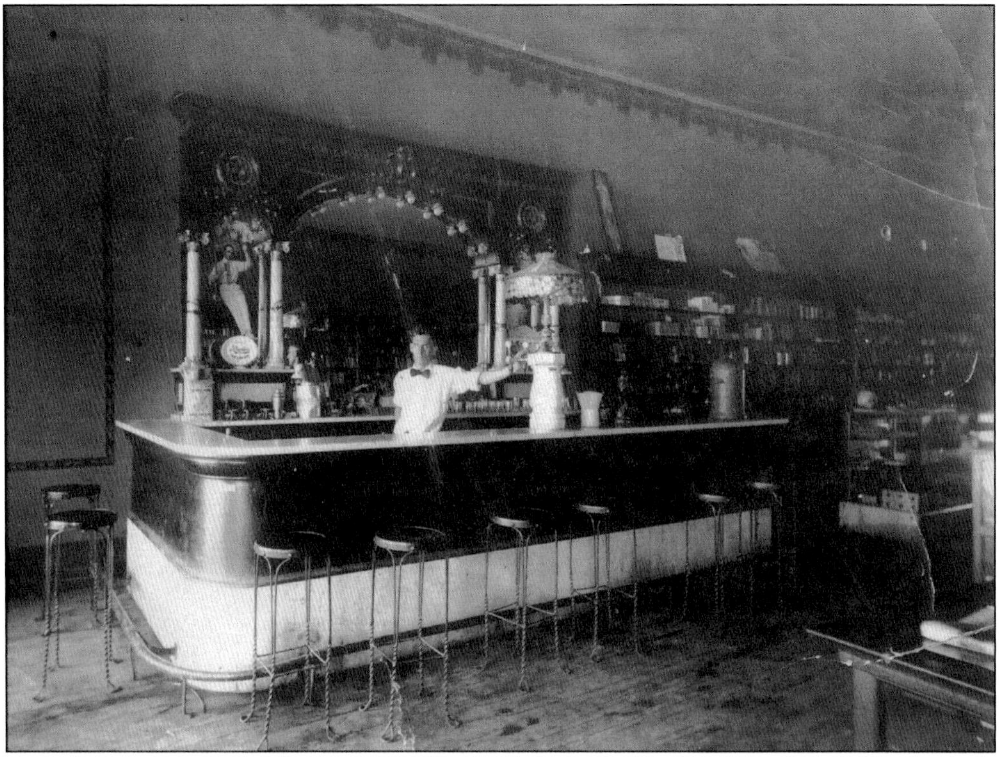

Here is the interior of the Guthrie Drug Store, which was located on the south side of the square. It was established by R. J. Knox in the late 1800s. Jim Guthrie bought it from Knox, years later selling to Raymond Kuykendall. Kuykendall operated it until his death in 1971. (Photograph courtesy of Bill Foulds.)

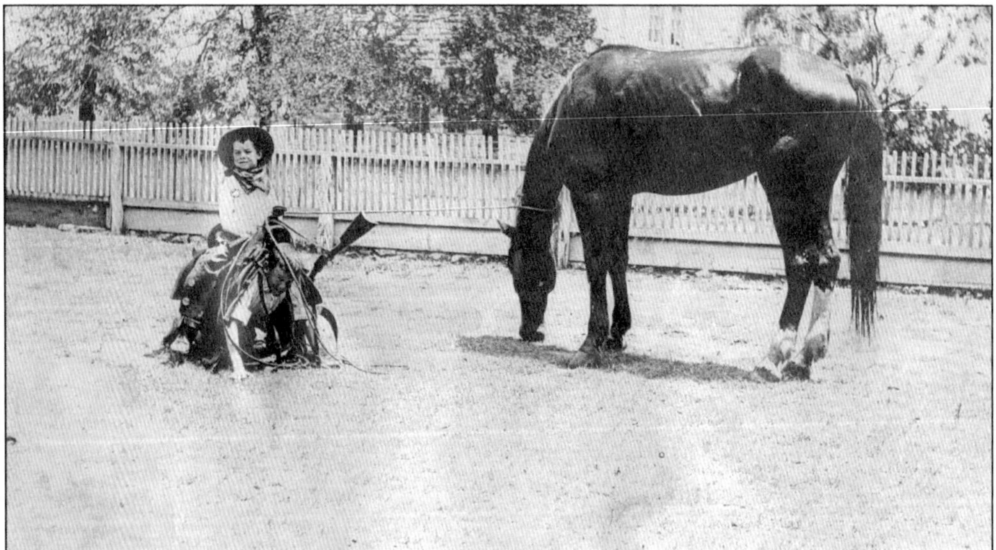

When one is too short to put the saddle on the horse, one must settle for a stationary ride. This photograph was taken on Main Street. The boy is unidentified. (Photograph courtesy of Milli Williams.)

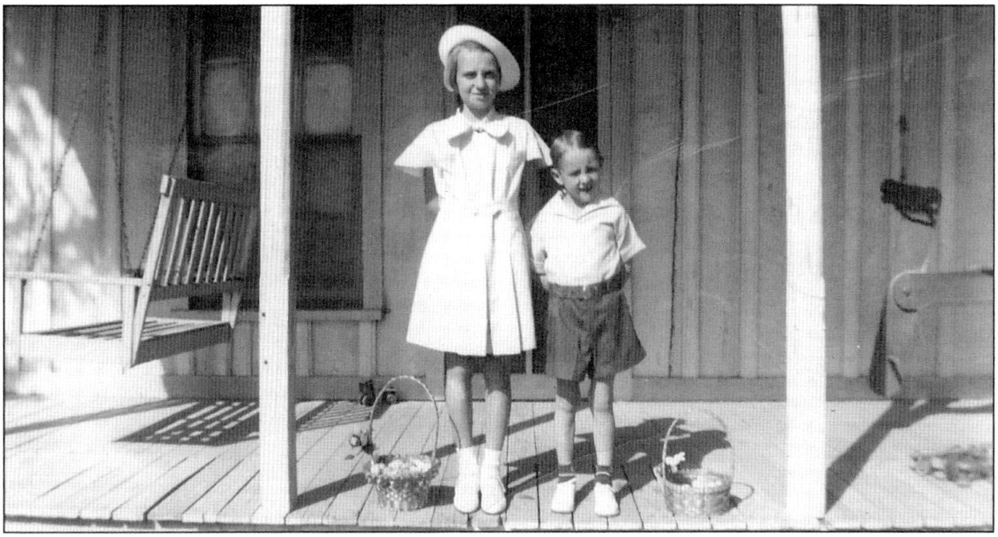

The Calvert house was home to Earl and Mattie Foulds for 13 years, and their two children were born there. This photograph was taken on Easter Sunday as can be seen from the baskets at the children's feet. The children are Martha Jo and Billy Earl. (This photograph courtesy of Bill Foulds.)

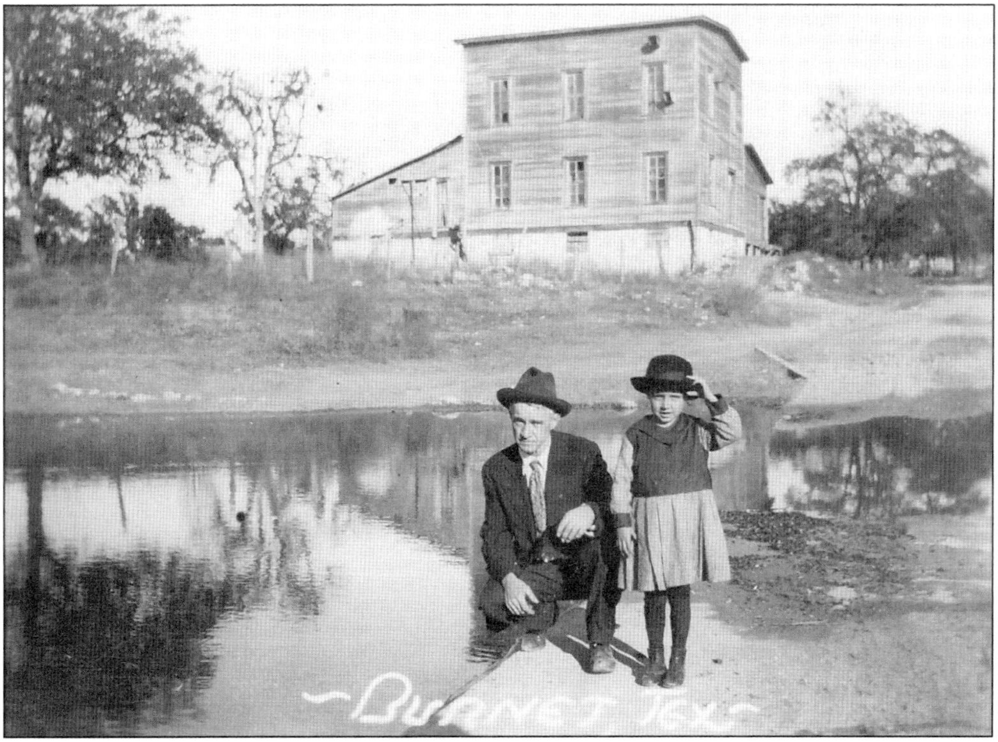

The Roller Flour Mill is in the background of this photograph. In the foreground are John Allen ("Al") Kinkead and his daughter Grace Elizabeth. Al Kinkead owned and operated a tin shop on South Main Street. Grace became the city secretary of Burnet, holding that position most of her working life. She loved the red poppies that annually covered her yard on U.S. 281 North. (Photograph courtesy of Bill Kinkead.)

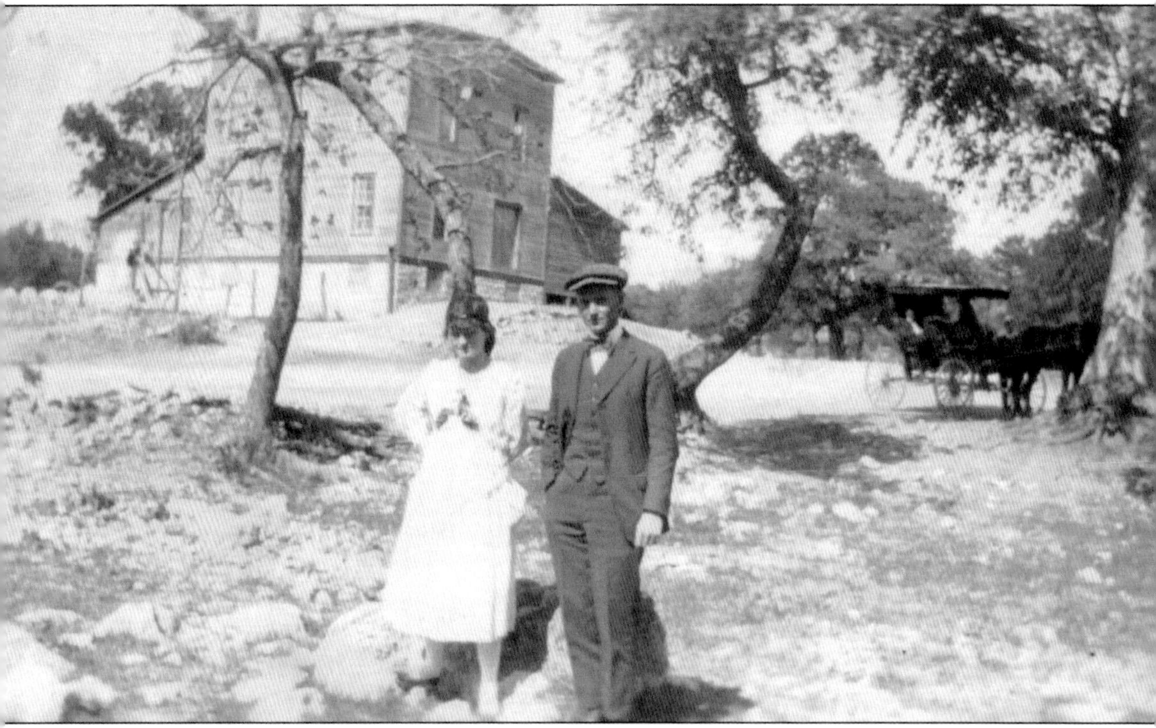

Minnie Peacock and her unidentified friend stand in front of the Roller Flour Mill on Hamilton Creek. The mill was owned and operated by John Smart. It was powered by steam generated by a large boiler and was considered a modern, efficient operation, using water from Hamilton Creek. It was located on the old Austin to Llano Road near the old stagecoach stop. This mill operated until early in 1920, when it was sold and razed. The boiler exploded in 1880, killing three people. John Smart, the owner, was at home sick, so his father was working in his place. The father, Bryce Smart; a worker, H. H. Hall; and Johnny Blackburn, the 13-year-old son of Judge Blackburn, were all killed. Johnny was running an errand for his mother and had momentarily stopped to watch the machinery. (Photograph courtesy of HBFL.)

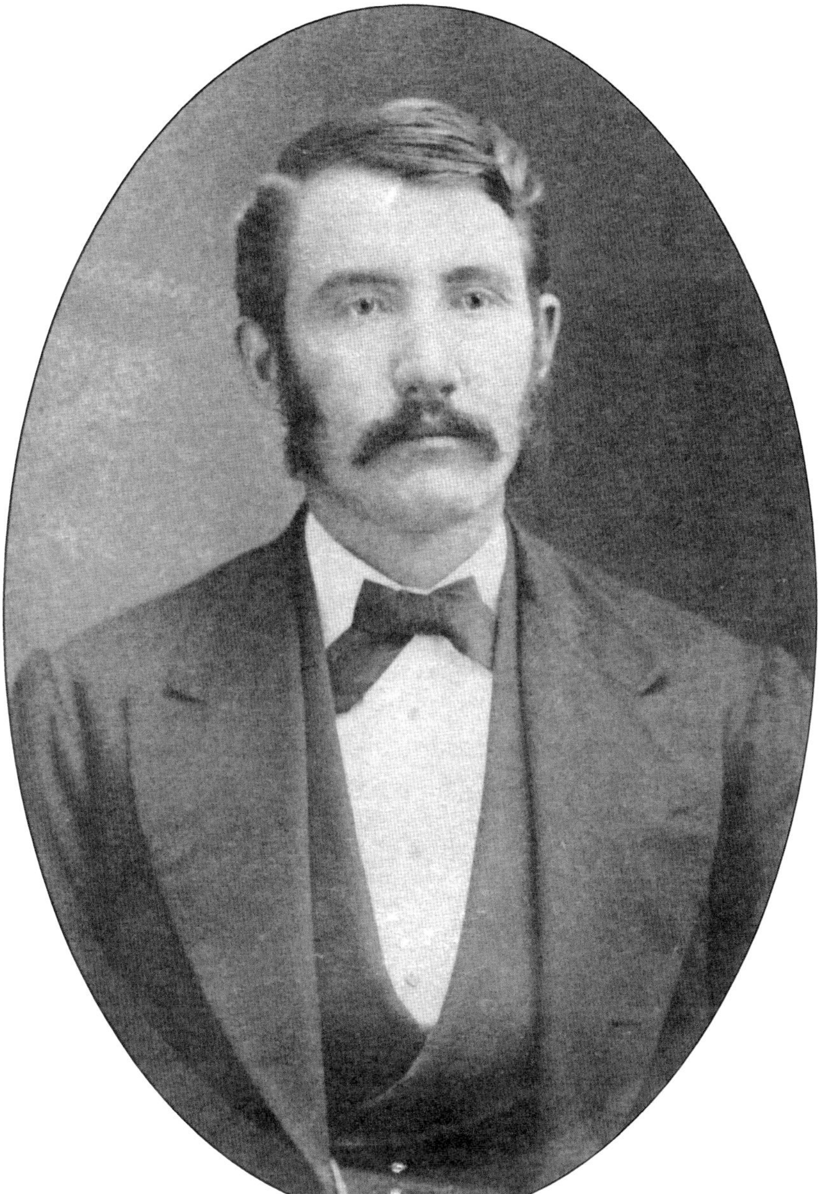

John White Smart (1838–1903), the owner of the Roller Flour Mill, came to Texas from Missouri with his parents about 1851. Smart joined the Burnet Christian Church in 1860 and was baptized in Soldiers Hole on Hamilton Creek. After operating a gristmill in Williamson County, he managed a tanyard for his father and partner, Tom Reddin. The tanyard made shoes for the Confederate army. More than a year later, Smart enlisted as a Confederate private and served until the war was over. He bought a drugstore in Florence, which he operated for several years, and later built a hotel in Lampasas. He ran a general merchandise store on the west side of the Burnet square either before or after operating the mill on Hamilton Creek. Smart held two patents. The first, Patent No. 478,720 dated July 12, 1892, was a device for cooling and preserving milk, butter, meats and vegetables. The second, Patent No. 513,657 dated January 30, 1894, was for "new and useful improvements in car-coupling devices." (Photograph courtesy of Sarah Douglas.)

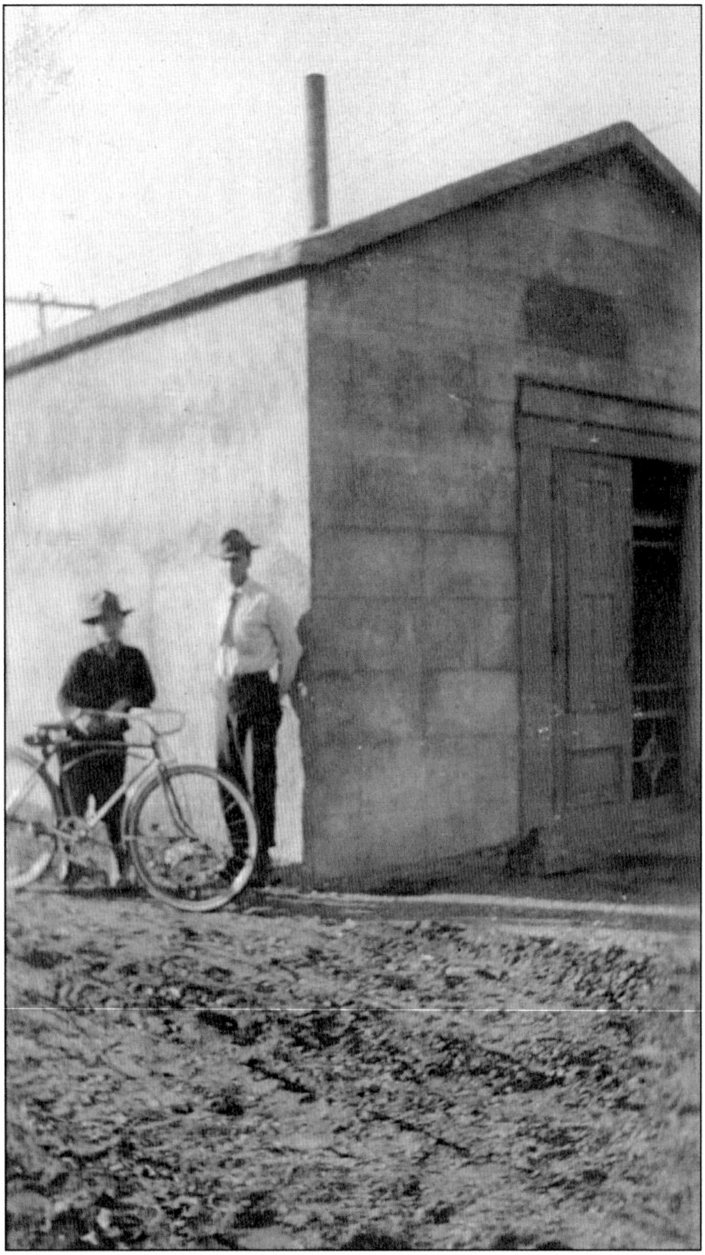

This small concrete building housed Burnet's first electric plant. On July 3, 1919, the city council granted W. C. Galloway a 50-year contract to provide the city with electric power. Galloway and Oscar Marek formed a partnership in which Galloway funded the project and Marek built and operated the plant. The company was named Burnet Power and Light. In order to build it, Marek borrowed an instruction book from Samuel McFarland. There were two dynamo engines, one to use and one for a backup. The plant provided power to each of four city districts in rotation. The entire city received power from sundown until 10:00 p.m. The city began buying additional power from Lone Star Power Company in 1926. In 1945, the city purchased a power distribution system from the Lower Colorado River Authority and the little plant was shut down. (Photograph courtesy of COB.)

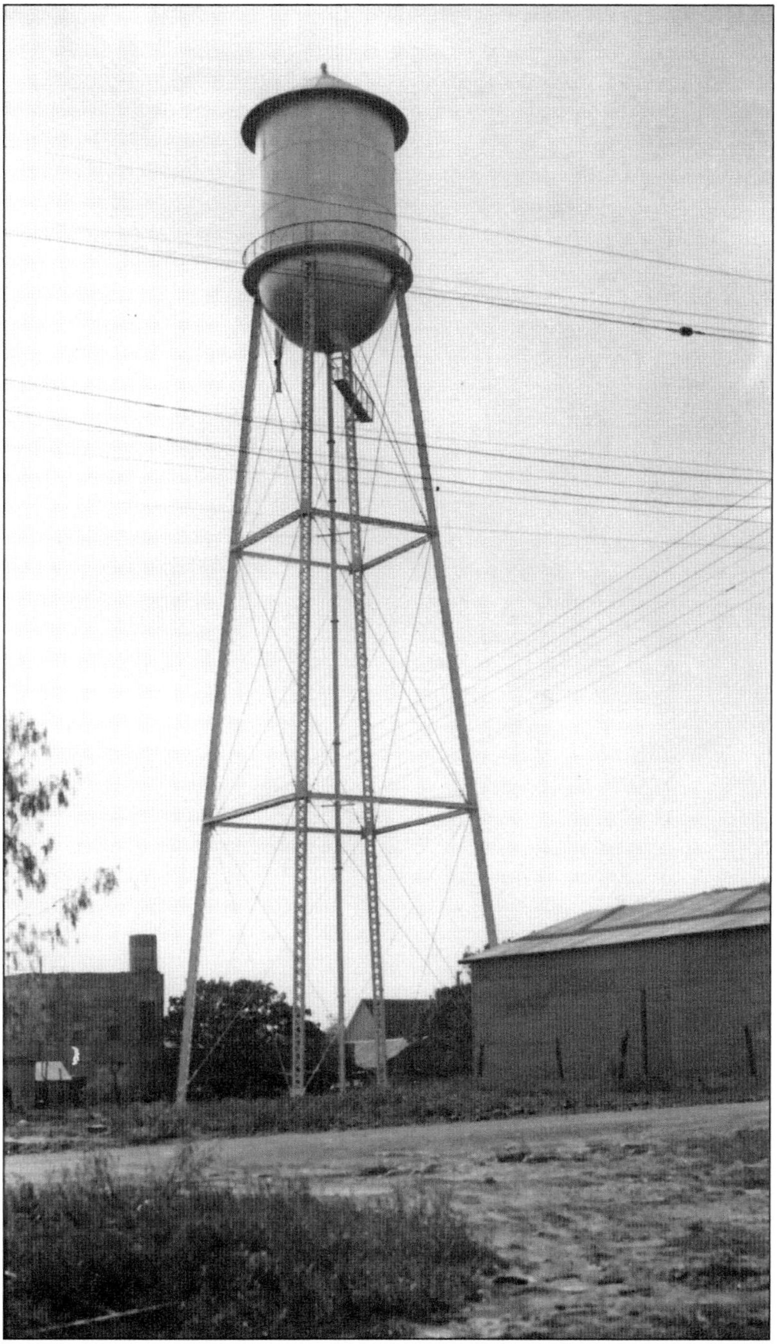

Here is a photograph of Burnet's first community water storage tank. Answering citizen demand, a grant for building a public distribution system was applied for and approved by the Public Works Administration in 1933. The City of Burnet voted $45,000 in bonds to be paid by charging for water. The city benefited, but the project also provided much-needed jobs. Seven wells were eventually drilled to meet the demand for water and were used exclusively until the city began pumping water from Inks Lake in 1987. The wells, though not currently used, are kept on line for emergency purposes. (Photograph courtesy of COB.)

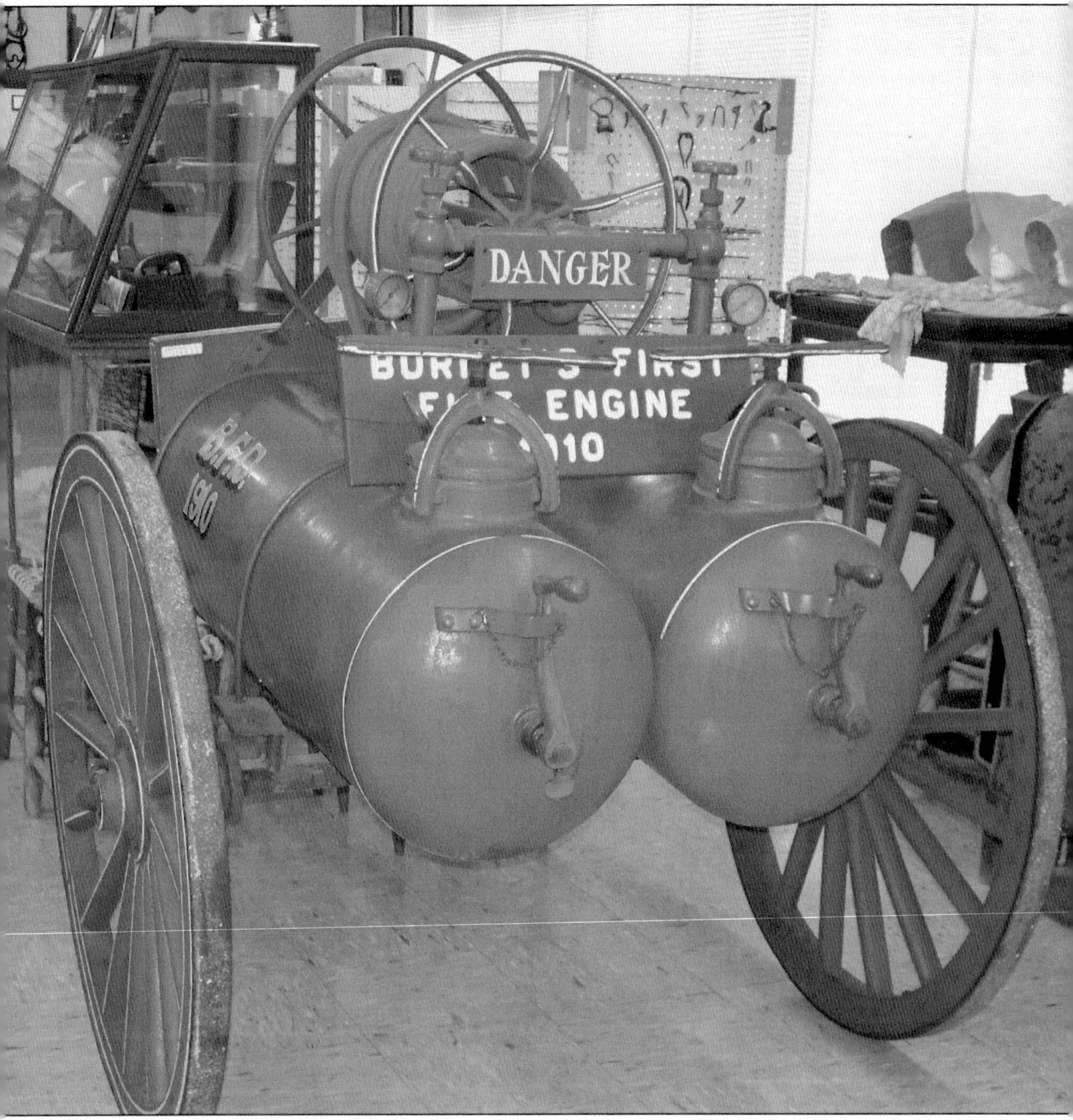

This small vehicle, acquired in 1910, is commonly called "Burnet's first fire engine." It is actually two chemical tanks with hoses mounted upon a buggy axle. Firefighters pulled it to the fire by hand. The citizens were proud of it. They are still proud of it, and it is on permanent display at Fort Croghan Museum. The first official volunteer fire department was organized January 27, 1932, with John Olney as president. When he passed away, Ross Johnson was elected in his place. Later Herman Schnabel was elected fire chief and held the office for 27 years. Burnet's first booster fire truck had a capacity of 380 gallons of water and could pump 55 gallons per minute.

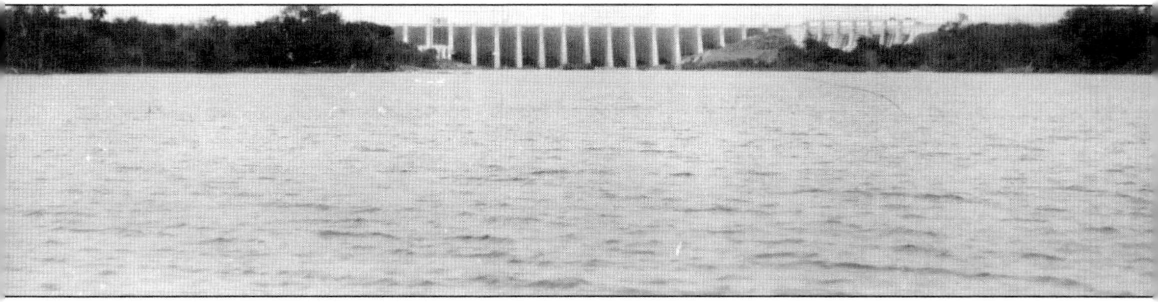

Buchanan Dam is 10,987.55 feet long, creating a lake 30.65 miles long and 4.92 miles wide. It was first envisioned in the early 1880s by Adam R. Johnson and surveyor Tom Chamberlain. Chamberlain drew a version of a finished dam that is on view at Fort Croghan Museum. In 1931, Emery, Peck, and Rockwood Development Company of Chicago became general contractors for building the dam and awarded a contract to Folgles Construction Company of Minneapolis. Work on Hamilton Dam was begun but went into receivership in 1932. Some 800 workers lost their jobs. Due to the efforts of state senator Houghton Brownlee and U.S. Congressman James P. Buchanan, both the state legislature and U.S. Congress became interested. On November 13, 1934, the 43rd Texas Legislature created the Lower Colorado River Authority. The authority applied for and received a federal grant to finish Hamilton Dam. The name was changed to Buchanan Dam in honor of the congressman.

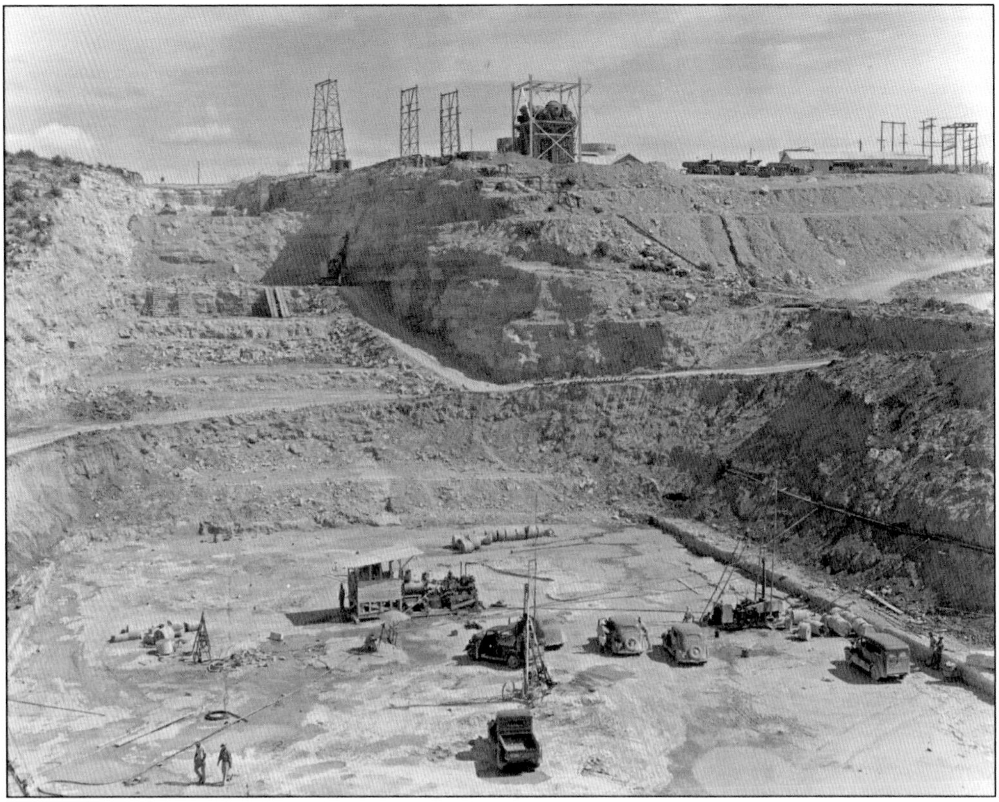

Buchanan Dam was 40-percent complete when the LCRA began construction again in July 1936. This photograph shows part of the immense amount of dirt work that had to be completed as part of building the foundation. The dam was built for two purposes: to eliminate the inevitable flooding along the banks of the Colorado River and to provide electricity to the area. This project helped considerably to bring Burnet County out of the Great Depression. Workers numbered 1,900 men at the peak of construction. Most of them lived in provided temporary housing, but some preferred to camp with their families in tents along the river. The photograph below shows some of the workers. (Photographs courtesy of the Lower Colorado River Authority.)

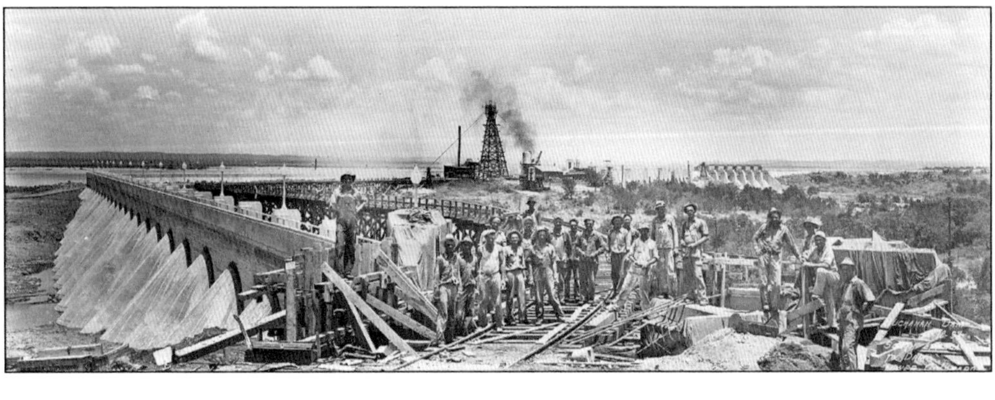

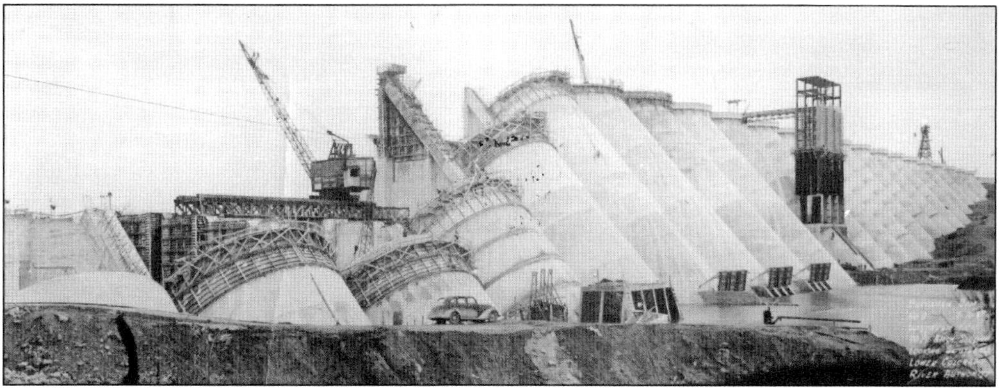

Buchanan Dam, with its 52 gigantic arches and 455 feet of Taintor gates along with the north spillway and rolled earth dike, is the longest multiple-arched dam in the world. The construction used 816 million pounds of concrete. The concrete mix required 4.5 million pounds of reinforcing, 473,620,000 pounds of crushed rock, 236,106,000 pounds of sand, 96,482,628 pounds of cement, and 2.1 million pounds of structural steel. The dam was completed in 1937, and the lake began filling. The power plant began operating in January 1938, sending 138,000 volts of electricity over the transmission lines. The photograph below was taken before the dam was complete. (Photographs courtesy of the Lower Colorado River Authority.)

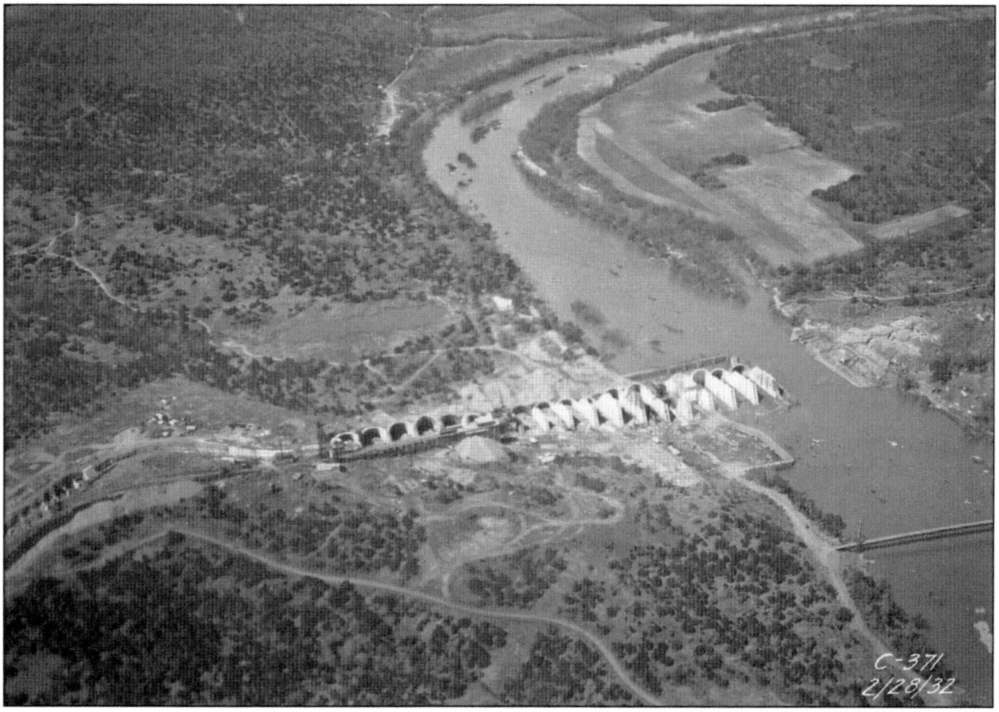

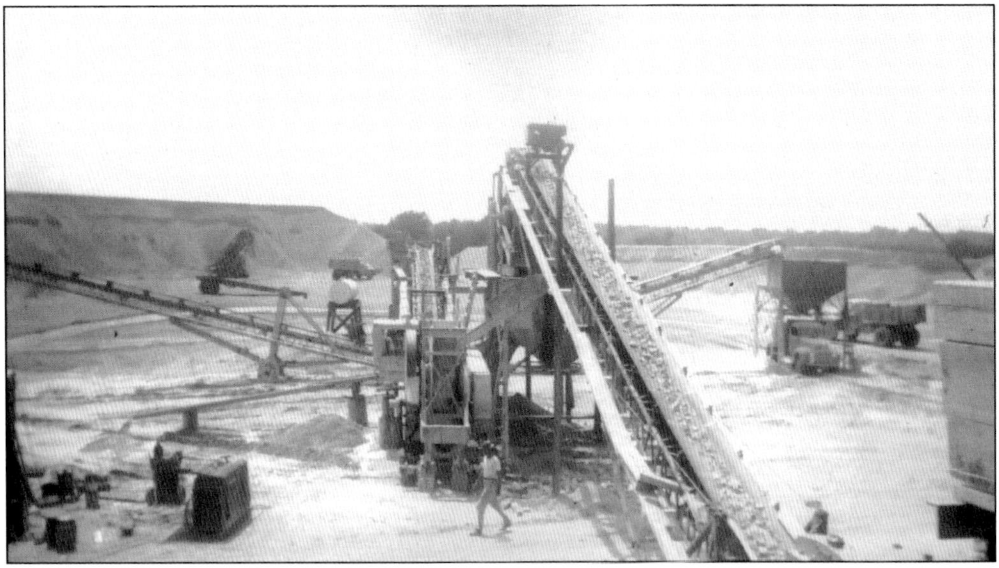

Houston Clinton and Company near Burnet provided crushed rock for the building of Buchanan Dam. Ramsey Clinton, Houston's son and partner, ran the operation. The photographs on this page were taken later but show how the stone was handled. The photograph above is the view from the top of the crusher and shows the crushed rock being moved on conveyers to hoppers. The truck on the right is being loaded from a hopper while the trucks in the photograph below are waiting to be loaded. The rotation of trucks carrying stone to the dam site was continuous daily until the structure was completed. (Photographs courtesy of Ramsey Clinton.)

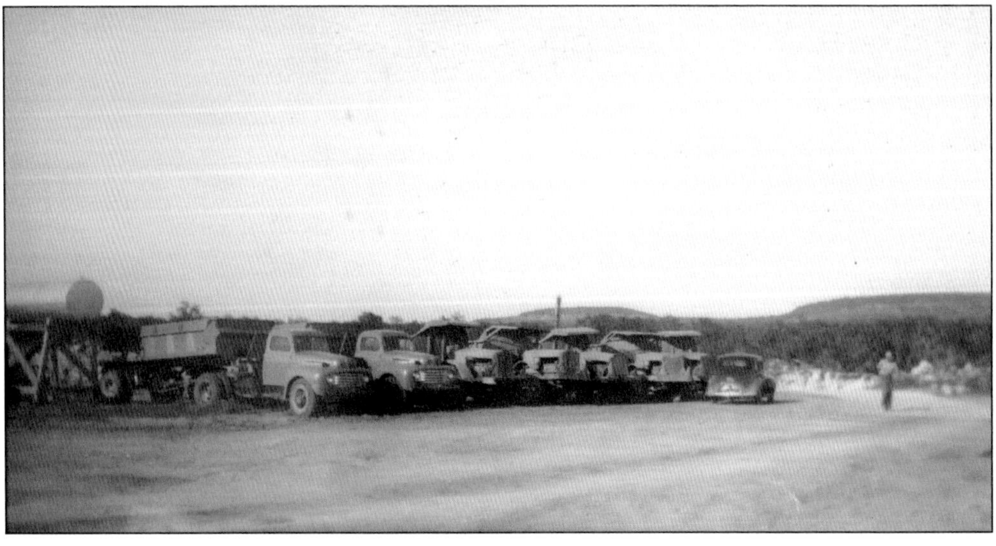

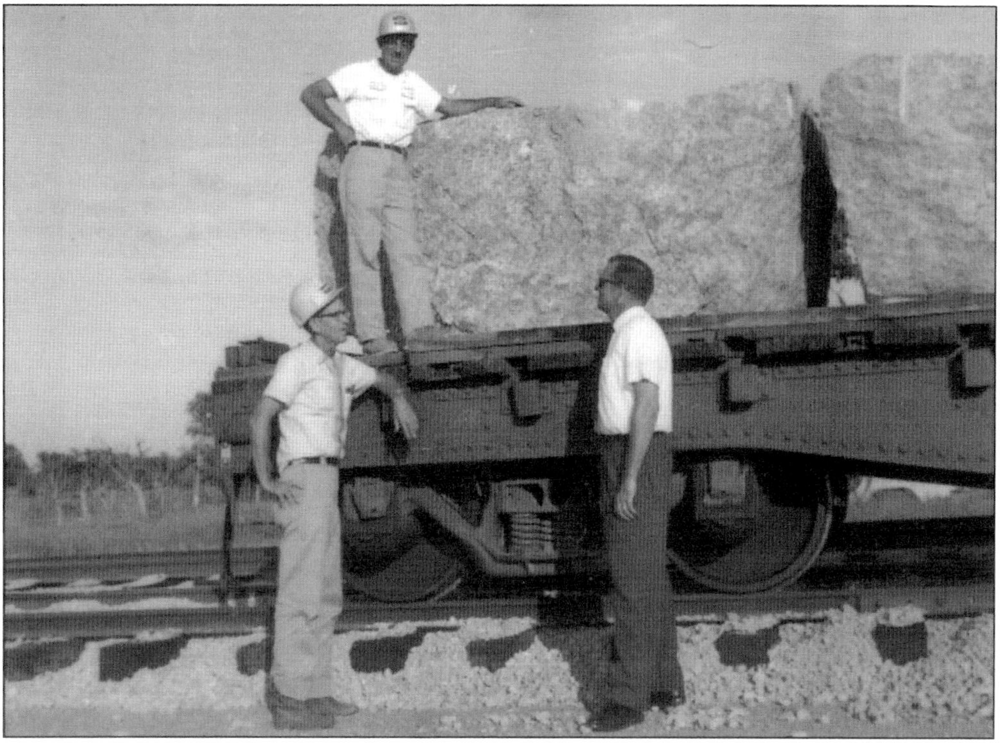

These huge blocks of granite were on their way to the Texas coast to be used for building jetties in the Gulf of Mexico. The jetties were needed to protect the shoreline and coastal cities from future storm damage. Ramsey Clinton stands on the right in this photograph. The Clintons sold the rock-crushing company to Texas Construction Material Company of Houston in 1957. The quarrying of rock has become the leading industry in the area, and Texas stone is shipped all over the world. Marble from the Holland quarry near Burnet was used in the building of the Washington Monument. A scene from that quarry is shown below. (Above, photograph courtesy of Ramsey Clinton; below, photograph courtesy of BCHS.)

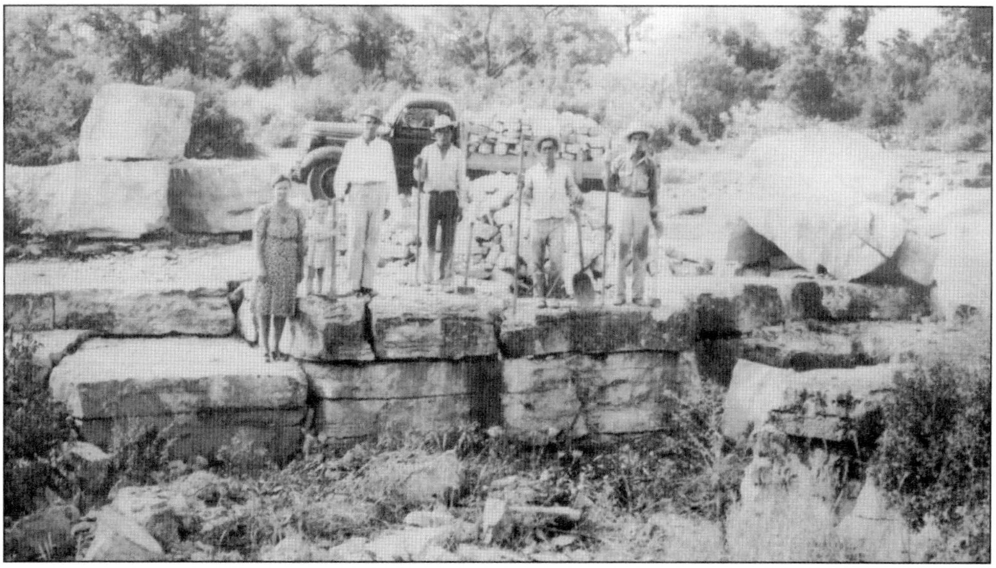

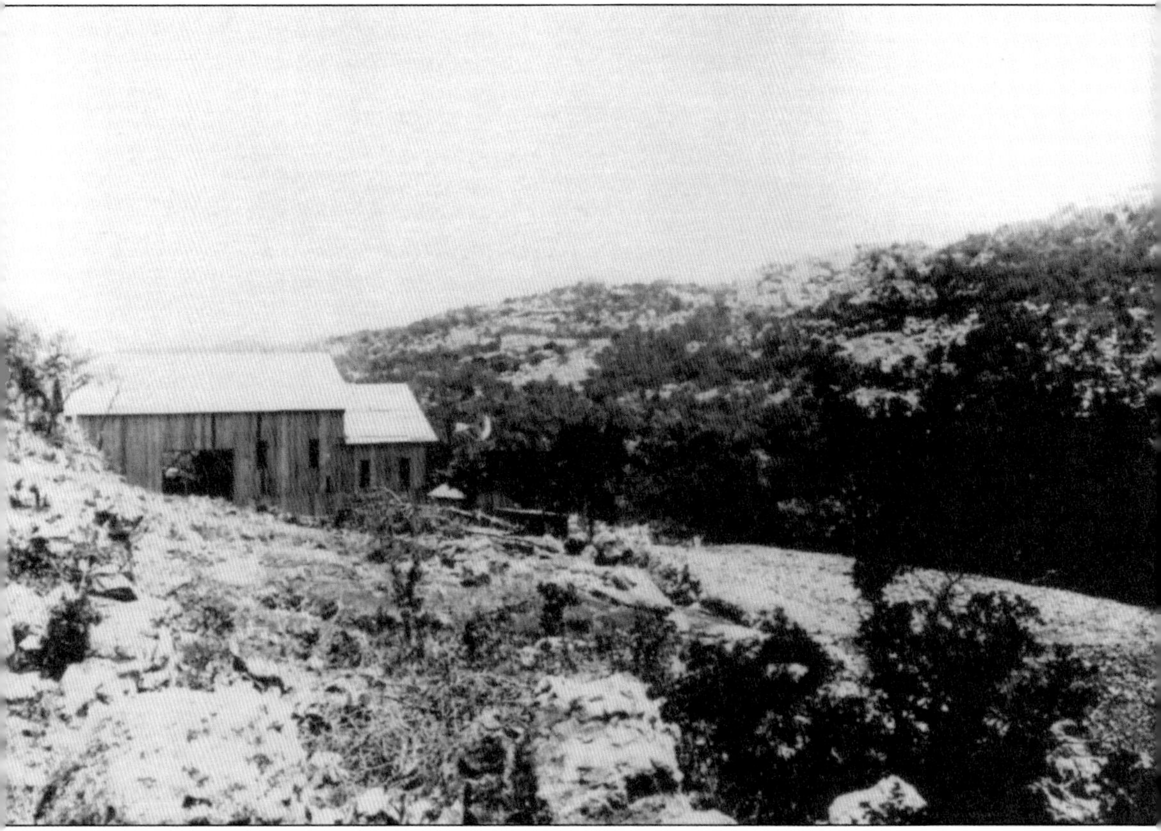

It is said that Texas has everything and Burnet County has most of that. This is a photograph of the old graphite mine located on the Dorbandt ranch near Lake Buchanan. The graphite was discovered in 1914, and the Southwestern Consolidated Graphite Company began mining it in 1916. This mine is the only source of fully integrated graphite in this hemisphere. In addition to use as lead in pencils and the production of art materials, graphite is used to slow down neutrons in atomic piles. During World War II, the War Production Board requested that this mine produce graphite for the war effort. Some minerals mined in Burnet County to less success were copper, zinc, lead, and iron. (Photograph courtesy of HBFL.)

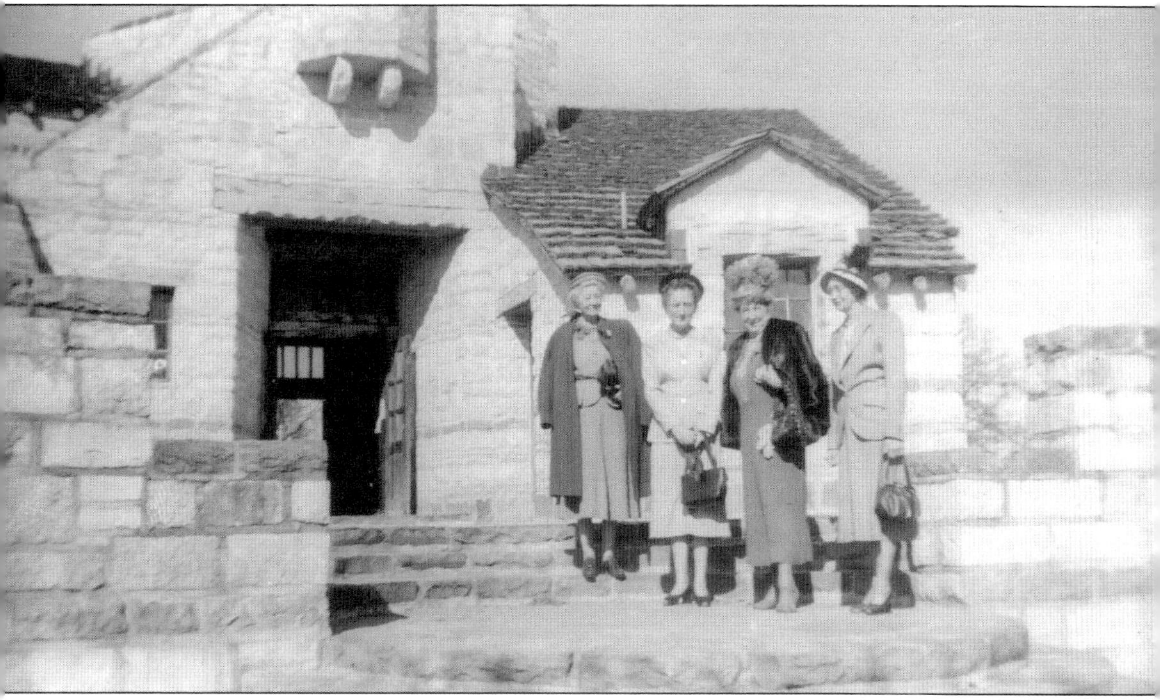

Tradition says that Longhorn Cavern has been shelter to Native American tribes, cowboys, and outlaws, including Sam Bass. Stories abound to support the claims. Formerly known as Sherrord's Cave for the rancher who owned the land where it was located, the cave entrance was only a hole in the ground. Around 1930, the Texas State Parks Board, in conjunction with the National Parks Service, built an entrance and placed lights inside the cave to accommodate tours. The name was changed to Longhorn Cavern. As part of his New Deal, Franklin Roosevelt created the Civilian Conservation Corps. One of the CCC mandates was to build or improve parks. Company 854 was moved to the park in 1934. There at different times, 1,600 young men built a road from U.S. 281 to the park and another from the park to Inks Dam. The CCC cleared out the cave, building lighted pathways throughout. They improved the entrance and constructed an administration building. These unidentified ladies from San Antonio are shown in front of that building. (Photograph courtesy of Milli Williams.)

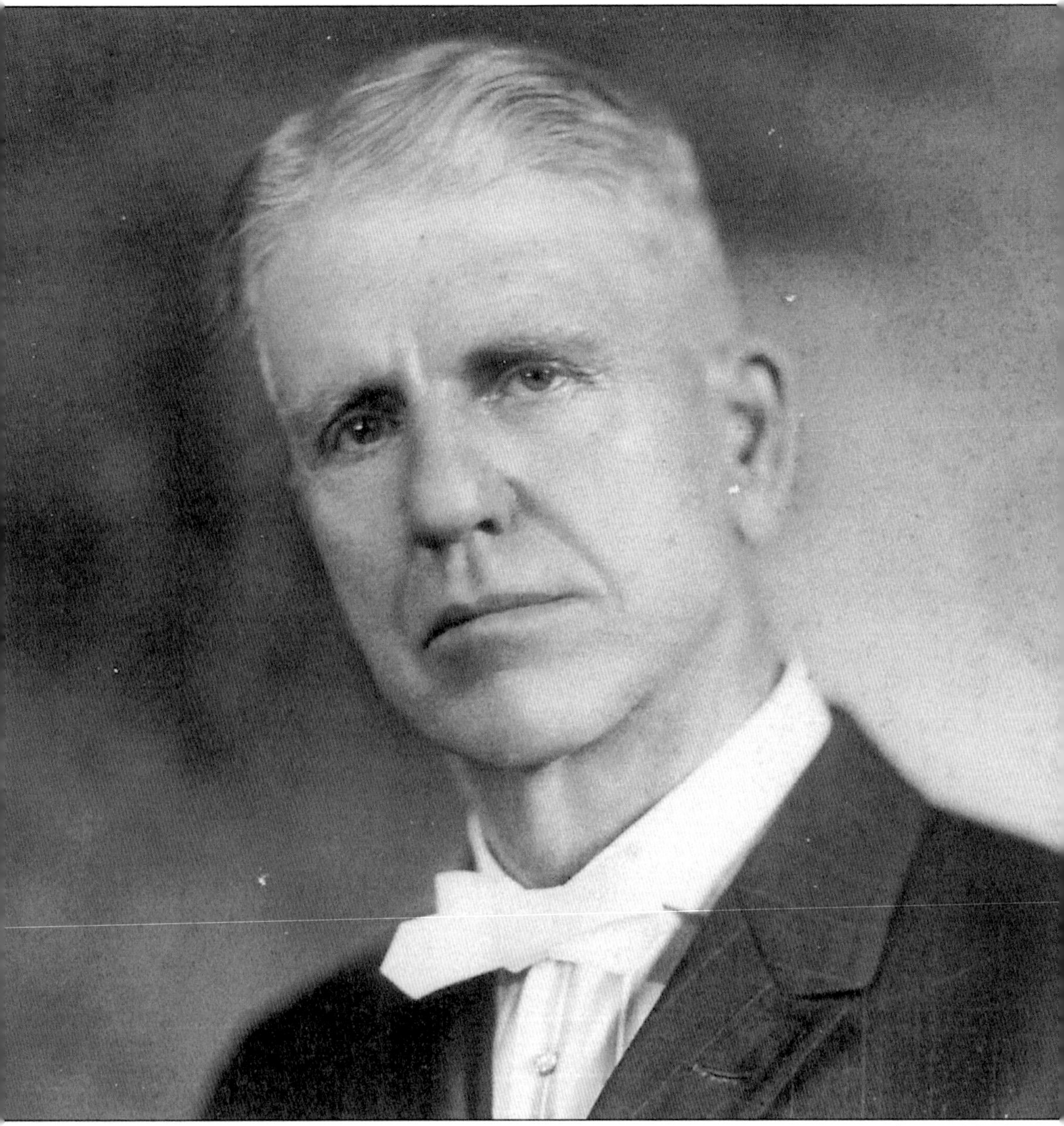

Warren Calvin Galloway (1856–1936) came to Burnet in 1882. A visionary in the world of business, he became one of the most influential persons in Burnet. He organized the First State Bank of Burnet, owned and financed the first electric plant, was Burnet County tax collector from 1904 to 1908, and served as mayor of the city for four months in 1925 and again from 1931 until his death in 1936. He was mayor when the public water system and later the sewer system were installed and paving of the streets began. Galloway and his wife, the former Mary B. Clark, were the parents of six children, but only three lived to be adults. They were Warren Calvin Jr., Harry Hobson, and Marie Clark. Harry and Marie eventually followed their father into the banking business at First State Bank. Warren Jr. served in the army during both World War I and World War II, rising to the rank of major. He took over the Galloway Insurance Agency upon his return to Burnet in 1950. (Photograph courtesy of First State Bank of Burnet.)

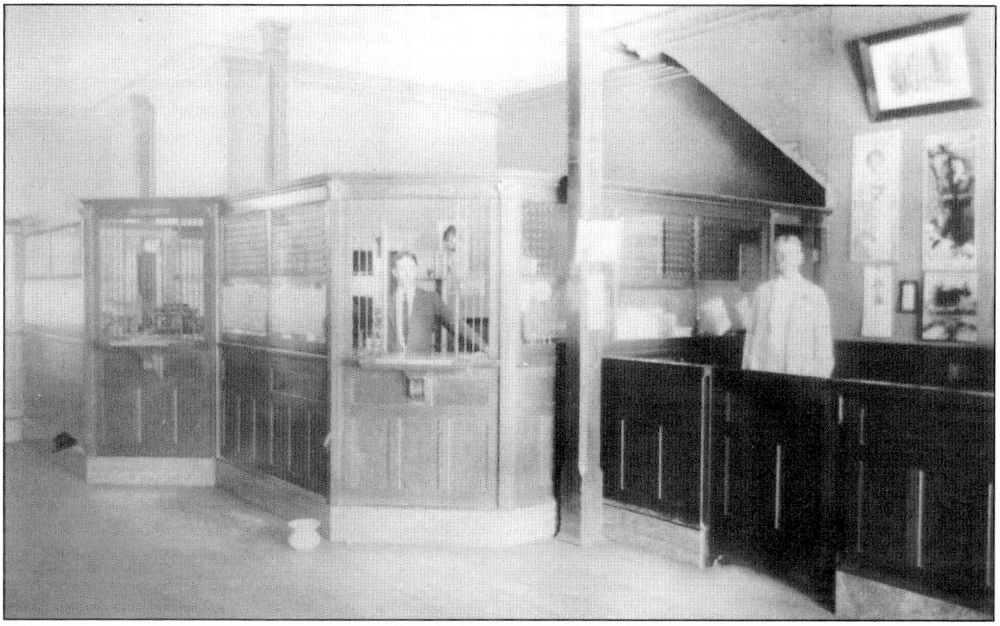

W. C. Galloway (right) and Charles Schnabel stand in the lobby of the First State Bank of Burnet in 1910. This was in the building on Jackson Street across from the Burnet Hotel. Except for a leave of absence from 1918 to 1919 to serve in World War I, Schnabel worked at the bank from 1908 until 1962. (Photograph courtesy of First State Bank of Burnet.)

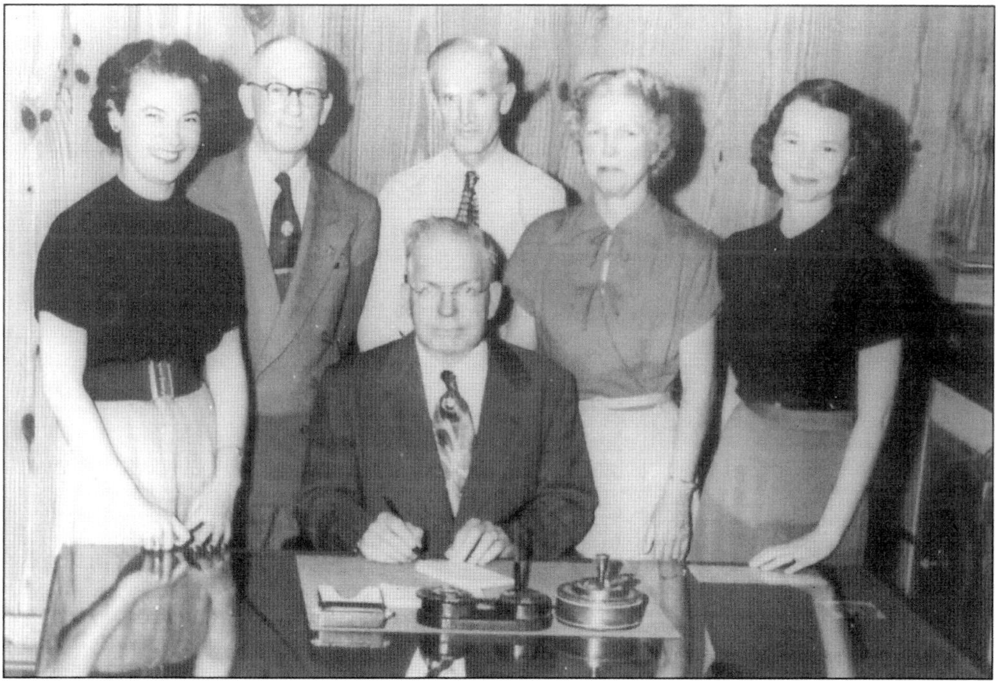

The First State Bank of Burnet staff is shown here with bank president H. H. "Hob" Galloway in 1951. They are, from left to right, Lois Hammett, W. D. Gardner, Charles Schnabel, Marie Clark Galloway, and Glendine Love. Both Schnabel and Marie Clark Galloway worked for the bank for more than 50 years. (Photograph courtesy of First State Bank of Burnet.)

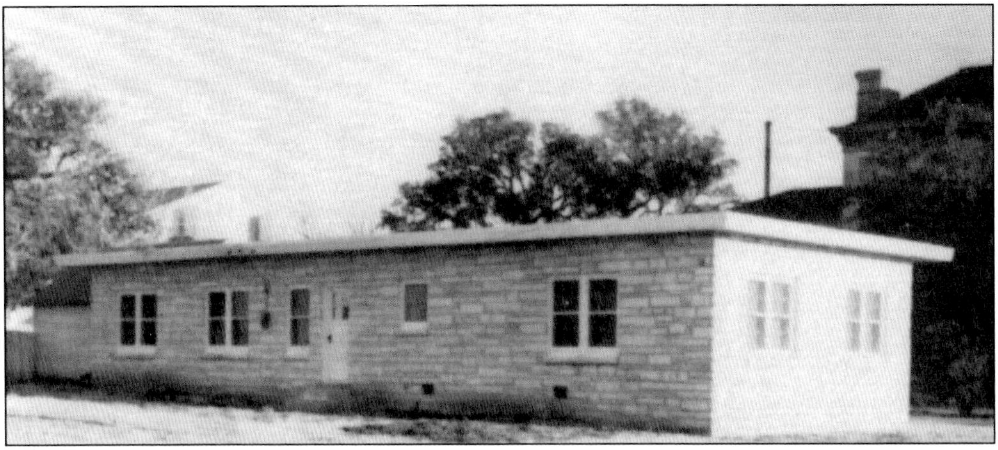

This building was the first freestanding library in Burnet. A frame building was bought in 1949 as World War II surplus and placed on county-donated land adjacent to the jail. By 1951, renovation was complete. The first Burnet library was established in 1904 and shared space in several buildings until 1948, when the Burnet County Free Library Board was officially organized. The library was located on the upper floor of the Burnet County Jail. Books totaling $500 were purchased, and 1,000 books were loaned by the Texas State Library. Nina Daugherty was hired as librarian at $50 a month but resigned in 1949, and Sue Goree was hired at $125 per month. The present Herman Brown Free Library, on the northwest corner of the square, was built in 1976. (Photographs courtesy of HBFL.)

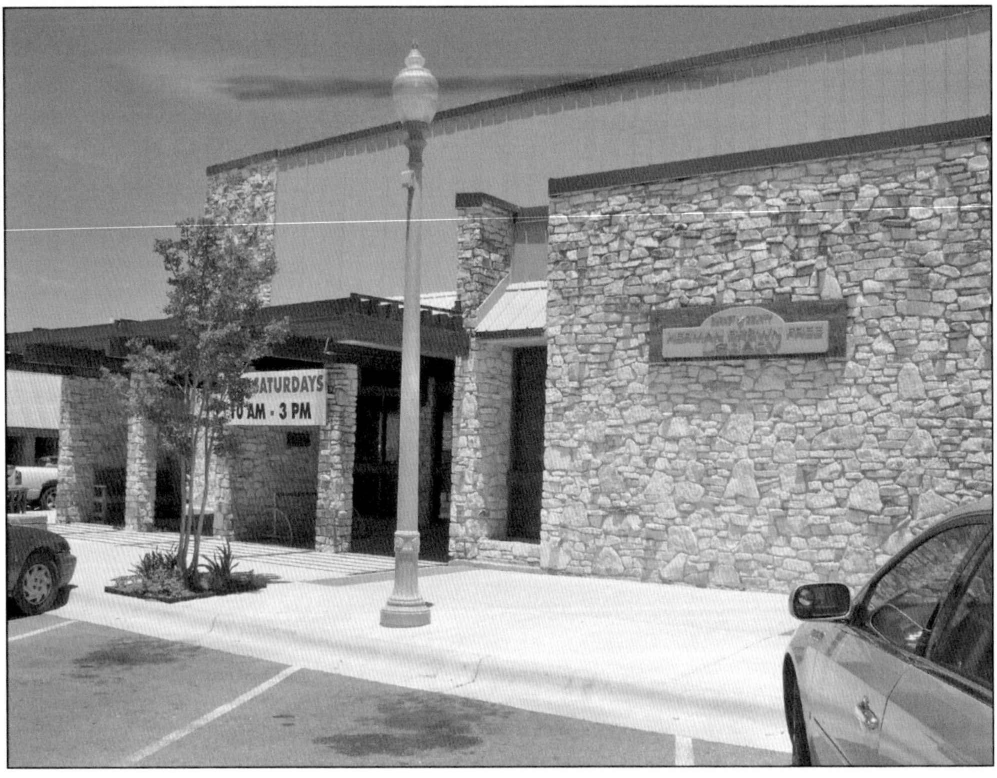

Four

Modern Burnet

During the Great Depression and World War II, the population of Burnet declined. The Depression caused some people to move in search of a job. During the war, people moved to work in defense plants. Almost all of the able-bodied young men were in the armed forces. However, the electricity produced by the damming of the Colorado River eventually brought in new businesses. Burnet became the "Gateway to the Hill Country." Tourists came to fish and play in the new lakes. Motels were built along the highways in Burnet, and new cafés and restaurants opened. The economy revived and the population grew again. The federal government passed the GI Bill to help veterans with education, job training, business startups, and home buying. People were looking to the future with confidence, and that translated into progress for Burnet.

The years following World War II were prosperous ones. The men who came back from the war married the girls who had waited for them, bought houses to live in, and started raising families. Hospitals were built, and so were new schools. The city built an airport and a swimming pool. A rodeo arena and a barn were erected for the 4H youth to show their animals. A new fair association was organized, and now the county fair had a home.

In 1973, a tornado ripped through the town, causing rampant destruction. Businesses, homes, and schools were destroyed. It was considered a miracle that no one was killed. The damaged buildings gave way to new ones, and the people of Burnet forged ahead.

This last chapter will show how forging ahead translated into improvements and amenities that make modern Burnet a wonderful place to live or visit and a place its citizens rightfully take much pride in.

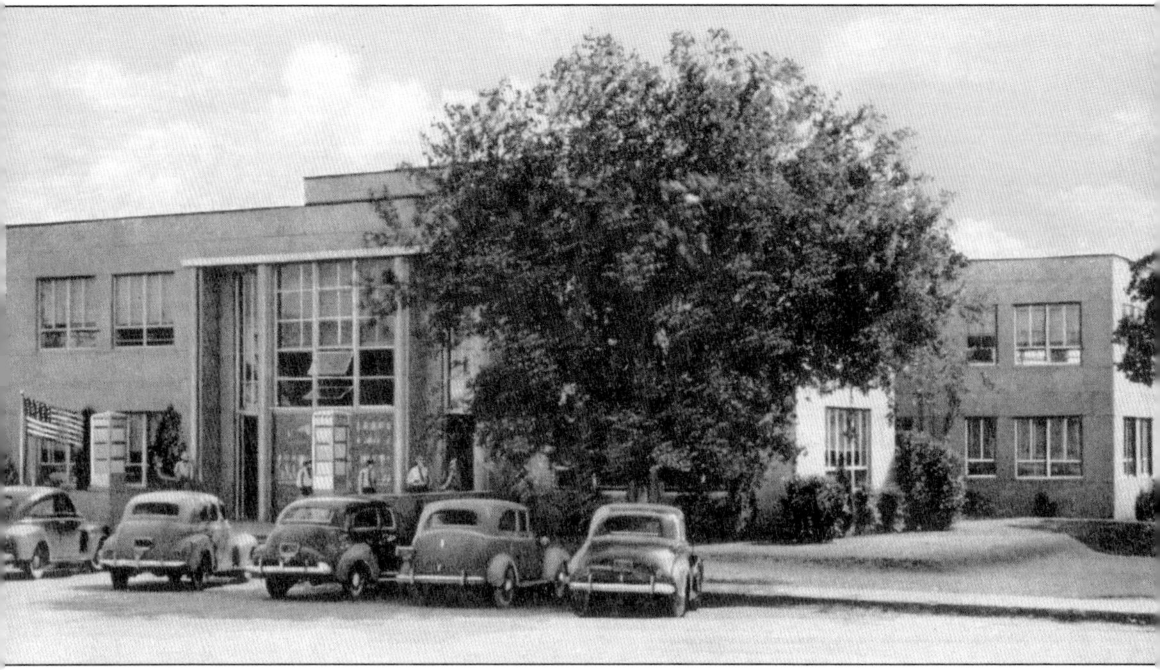

By 1935, it was evident that Burnet County needed a larger, more efficient courthouse. The Commissioners Court requested a grant from the U.S. Public Works Administration. On November 18, 1935, the county received a loan and a grant totaling $135,000 for the construction and furnishing of a new courthouse. The Commissioners Court held a bond election to cover the $75,000 loan part of the grant. It passed, and the construction began in February 1936 and was completed in August 1937. The 10,000-square-foot building was constructed of granite from the quarry at Marble Falls, and the floors were paved with terrazzo from the Magill place south of Burnet. The state capitol is built from granite and terrazzo from these same quarries. The ultramodern new courthouse was the pride of the county. (Photograph courtesy of COB.)

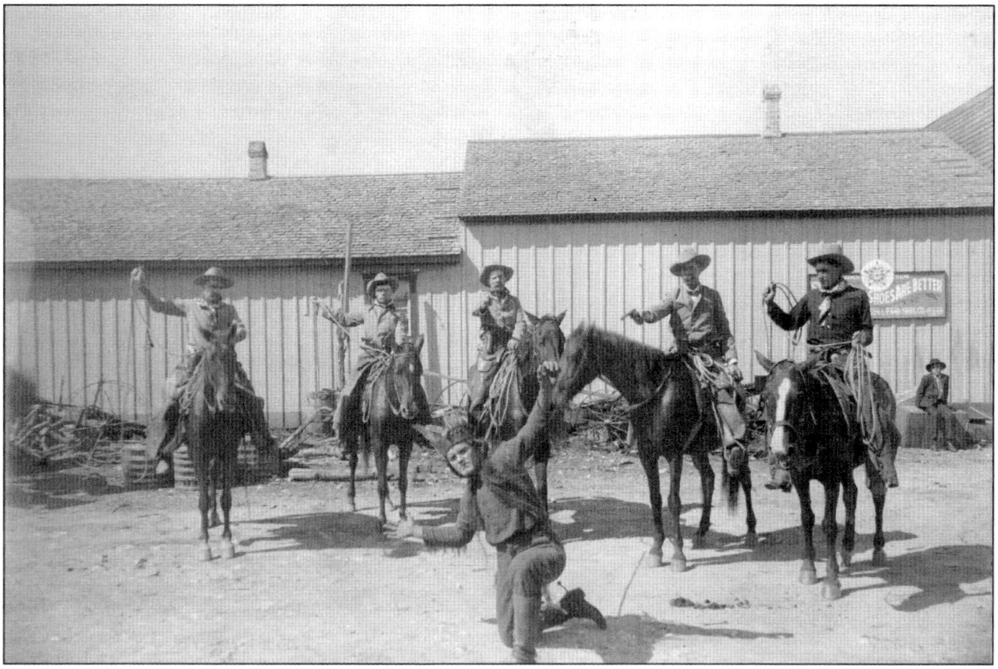

The fellow on his knees in this photograph is Burnet County sheriff Andy Ray. He and his posse presented a mock "cowboys and Indians" skirmish at the Burnet County Fair. Sheriff Ray dressed and played the part of a tribal chief. Ray was sheriff from 1926 to 1932. He was also county tax collector until that position was separated from the sheriff job in 1930. (Photograph courtesy of Maxine Glimp.)

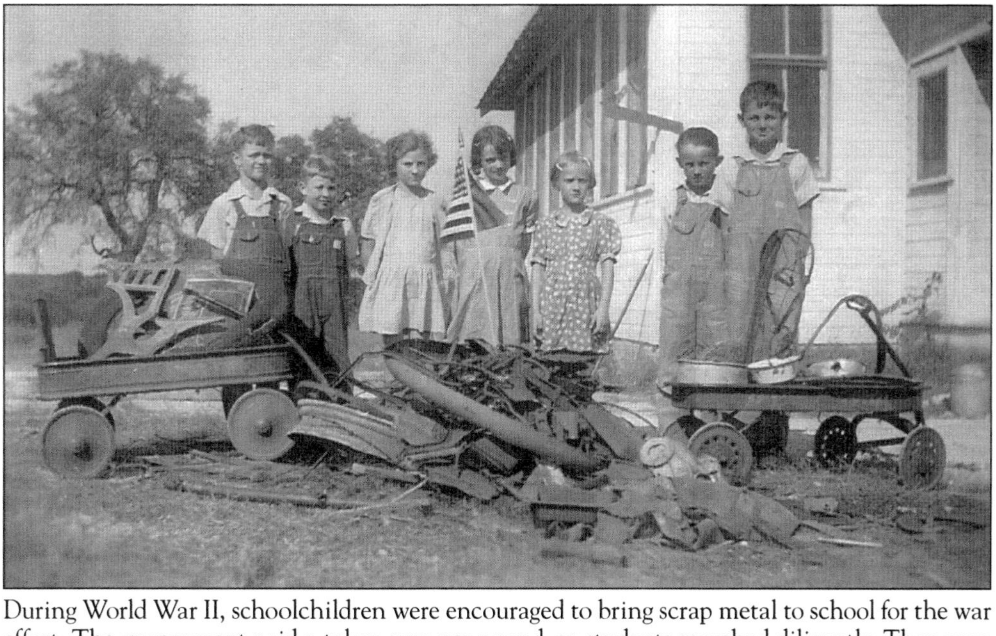

During World War II, schoolchildren were encouraged to bring scrap metal to school for the war effort. The government paid a token sum per pound, so students searched diligently. They were also praised for their patriotism, so a lot of pride was felt. This is a group of Mount Blanc students showing off their pile of metal. (Photograph courtesy of HBFL.)

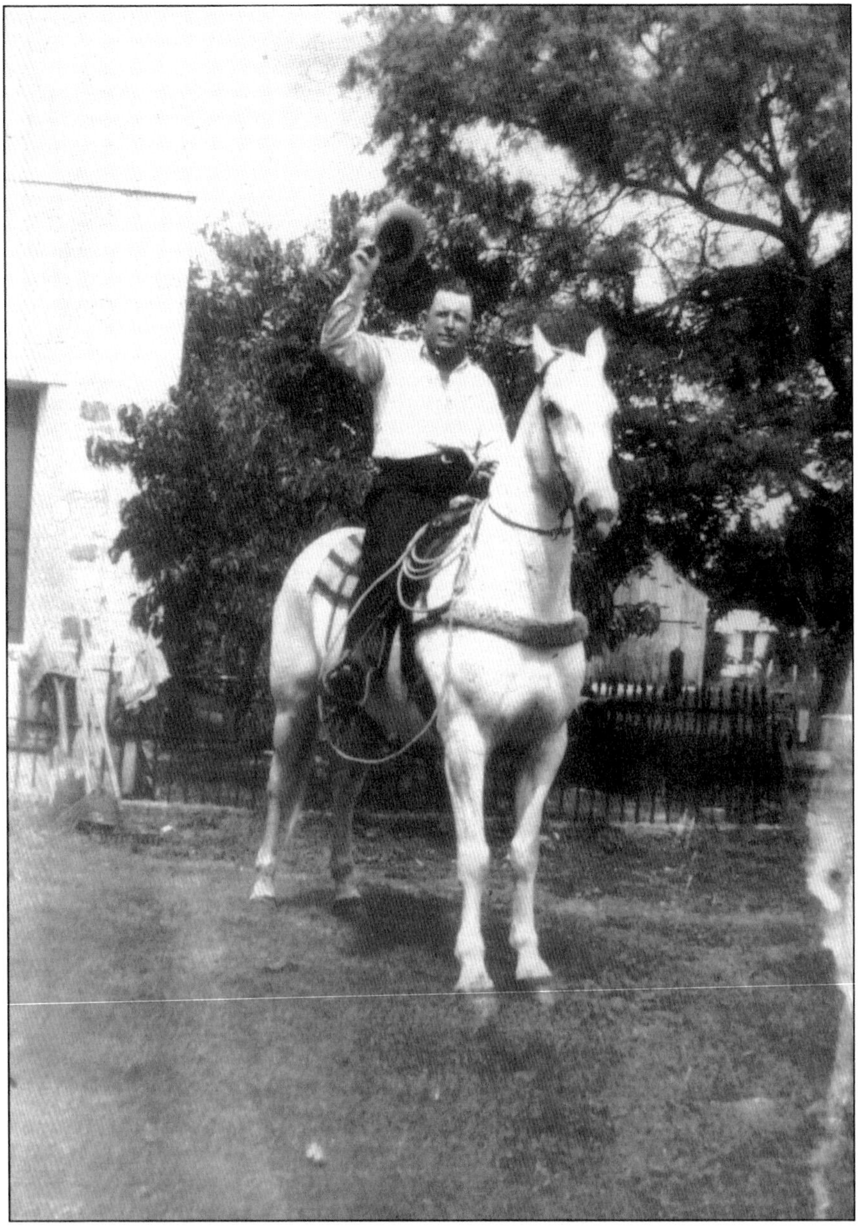

Wallace Riddell (1899–1978) was elected Burnet County sheriff in 1939 and became the most reelected sheriff in Texas. He was still in office when he died. Wallace, as everyone called him, was known for his even-handed toughness and dedication to duty. His vast knowledge of people and law enforcement was legendary. He treated young offenders with an eye to setting them on a straight path for the future, and there are citizens today who say Wallace saved their lives. He was often called a "cowboy sheriff" because of his love for the sport of rodeo. He was an accomplished calf roper and in 1976 was inducted into the Central Texas Cowboy Hall of Fame. In this photograph, Wallace sits astride his talented mount, Eagle. Eagle was famous as a rodeo horse. During rodeos, Wallace picked up bronco riders and roped "off of him." Other cowboys roped and steer wrestled "off of him." A statue of Wallace stands on the courthouse lawn. (Photograph courtesy of Pat Riddell.)

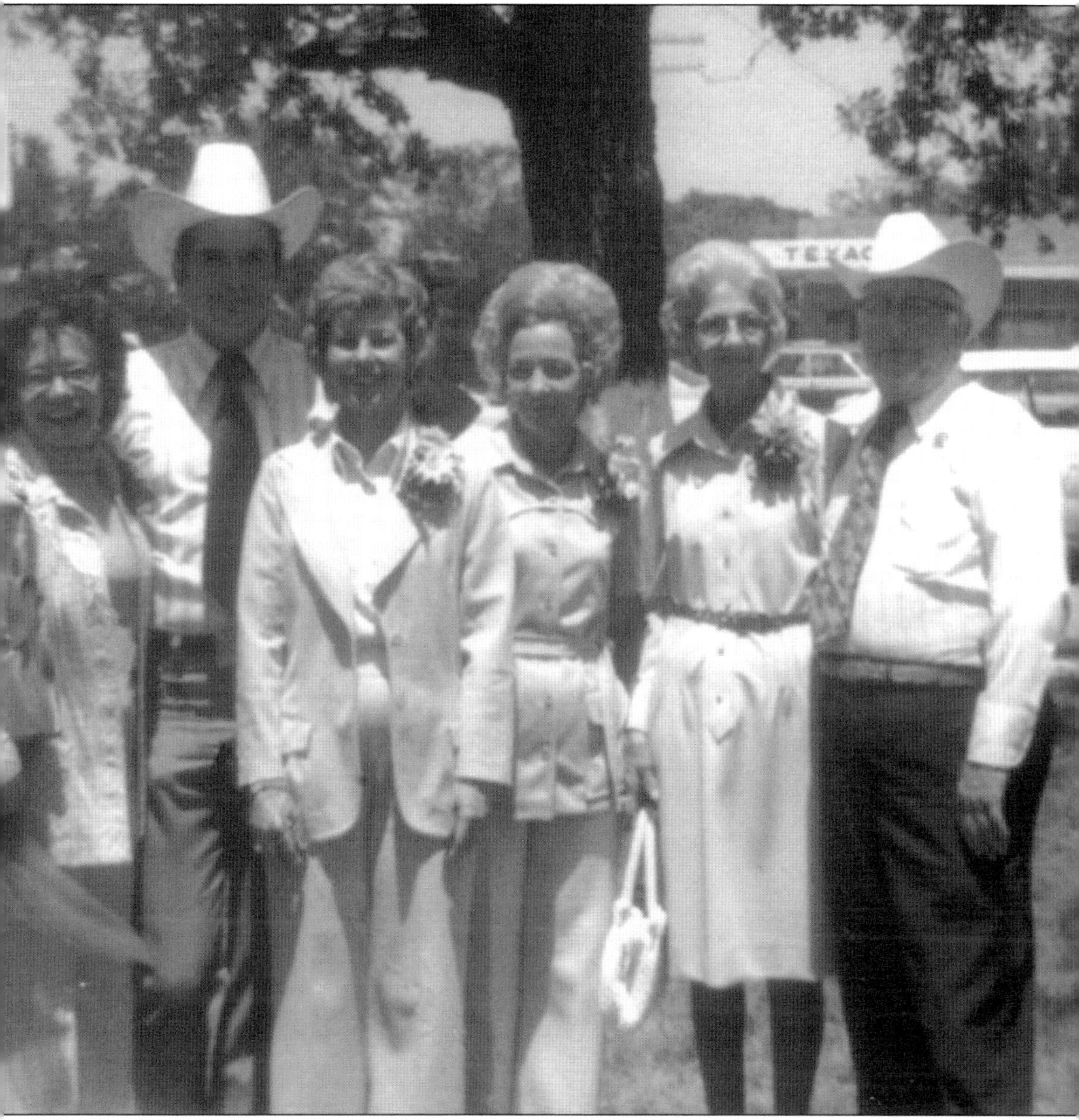

Here is the Riddell family: from left to right, Vonnie, Pat, Daisybel, and Modena, with their parents, Essie and Wallace. The sheriff was provided an apartment in the county jail, and that is where the children grew up. Essie cooked all of the meals for the prisoners, and legend says that some got themselves arrested just to eat her excellent food. The siblings all serve their community. Pat is serving his second term as city alderman, and Modena was district court clerk from 1975 to 1998. Vonnie and her husband, Billy Joe Fox, developed Delaware Springs and Oak Vista subdivisions. (Photograph courtesy of Pat Riddell.)

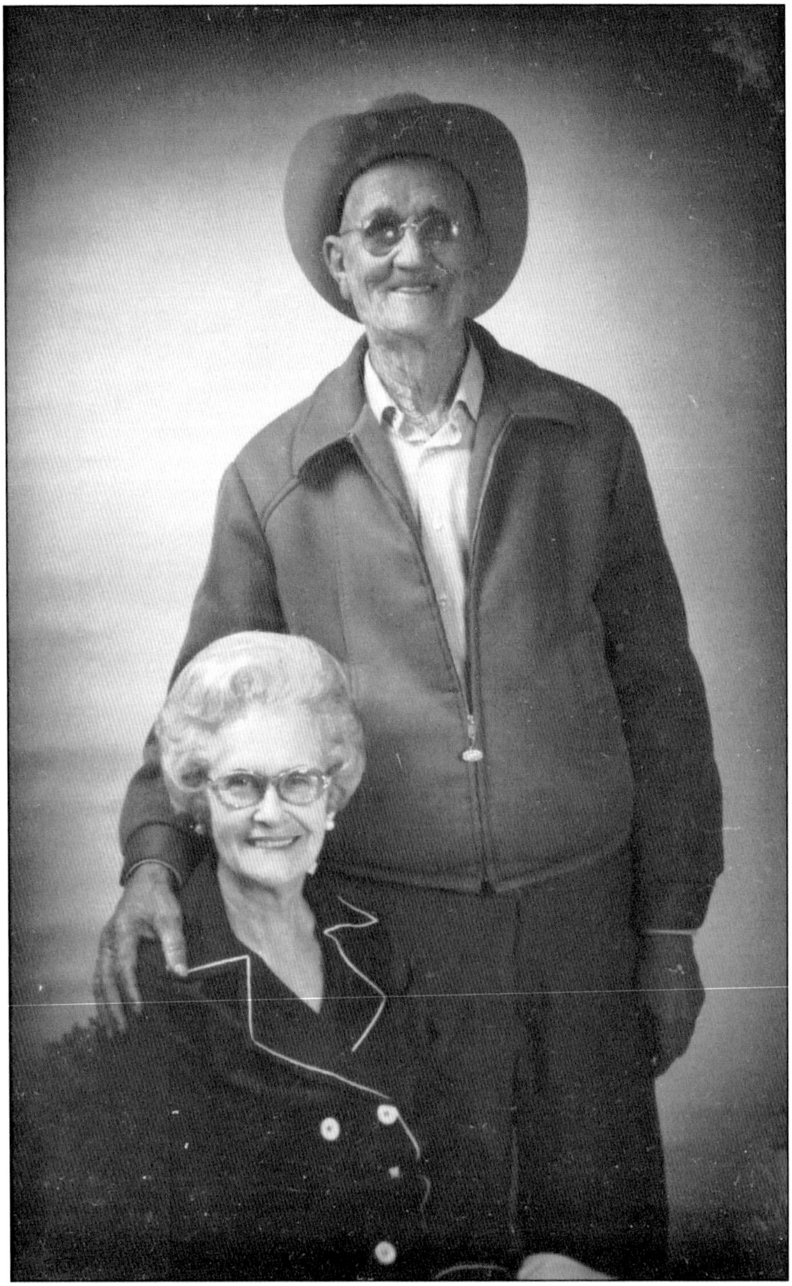

Arnold T. "Mutt" Atkinson was a rawhide-tough ranch hand cowboy all of his life, and he knew everything there was to know about handling horses and livestock. He was full of bits of wisdom and tales that came to be affectionately called "Muttisms." Mutt said, "I came to Texas with a ten dollar hat and a fifty dollar saddle and started punching cattle. I brought half a plug of tobacco and a box of Black Draught [laxative]. The tobaccos all gone but I still have all the Black Draught." He was gored by a cow once and upon arriving at the hospital told the doctor, "Hurry up with the stitching doc, 'cause I got to get back and saw the horns off that fool cow before she hurts somebody." He was serious. Mutt married Hazel Goble, and together they raised 12 children. (Photograph courtesy of Lila Atkinson Lewis.)

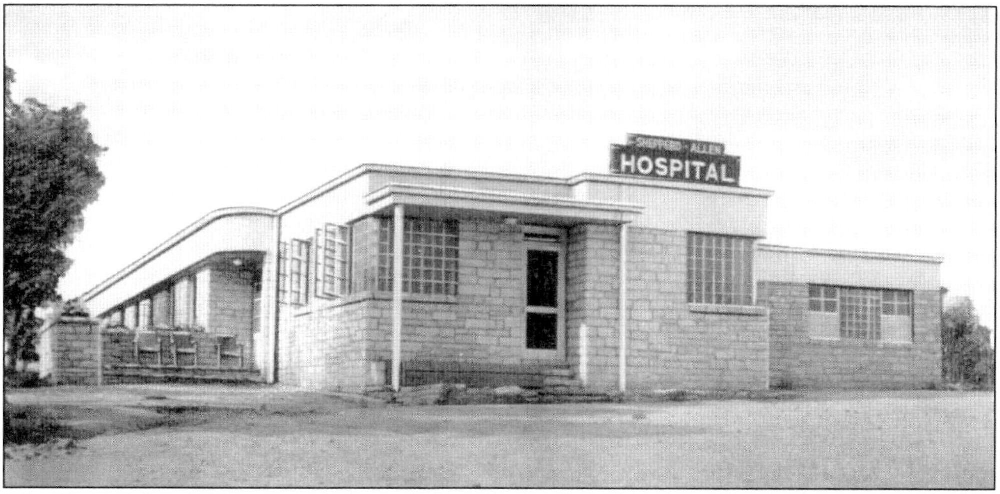

The Shepperd and Allen Hospital was the first hospital to be built in Burnet. It was a partnership between Dr. Joe Shepperd and Dr. George Scott Allen. They built a 17-bed hospital and clinic. The partnership was dissolved when Dr. Allen was called to serve with the army medical corps during World War II. During that time, Shepperd's brothers, Dr. Ray and Dr. Roy Shepperd, joined the hospital staff. An additional wing was added in 1950 and still another after that, which brought the hospital capacity to 60 beds. The Shepperd Memorial Hospital eventually built a much larger and better-equipped hospital on U.S. 281 South. The Shepperd family in this photograph included, from left to right, doctors Ray and Joe; their mother, Ivy; and doctors Ivan and Roy. Another son died at the age of 16. (Above, photograph courtesy of HBFL; below, photograph courtesy of Fannie Shepperd.)

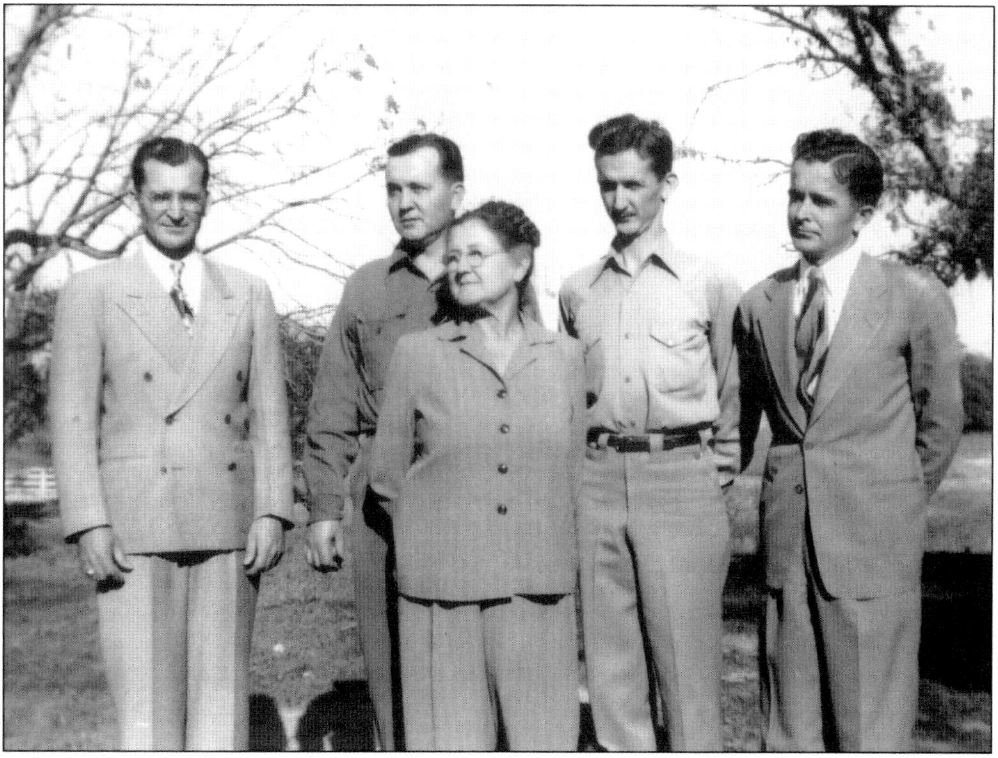

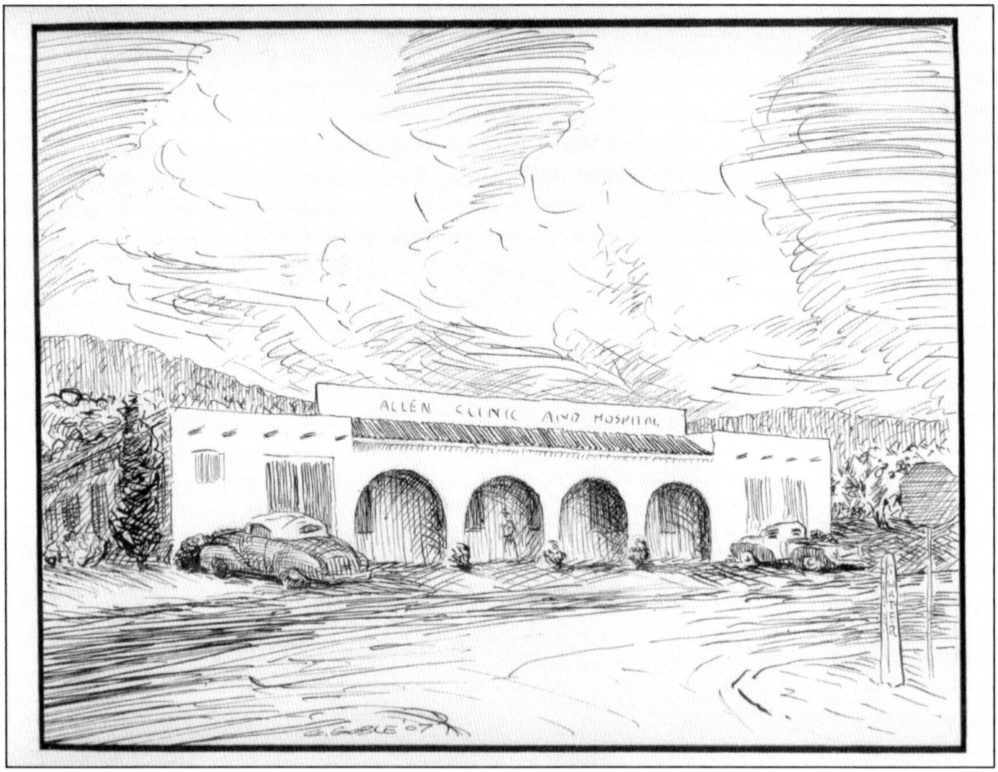

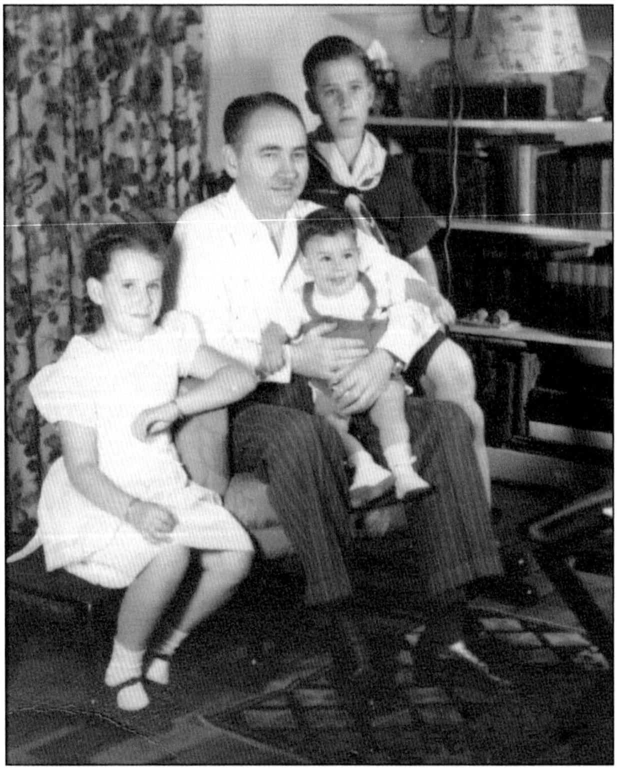

Dr. George Scott Allen built the Allen Clinic in 1946 with 25 beds and a clinic. Doctors J. Campbell Kern and Bill Ozier were associated with Dr. Allen at the hospital. The bed capacity was later increased to 35, and when the hospital closed in 1974, there were five doctors practicing there. They became affiliated with the Shepperd Memorial Hospital staff, although the Allen Clinic remained open for outpatient care until Dr. Allen retired. It became an office building for some years before it was demolished. The photograph at left shows Dr. Allen holding son George with daughter Alice and son Thrasher beside him. Dr. Allen and his wife, Mary Jane, had five children. The others are Johnathan and Sarah. (Above, drawing courtesy of Guy Goble; left, photograph courtesy of Thrasher Allen.)

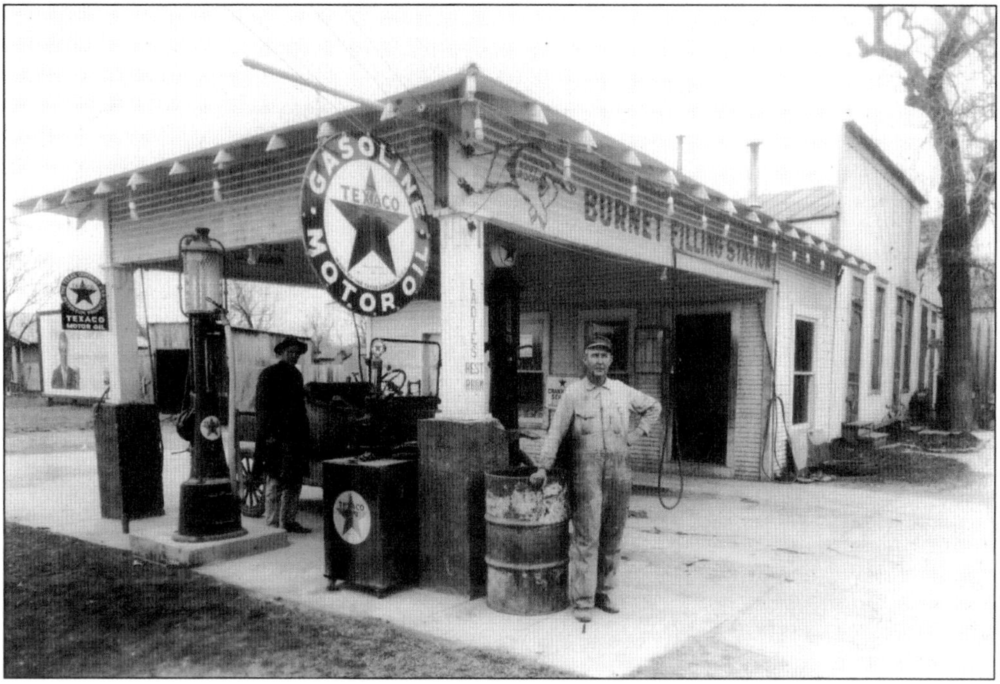

The Craddock service station was located at the northwest corner of the courthouse square. It is very typical of the stations of the 1920s. Craddock's service consisted of pumping the gasoline, wiping the windshield, and checking the oil and the air in the tires, usually with a few friendly comments. One might drink a 5¢ soda pop while the car was serviced and pick up a free map before leaving. There were no credit cards then, but Craddock ran a tab for trusted regular customers. The Tower Lodge can be seen in the photograph below. For years, the restaurant on U.S. 281 North was a popular place to dine, but fire destroyed the building in the early 1980s. (Above, photograph courtesy of BCHS; below, photograph courtesy of HBFL.)

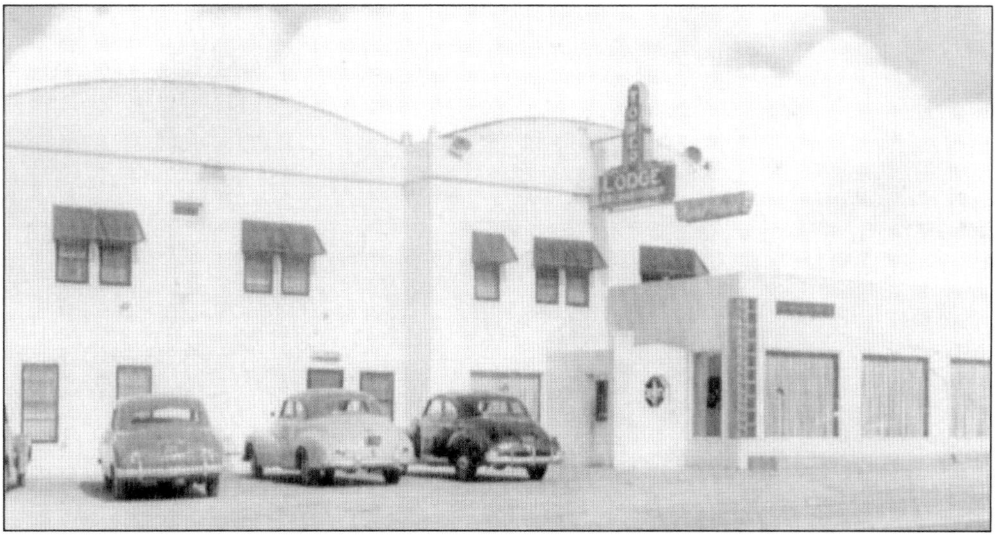

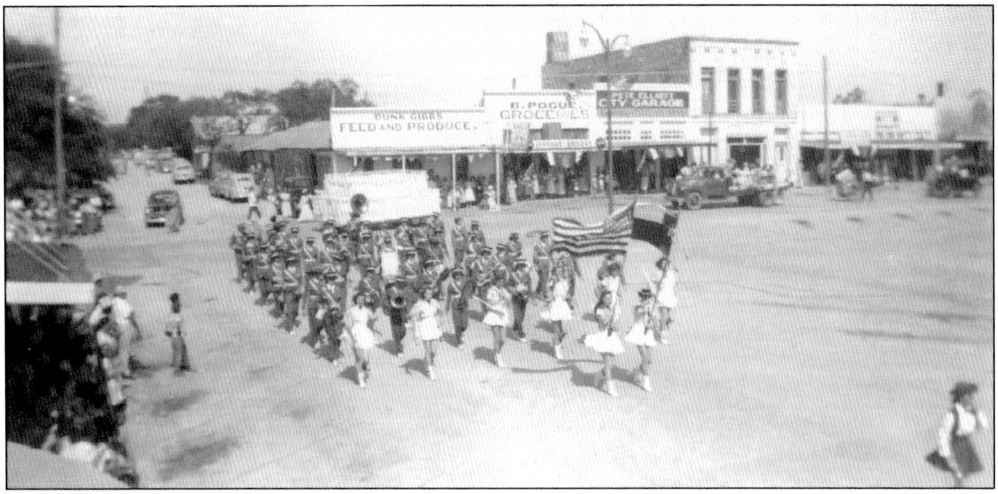

In 1952, Burnet County residents celebrated its centennial birthday with an all-out party. The many activities started with the parade and ended with music and dancing. The view in the photograph below is of the Fort Croghan parade wagon. It is all decked out for a journey across the country, 1800s style. (Photographs courtesy of Milli Williams.)

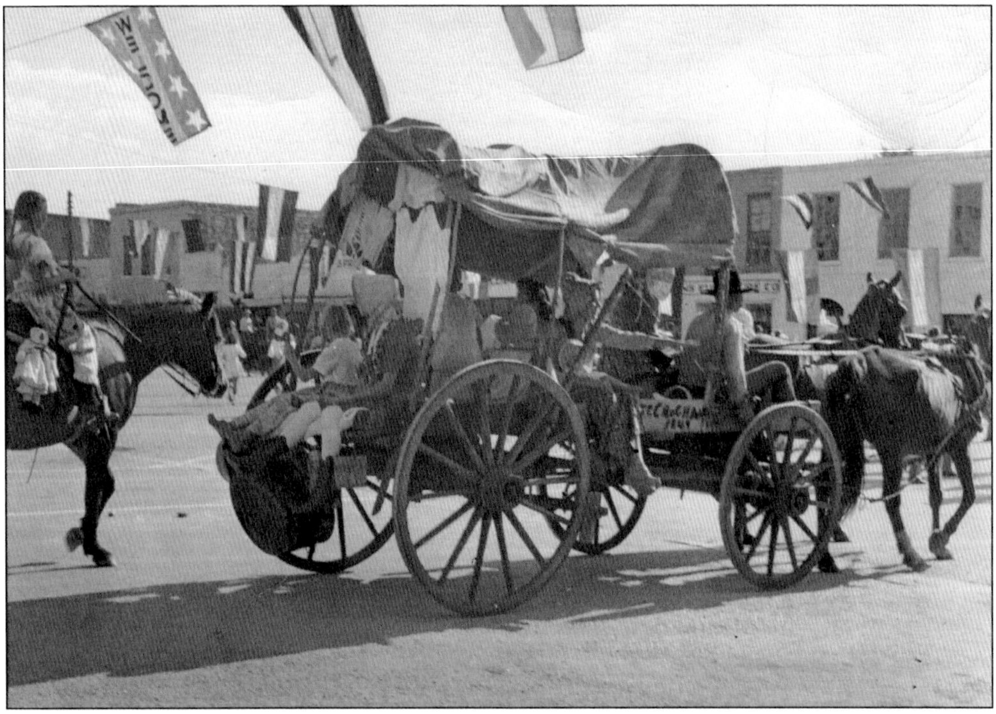

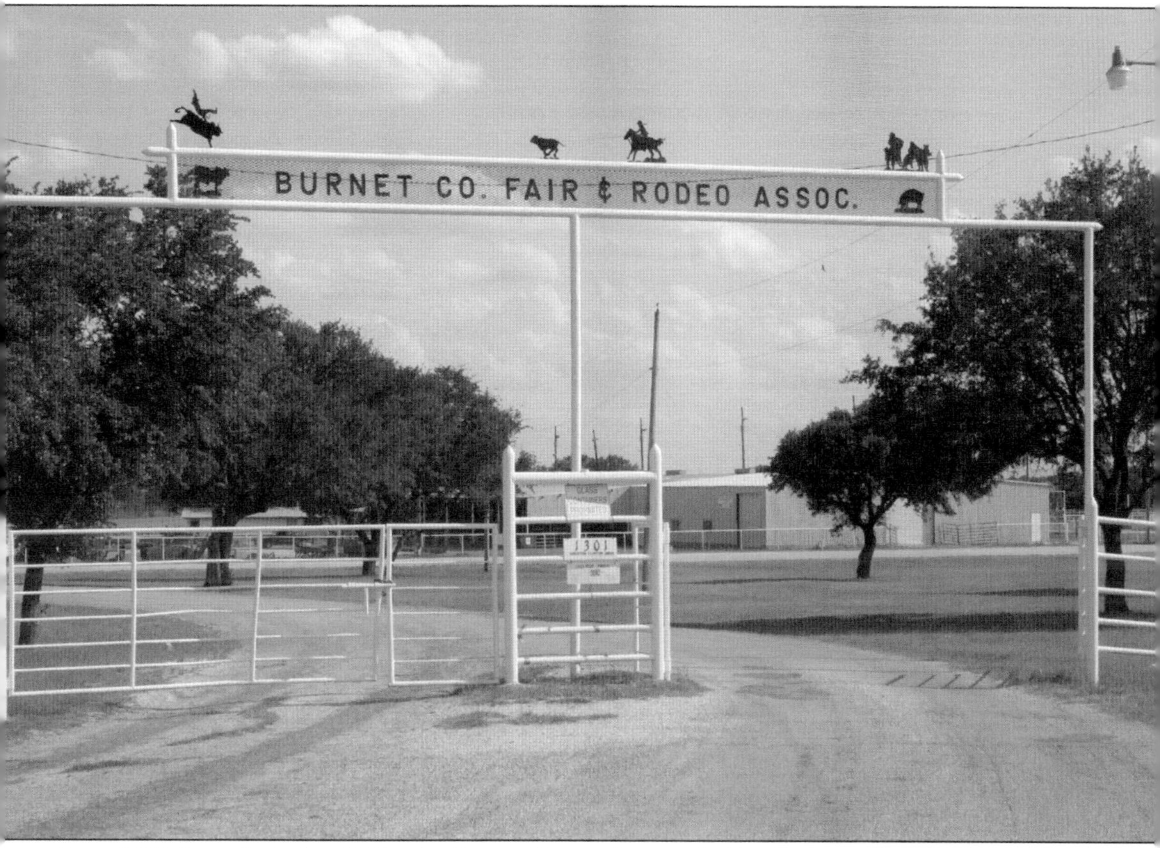

From 1907 through the late 1930s, the Burnet County Fair was held in Bertram. During the 1940s, it was held in such places as the American Legion Hall and the Burnet school cafeteria. The livestock show was held on the courthouse square. About 1950, the following citizens decided a central location was needed: Beck Hibler, Charley Taylor, Jim King, Lofton Meredith, Johnny Allen, Clay Lawson, Adolf Wall, Ira Lee Wall, LaVaughn Meridith, and Darryl Daniel. They borrowed $68,000 from the Farmers Home Administration and hired Lynn Willis as designer and Clyde Keele as general contractor. Houston Clinton and the city of Burnet donated land. The new barn accommodated its first show in 1967. The Fair Association and the Rodeo Association were combined in 1965 to become the Burnet County Fair and Rodeo Association. Ray Cagle and Jane Parker were county agents. Esther Warden was the first woman director of the association. On March 25, 1982, the arena was renamed for Houston Clinton, a dedicated supporter and participant of the rodeo. (Photograph courtesy of Kina Cockroft.)

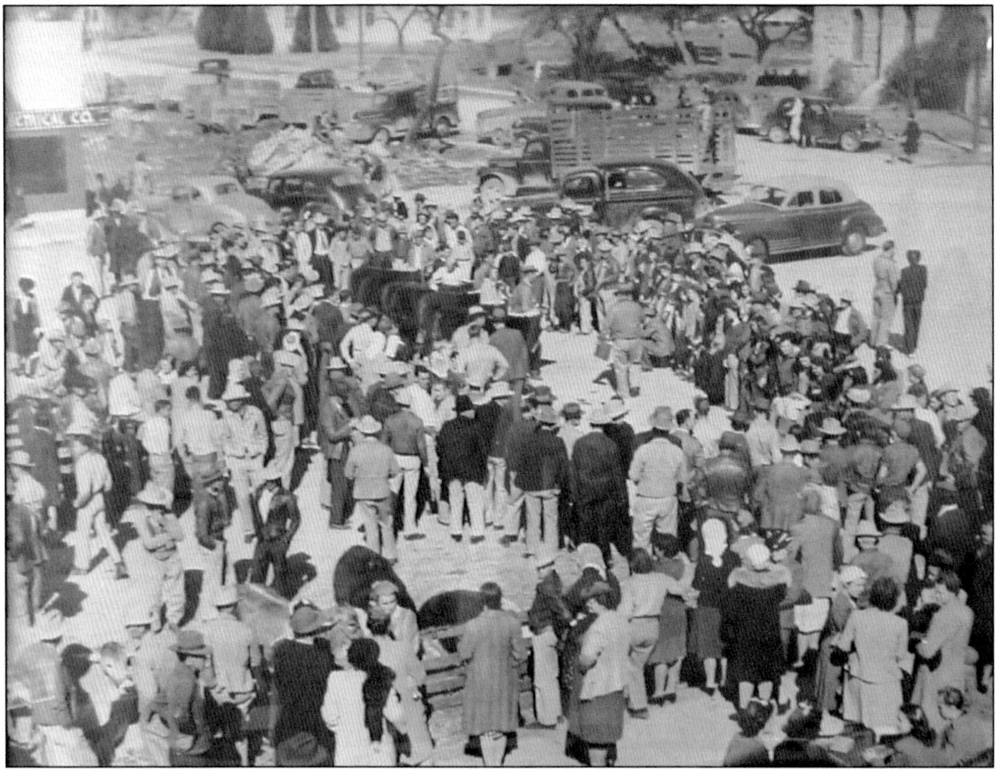

This is a view of the livestock show being held on the courthouse square sometime in the 1940s. The shows were always well supported by the community. Both businesses and individuals bid on the livestock so the 4H youngsters could receive compensation for raising their livestock.

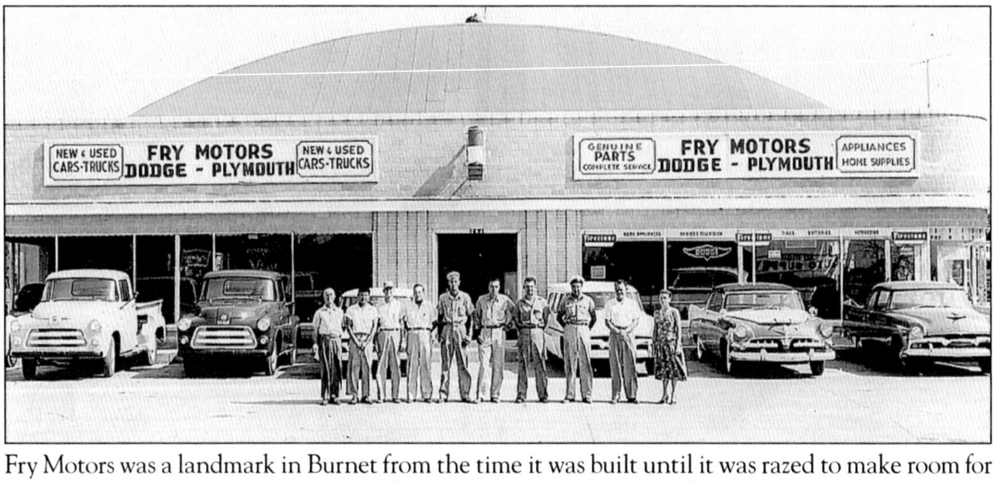

Fry Motors was a landmark in Burnet from the time it was built until it was razed to make room for the new Walgreen's drugstore in 2009. This 1956 photograph shows all of the personnel standing out front. From left to right are owner Arthur "Ted" Fry, mechanic Johnny Escamilla, service manager Weldon B. Cole, mechanic Harry Smith, mechanic C. O. Mills, television/radio technician C. B. Marx, mechanic Bobby Roberts, body and paint technician Joe Martinez, salesman Howard Stewart, and bookkeeper and secretary Ethel Lock. (Photograph courtesy of COB.)

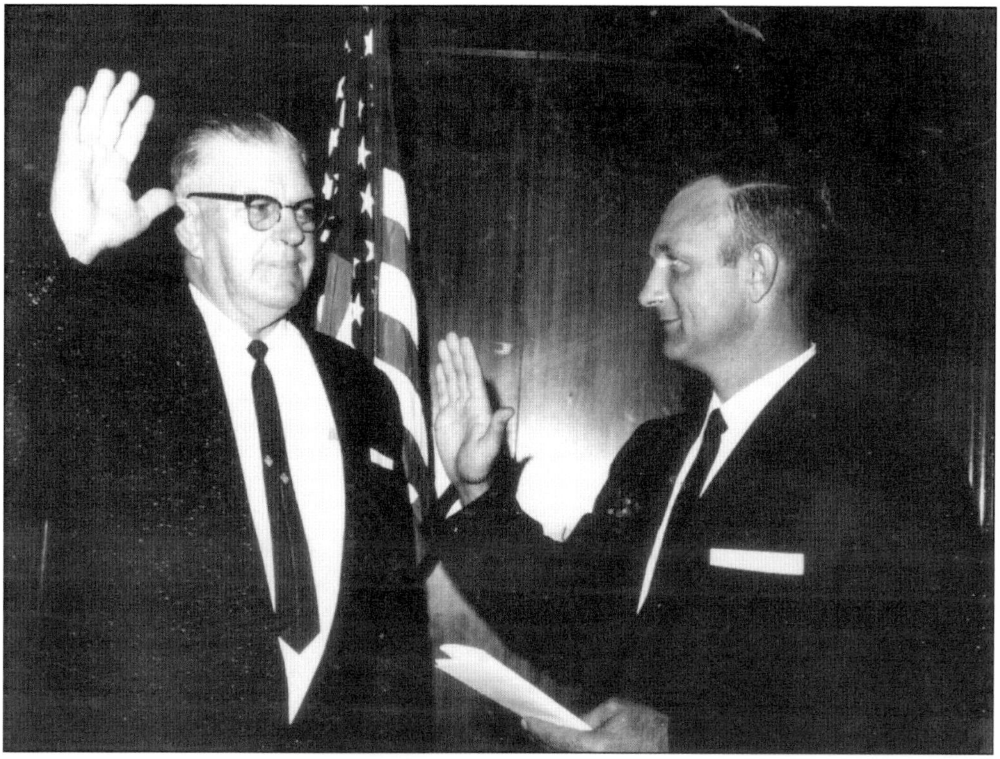

Here is Burnet County judge Joe Evans, who served from 1955 to 1963, swearing in Judge Tom O'Donnell Sr., who served from 1963 to 1970. In the photograph at right, Judge O'Donnell is swearing in Judge B. Pogue, who served from 1970 to 1978. (Photographs courtesy of Milli Williams and Frances O'Donnell.)

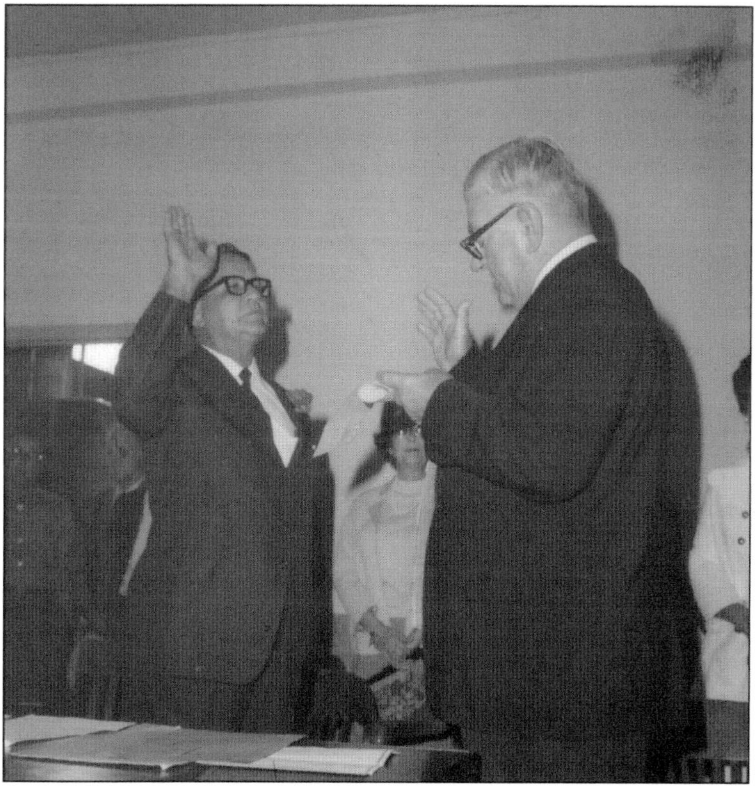

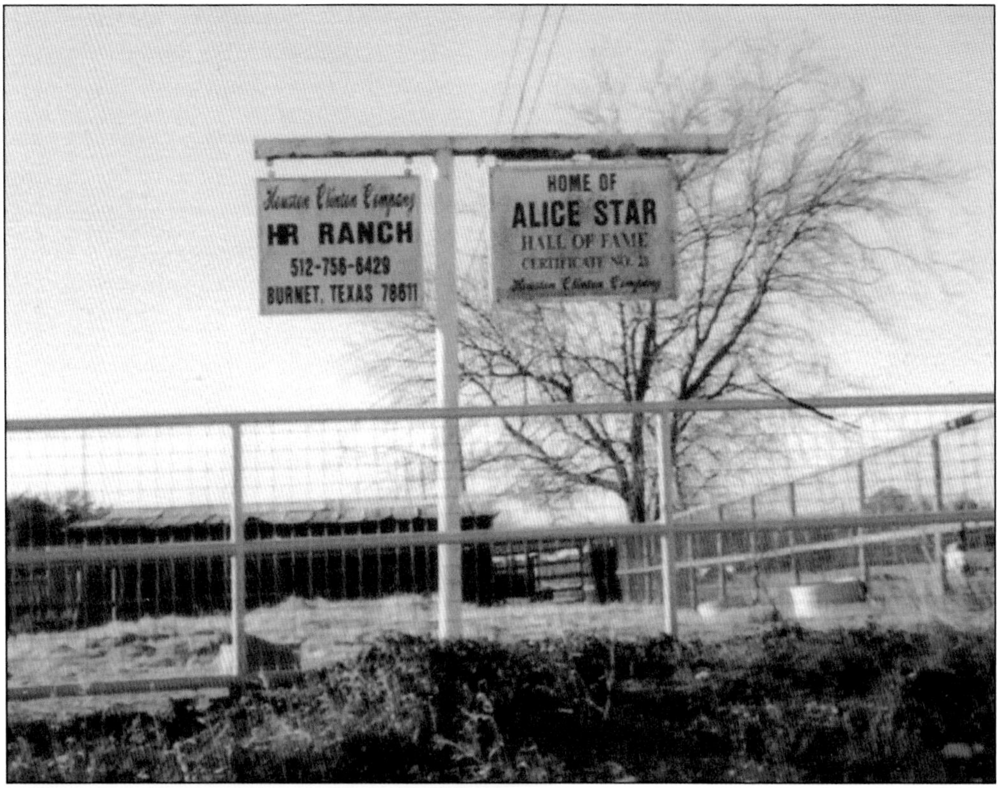

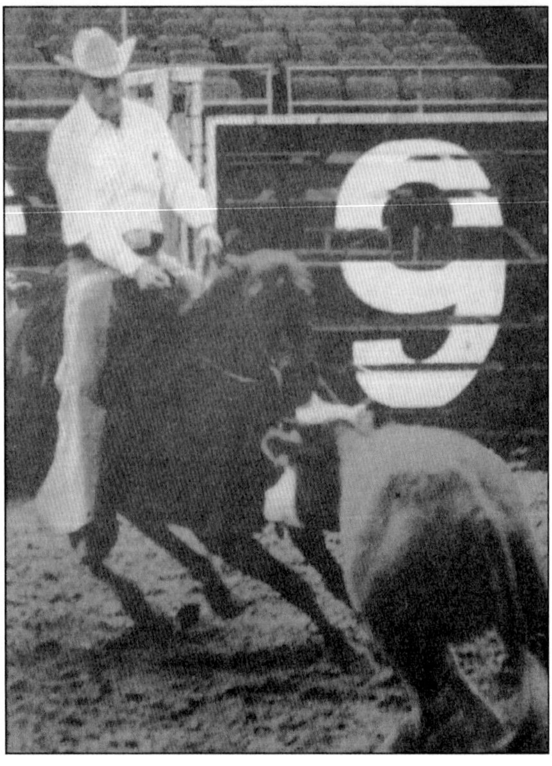

Just a few miles from Burnet on U.S. 281, there is a sign that says "Home of Alice Star." She was famous throughout the entire world as a champion cutting horse. She possessed intelligence, great strength, speed, balance, and a lot of heart. Houston Clinton, who knew horses, expected she would be a champion when he first purchased her at auction. He is shown training her as a rodeo cutting horse. She began winning the next year. Traveling to all of the top-level shows, Alice Star earned 390 performance points, 19 halter points, and $35,909 in championship money. She was inducted into the National Cutting Horse Association Hall of Fame in 1969. She was the American Quarter Horse Association champion in 1960 and twice named Reserve World Champion. It saddened the heart of many a rodeo cowboy when Alice Star passed away in 1969. She rests forever at her home on the Clinton ranch. (Left, photograph courtesy of Ramsey Clinton.)

Jim Morgan Cross was Burnet County attorney from 1985 through 1991. He was known for his joke repertoire and ability to put people at ease. Lieutenant Colonel Cross (U.S. Air Force Reserves) and his wife, Margaret Lillian, raised five children. His daughter, Carolyn, says, "He never preached but offered words of encouragement." He helped many persons in Burnet county find help with their alcohol problems. A recovering alcoholic himself, he was just short of 12 years of sobriety when he died. The photograph below is of Wayne Alton Barton (1919–1983), who was Burnet County clerk from January 1956 through June 1979. A graduate of Bertram High School and the University of Texas, Barton served in the U.S. Air Force from 1941 through 1945. (Right, photograph courtesy of Carolyn Cross; below, photograph courtesy of Arlee Barton.)

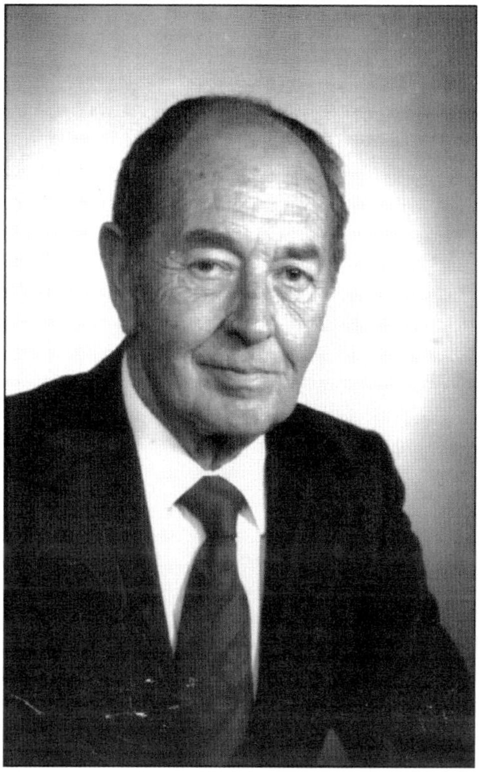

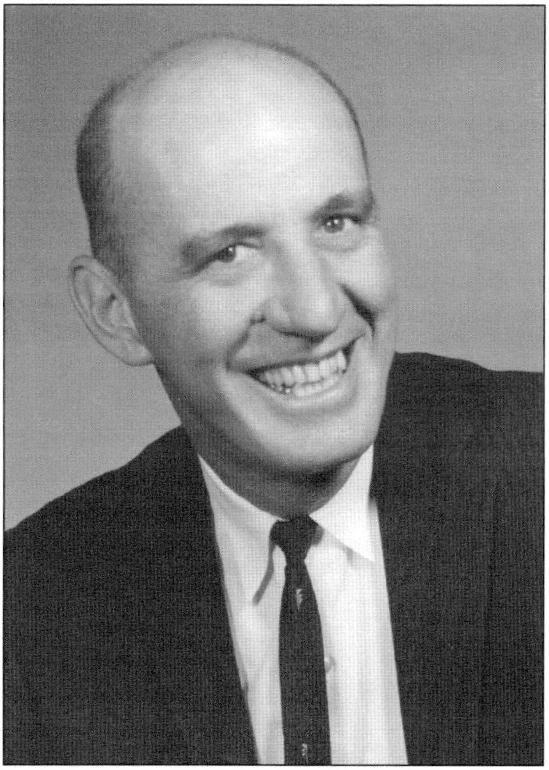

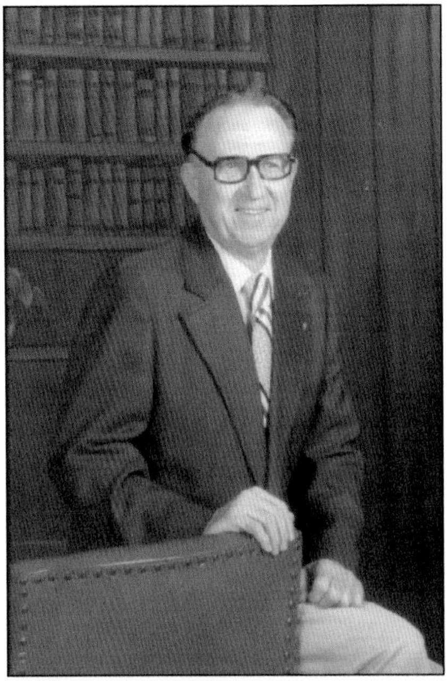

Chester Kincheloe has served in leadership roles with too many organizations to mention here. A graduate of Oatmeal High School, he worked with the county agent before World War II, then served with the U.S. Air Force in China with the "Flying Tiger Group." Back at home, he worked at the *Burnet Bulletin*, becoming owner/publisher in 1963 until 1970. He served as justice of the peace from 1973 to 1983, city municipal judge from 1978 to 1982, and Burnet County judge from 1983 to 1990. As county judge, he instituted the first computer system for the courthouse. Below is the Pen Chat Club in 1968. Only the last names are given. They are, from left to right, (first row) Reed, Adrian, Jenkins, Knox, and Kassaw; (second row) Rucker, unidentified, Larry, Bryant, Albritton, Debo, and Lucile O'Donnell. Lucille Frazier took the picture with O'Donnell's camera.

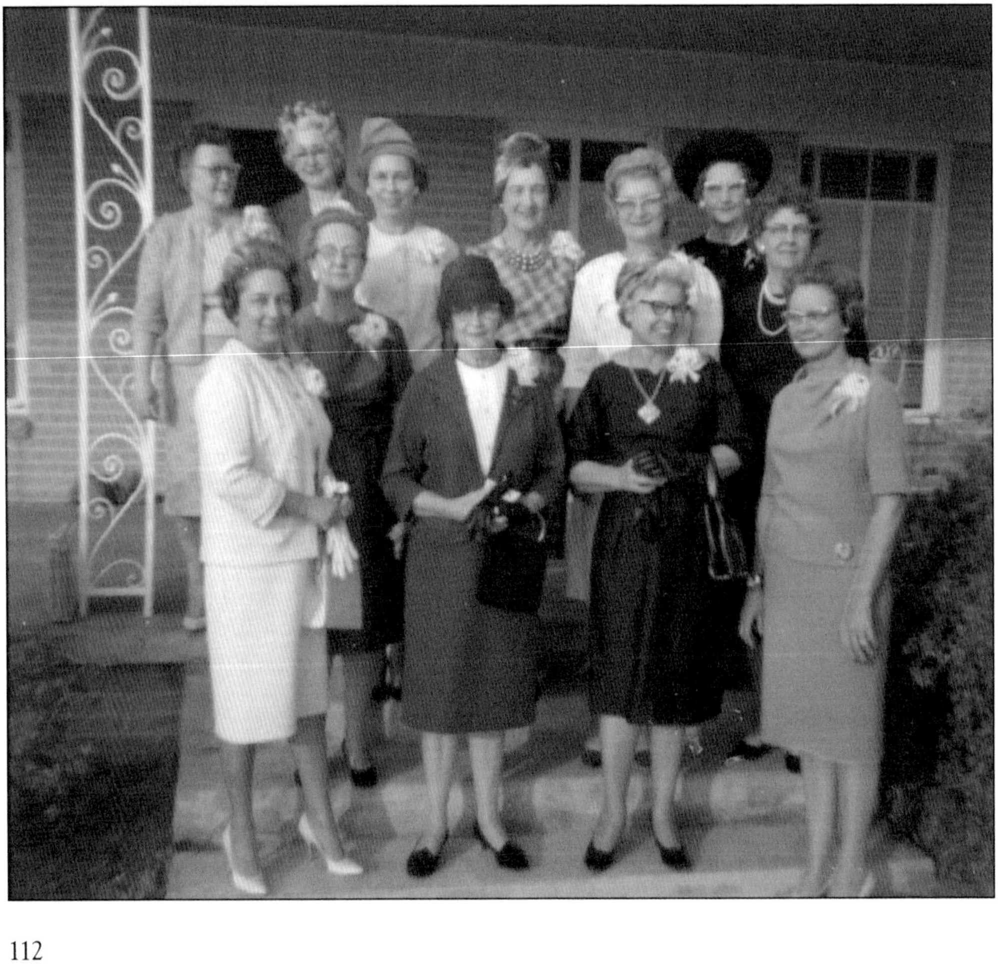

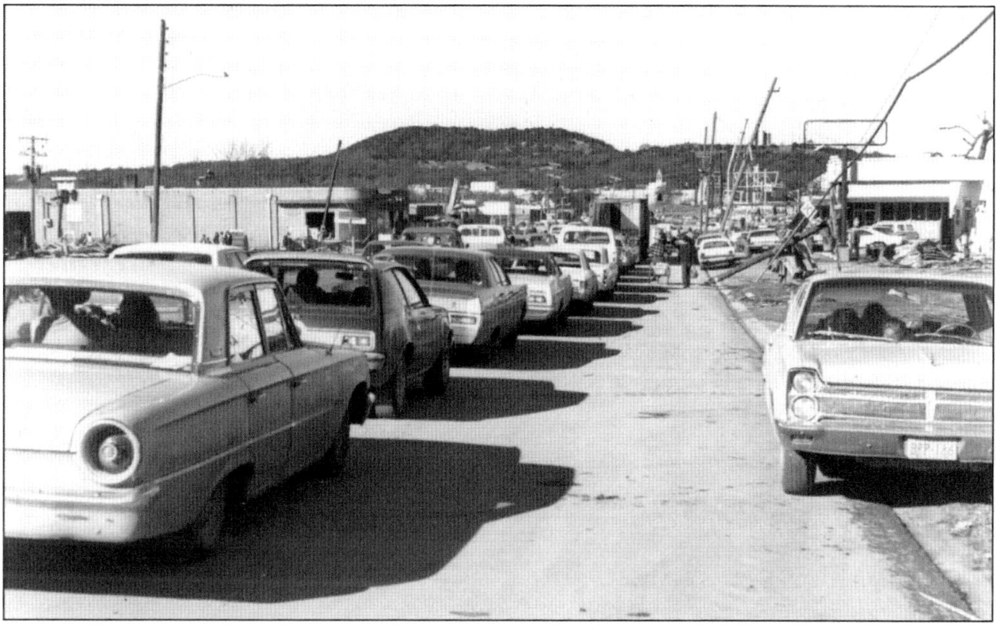

In 1973, a tornado roared through the town of Burnet before daybreak, wreaking havoc. It struck buildings along U.S. 281 and the intersection of U.S. 281 and TX 29 and continued northeast, destroying homes, schools, and businesses. Utility lines were ripped down. It seemed a miracle that no deaths occurred. This view is looking toward the highway intersection on TX 29 the morning after the storm. (Photograph courtesy of HBFL.)

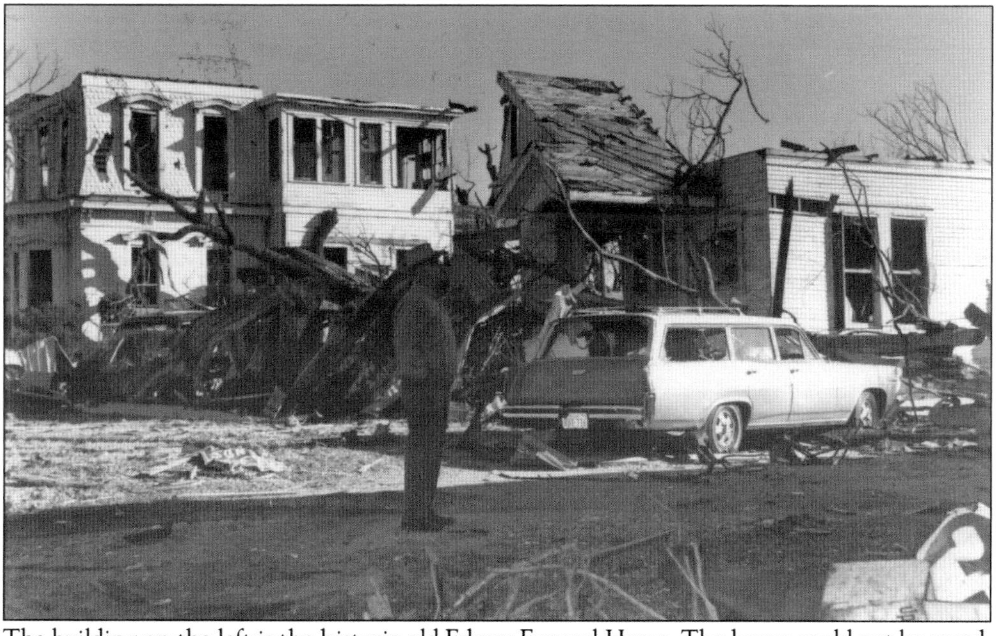

The building on the left is the historic old Edgars Funeral Home. The home could not be saved, so it was demolished and the present brick building was erected. The Red Cross came in to help those who had lost everything, and the federal government provided temporary housing by bringing in mobile homes. Neighboring towns sent utility workmen to help the city repair lines. (Photograph courtesy of HBFL.)

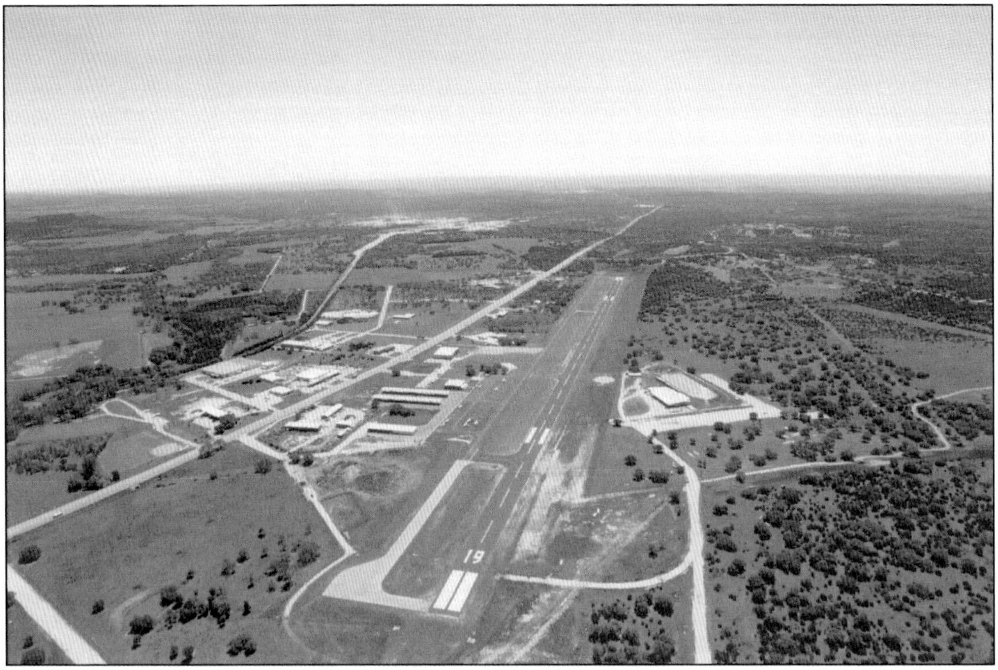

This is an aerial view of Kate Craddock Field, Burnet's municipal airport, with its 5,000 feet of lighted runway, instrument approaches, hangers, and major aircraft maintenance services. It is a busy airport. A view of the old Hamilton swimming pool in Tommy White Park is below. It was closed when the new one opened at the Galloway-Hammond complex. (Above, photograph courtesy of COB; below, photograph courtesy of Milli Williams.)

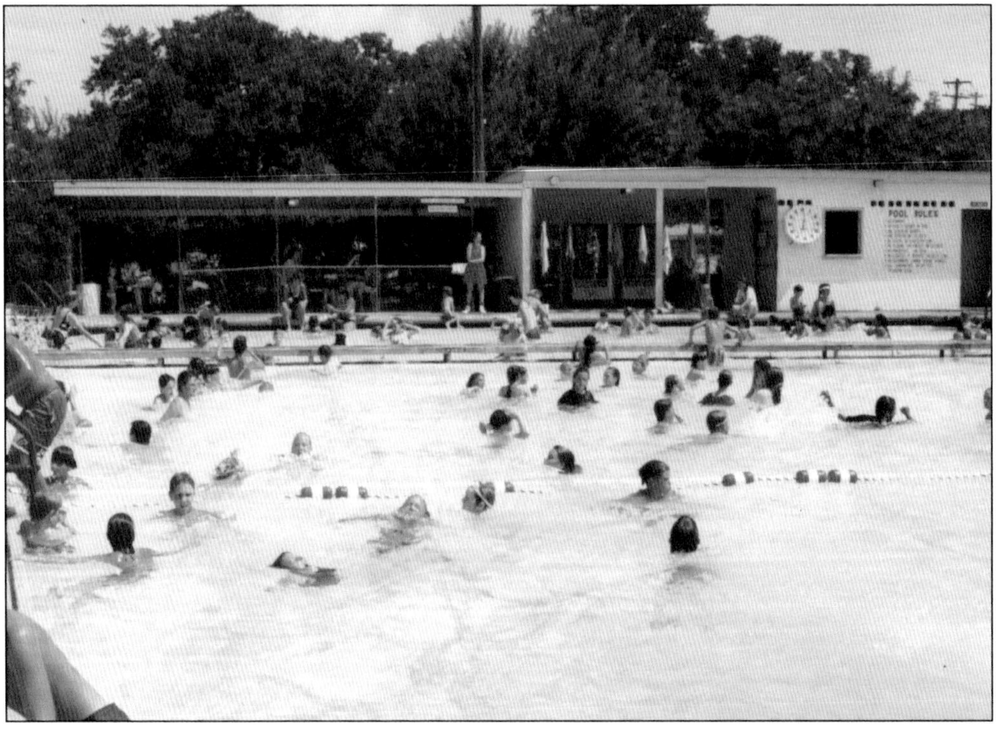

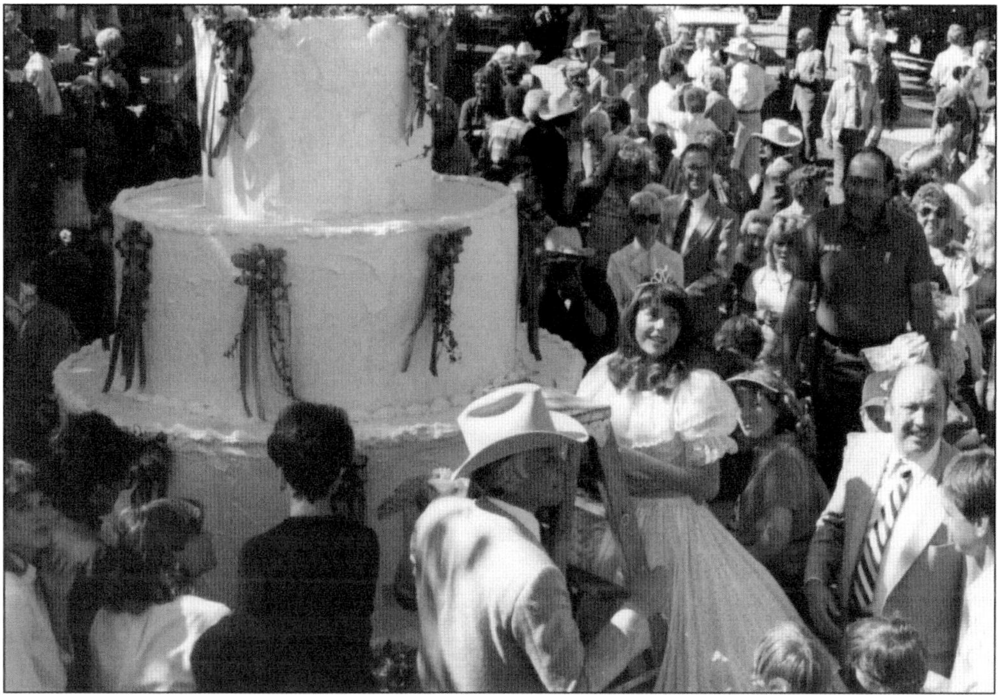

The huge cake in this photograph was part of the City of Burnet's centennial celebration of its incorporation in 1883. The cake was featured in the parade, and most of Burnet's citizens and dignitaries were present. (Photograph courtesy of Milli Williams.)

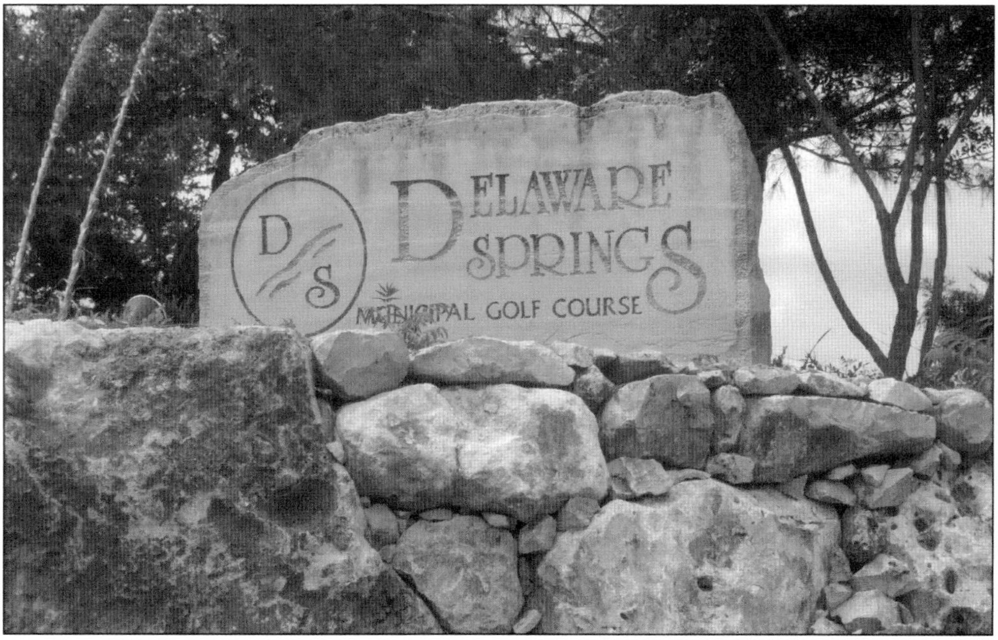

Delaware Springs is an 18-hole championship golf course. The course was voted four stars out of five by *Golf Digest*'s "Best Places to Play" and was listed in Jeff Barr's "1001 Golf Holes You Must Play Before You Die" in 2005. There is a pro shop, driving range, putting green, and dining room. (Photograph courtesy of Crista Fisher.)

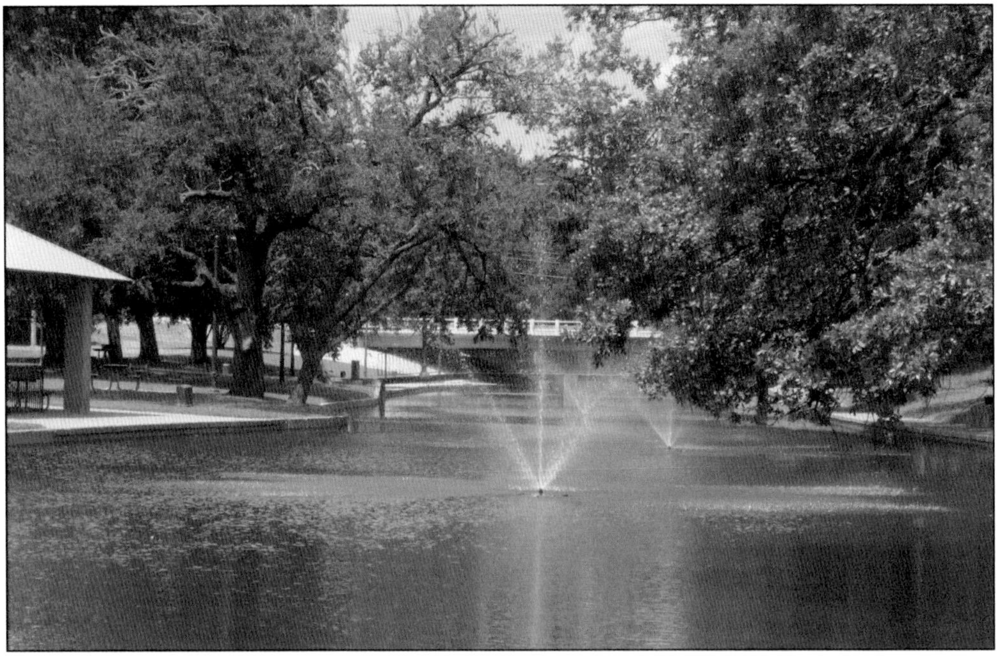

Hamilton Creek Park is just two blocks west of Burnet's historic courthouse square and offers lighted walkways, picnic areas, pavilion, gazebo, playscape, fountains, and a footbridge across the creek. Free movies are shown there on weekends during the summer months.

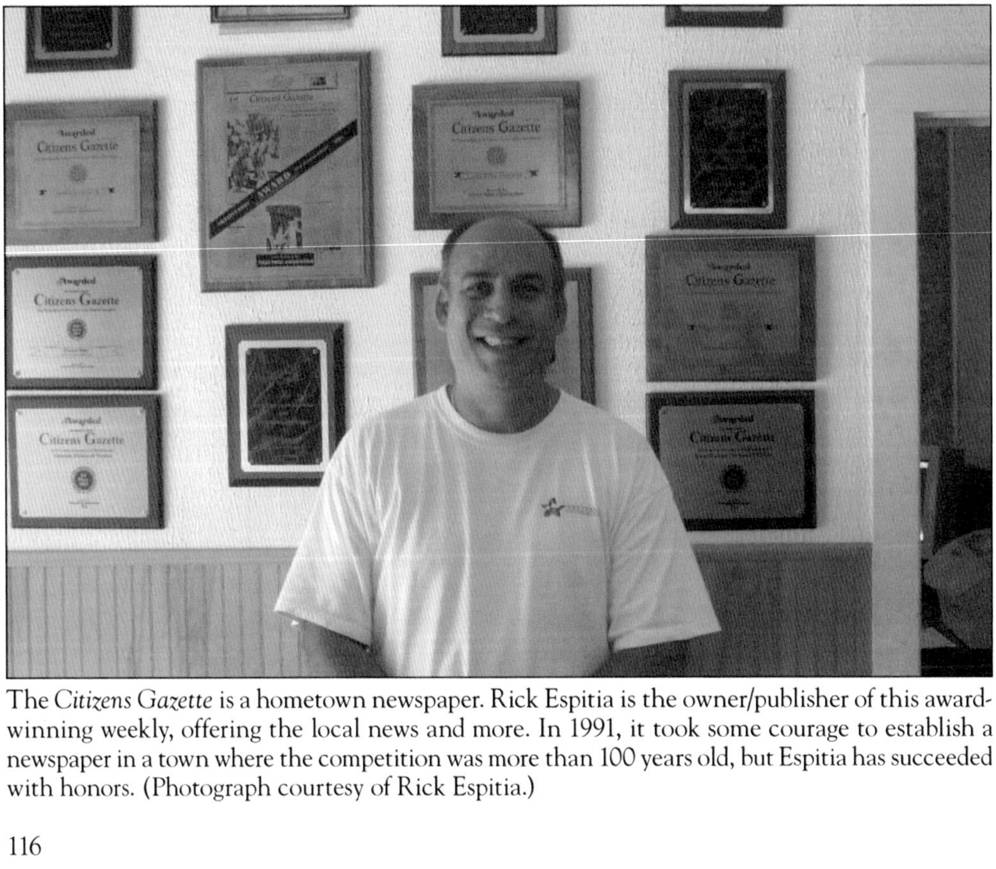

The *Citizens Gazette* is a hometown newspaper. Rick Espitia is the owner/publisher of this award-winning weekly, offering the local news and more. In 1991, it took some courage to establish a newspaper in a town where the competition was more than 100 years old, but Espitia has succeeded with honors. (Photograph courtesy of Rick Espitia.)

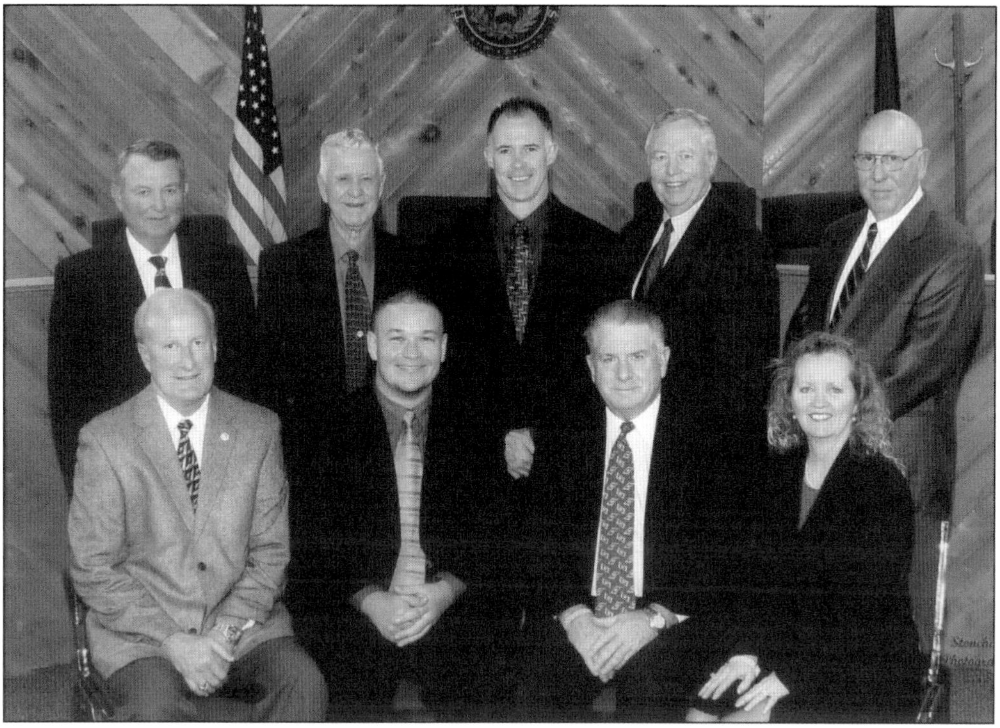

This is the Burnet City Council that, in 2005, launched a plan to renovate the courthouse square. They are above, from left to right, (first row) city manager Michael Steele, councilmen Zack Reed and Pat Riddell, and city secretary Crista Bromley; (second row) James Ritter, A. B. Daugherty, Mayor Dennis Kincheloe, and councilmen Ken Graham and Howard Benton. The photograph below is a view of Main Street looking south before the renovation began. (Photographs courtesy of COB.)

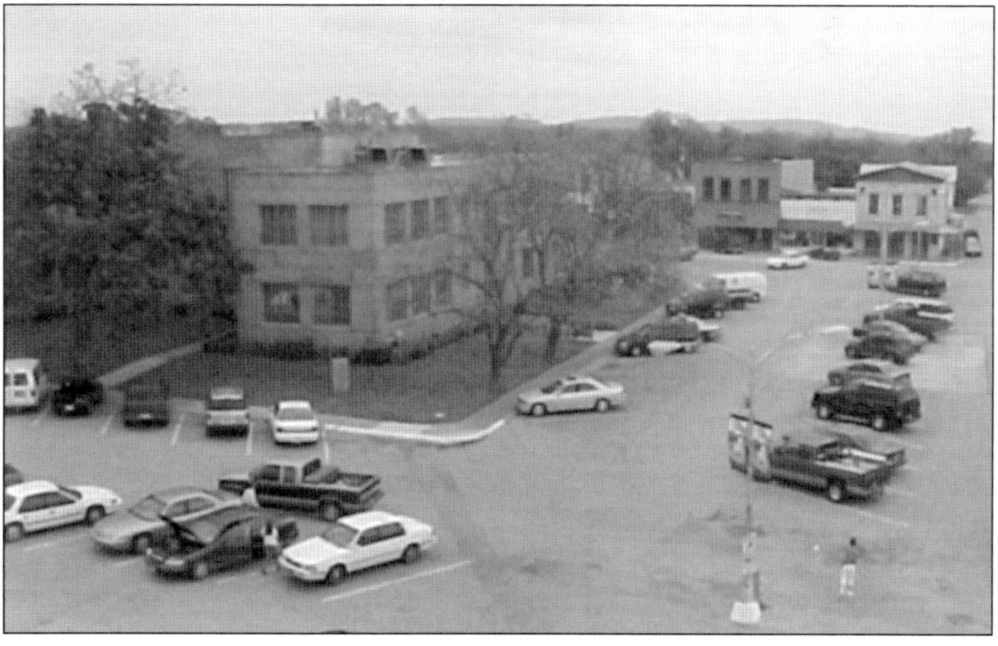

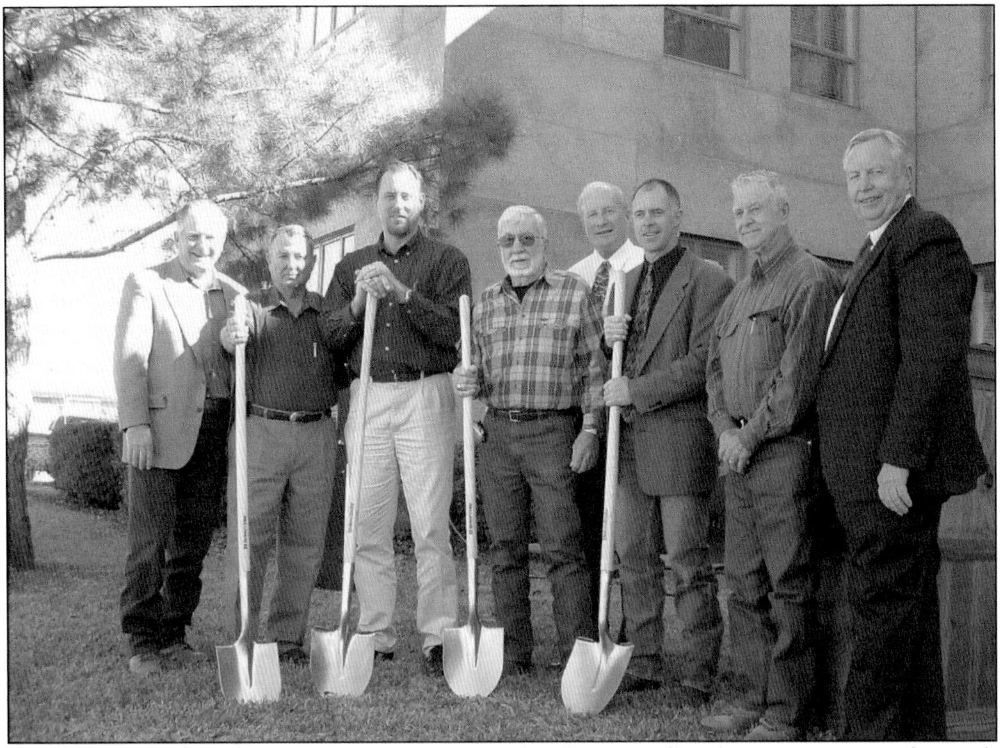

The work on the $2-million "Square Project" started with a groundbreaking ceremony on the south side of the courthouse lawn. Those present were, from left to right, Pat Riddell, James Ritter, TX DOT representative Howard Lyons, Howard Peabody (J. P. Contractors), Michael Steele, Dennis Kincheloe, A. B. Daugherty, and Ken Graham. The view in the below photograph is Jackson Street looking east after the renovation. Among many improvements, the sidewalks and businesses were made Americans with Disabilities Act accessible. (Photographs courtesy of COB.)

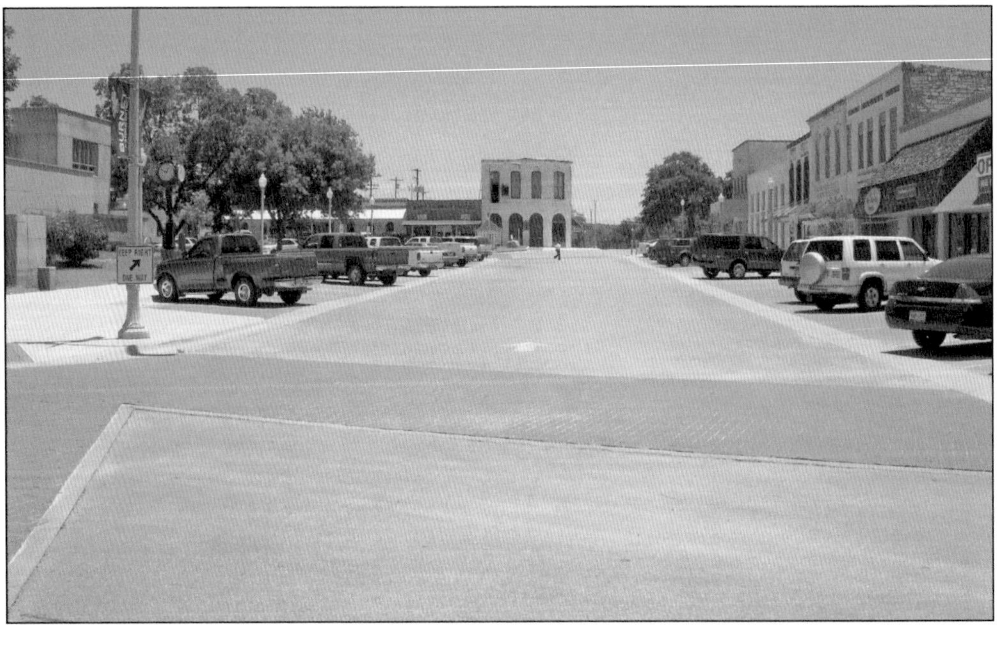

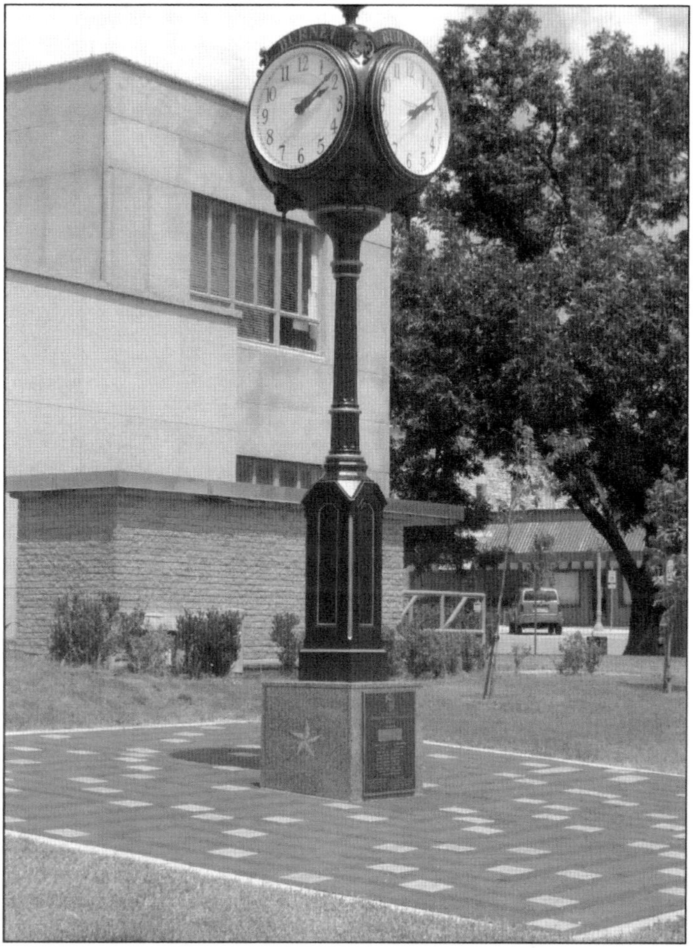

The History Plaza features a maze. As one follows the pathway, pavers tell the history of the county, ending at the clock tower in the center. Other engraved pavers honor individuals of past and present times. The square renovation was completed in 2007, and those present at the ribbon cutting were, from left to right, Michael Steele, project manager Crista Bromley, Linda Turner, Paul Shell, Howard Benton, Pat Riddell, James Ritter, grant writer Leo Wood, and Zack Reed. (Photographs courtesy of COB.)

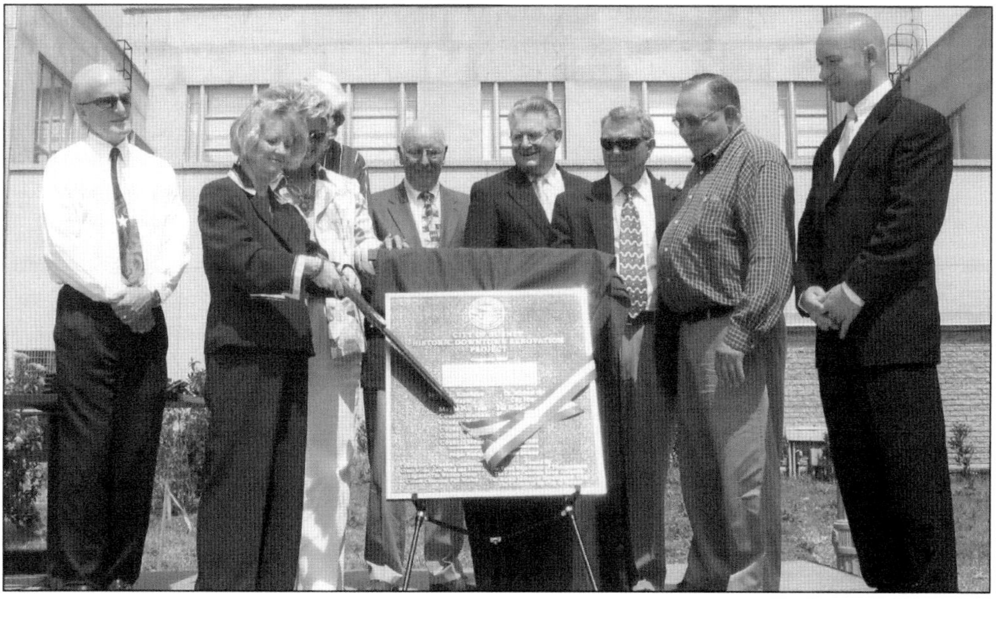

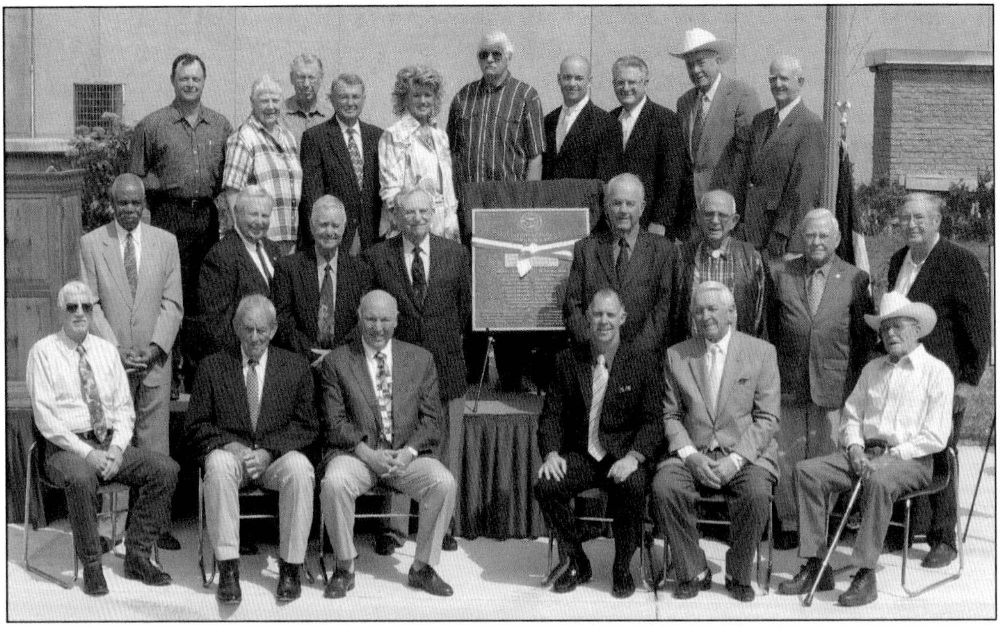

All except one of the living city mayors and councilmen were present for the square dedication. They were, from left to right, (first row) Bobby Bradshaw, Ramsey Clinton, Howard Benton, Dennis Kincheloe, Bill Wilcox, and Ronnie Waggoner; (second row) Richard Sanders, Ken Graham, A. B. Daugherty, Bob Wilkins, Howard Lange, Al Kroeger, James Fry, and John Sandner; (third row) Steven Palmour, Ina Cooper, Roy Oakley, James Ritter, Linda Turner, Paul Shell, Zack Reed, Pat Riddell, John Hoover, and Cecil Hester. Not present was former mayor Jerri Robinson. The photograph below is of the Burnet County Courthouse Annex on TX 29 East. It was built to provide more office and courtroom space not available in the main courthouse.

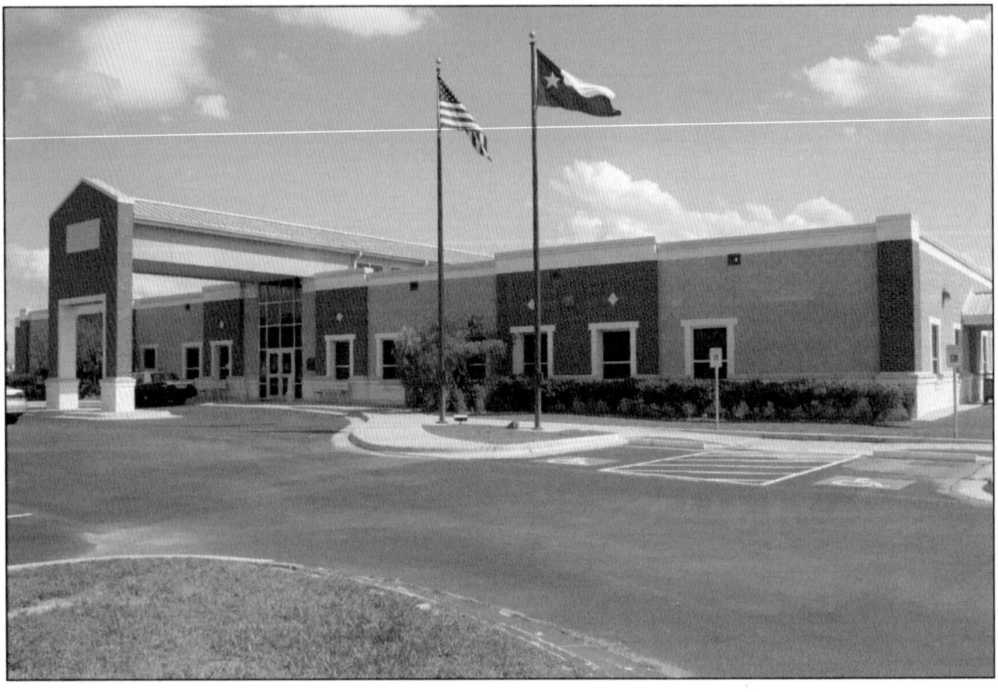

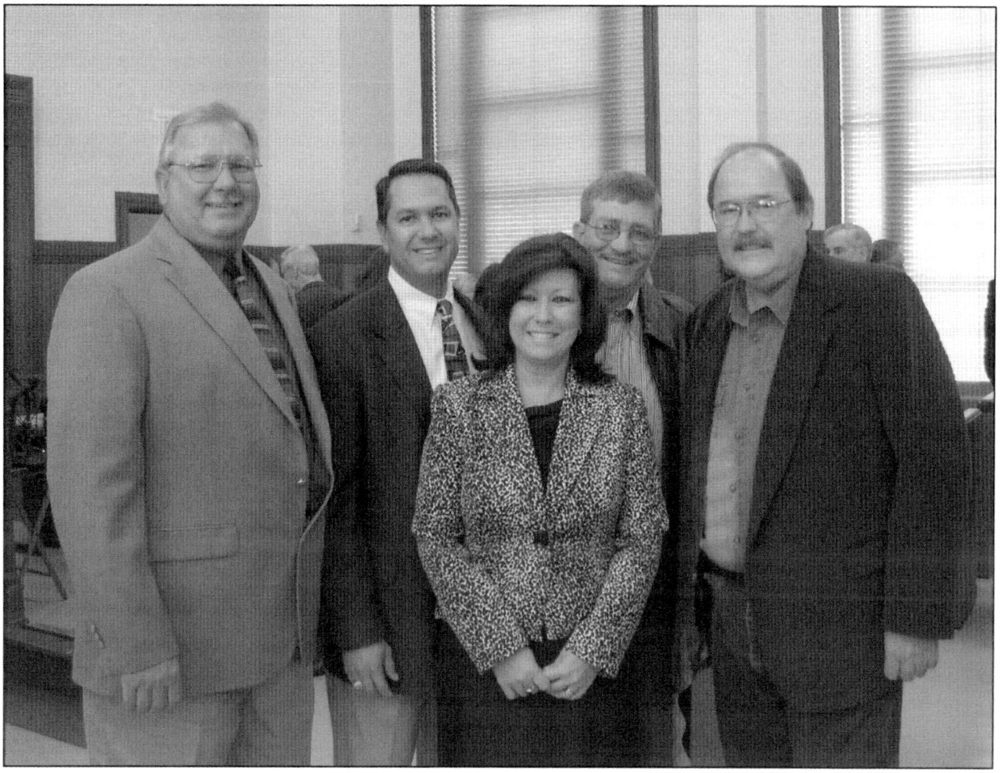

The 2009 Commissioners Court is shown in the above photograph. Commissioners are, from left to right, Russell Grater, Precinct 2; Joe Don Dockery, Precinct 4; Ronny Hibler, Precinct 3; and Bill Neve, Precinct 1. County judge Donna Klaeger stands in front. Klaeger is the first woman to hold the office. The Wallace Riddell Law Enforcement Center was built in 1982, but the jail eventually became inadequate, making a new one necessary.

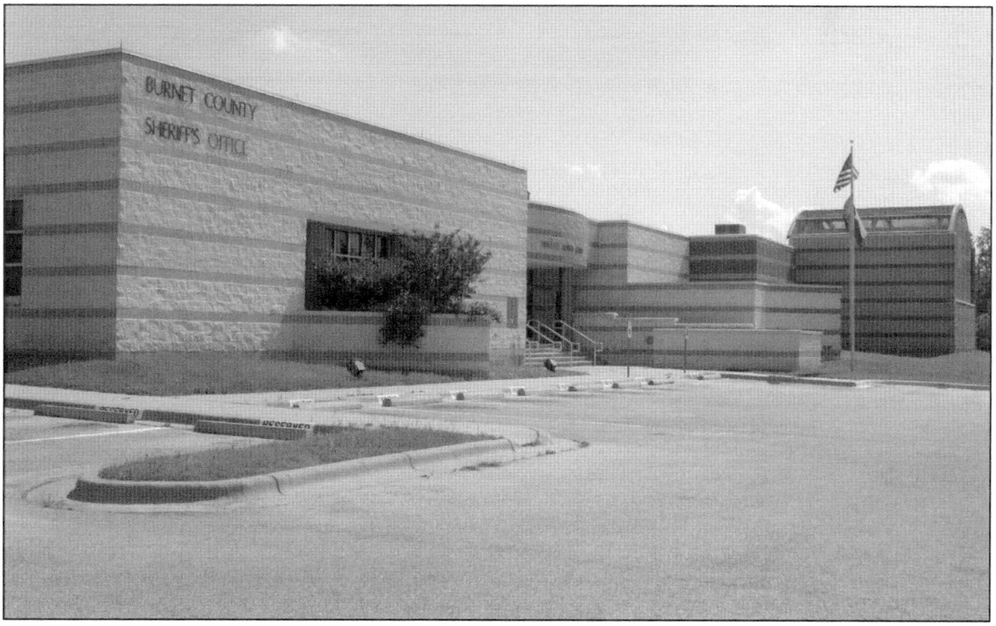

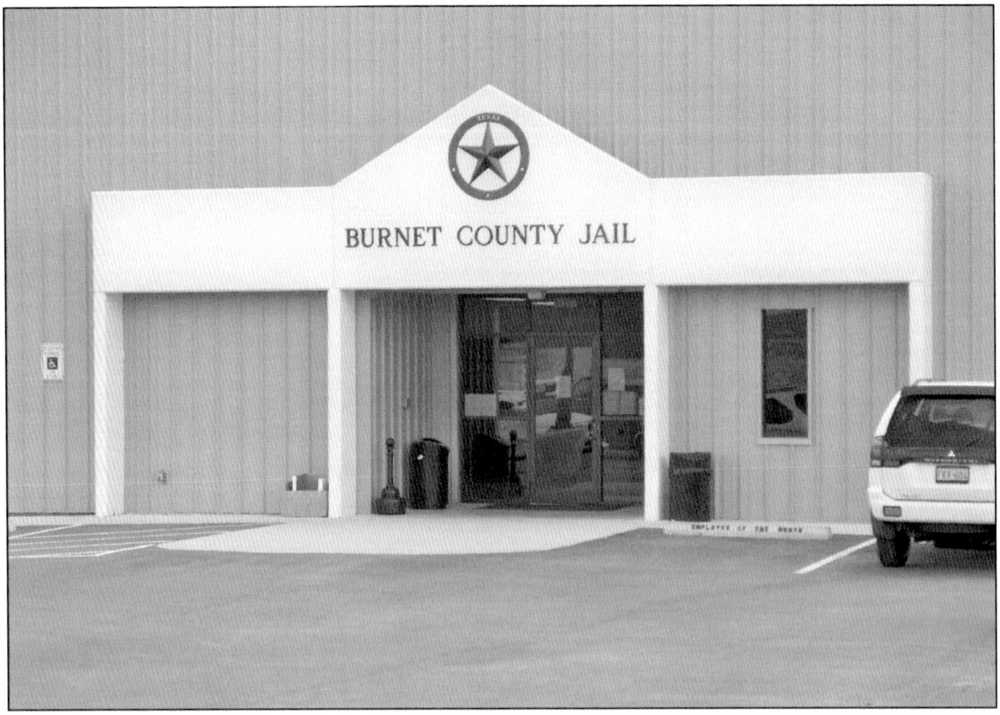

Burnet County built this new jail to alleviate crowding at the old one. This jail was completed in 2009, and the prisoners were transferred to it. The old jail will be refurbished for future use.

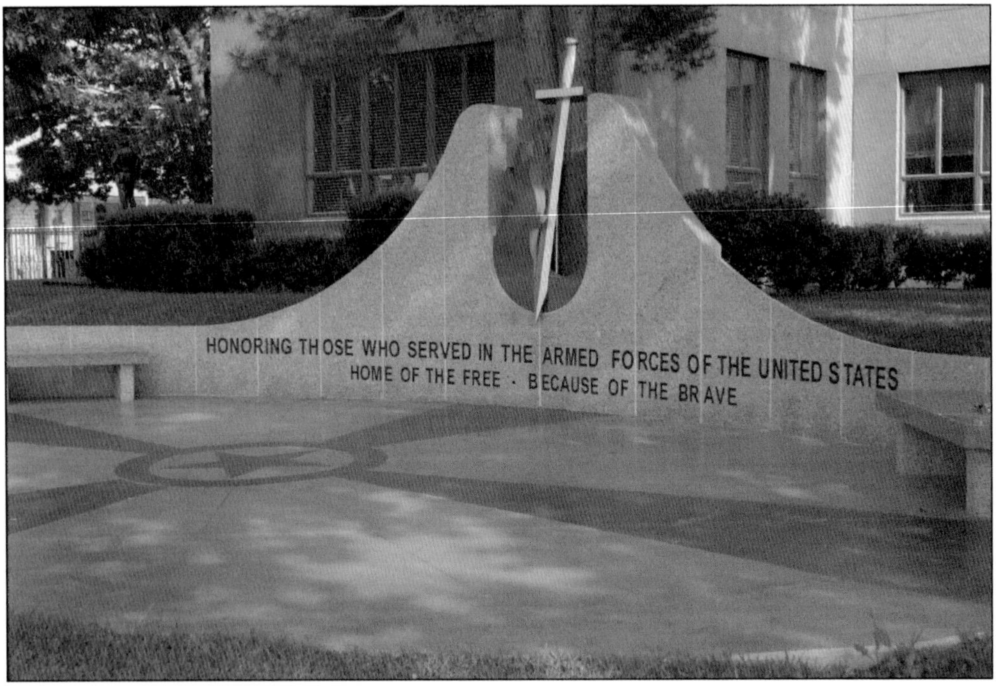

A group of citizens, businesses, organizations, and corporations worked together to raise funds and construct this Veterans Memorial on the north side of the courthouse lawn. The donors' names are inscribed there.

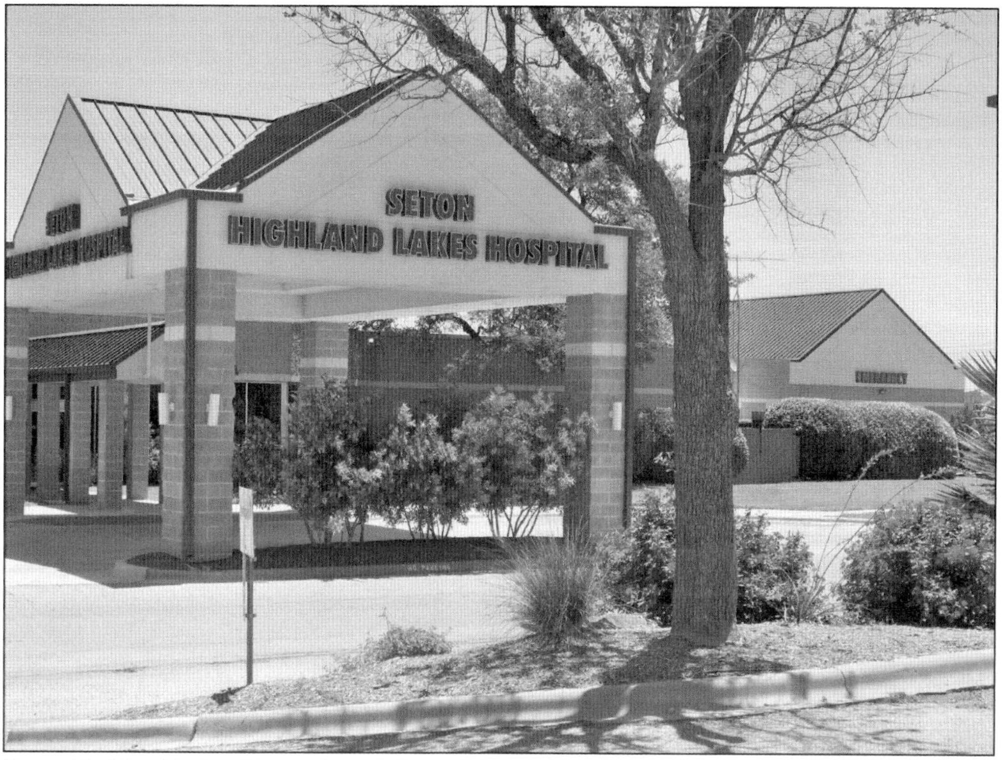

Seton Highland Lakes Hospital is a full-service acute-care hospital on U.S. 281 South in Burnet. The complex includes health care clinics offering primary and specialty care, such as home health, rehabilitation, and hospice services.

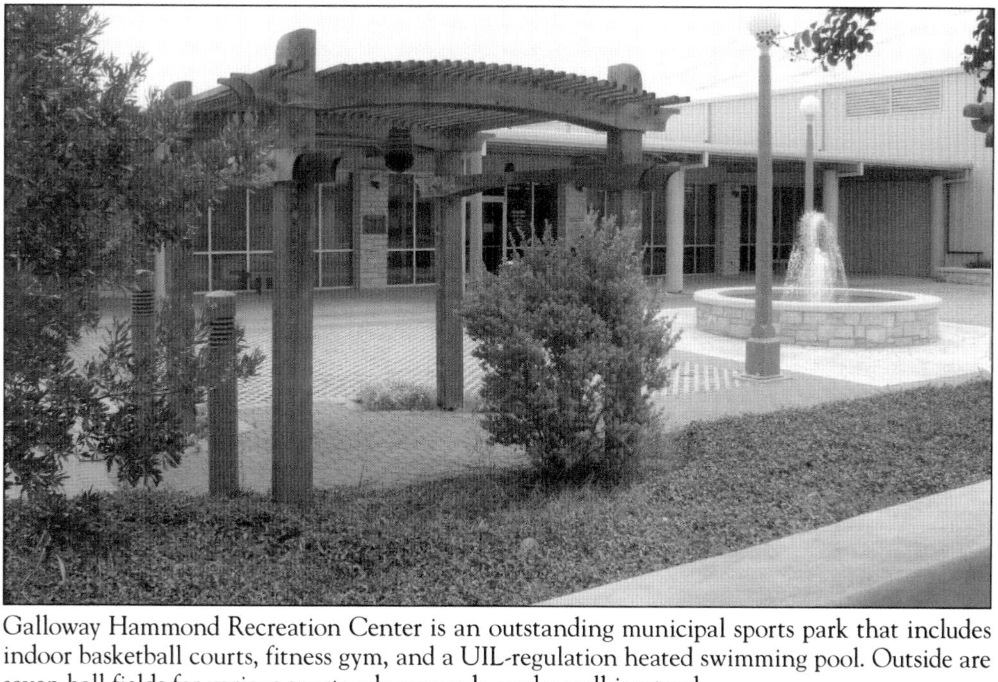

Galloway Hammond Recreation Center is an outstanding municipal sports park that includes indoor basketball courts, fitness gym, and a UIL-regulation heated swimming pool. Outside are seven ball fields for various sports, playgrounds, and a walking track.

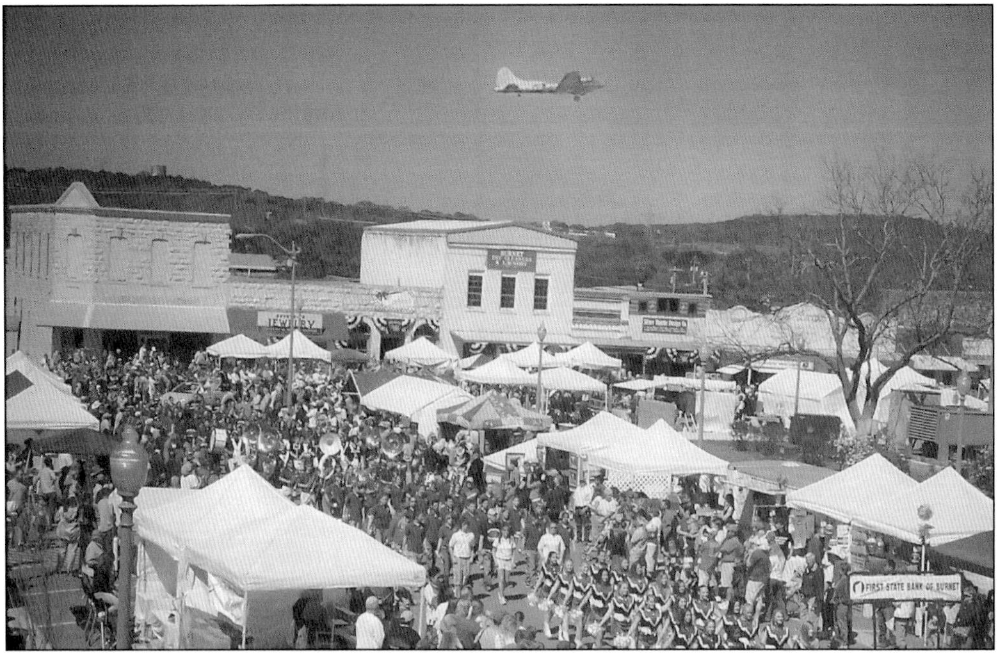

Every year in April, the chamber of commerce sponsors the Bluebonnet Festival. The festival features a parade, races for all ages, live music, Miss Burnet competition, vendors, and more. It draws some 30,000 people to the festivities. This photograph is a view of Washington Street during the 2009 event.

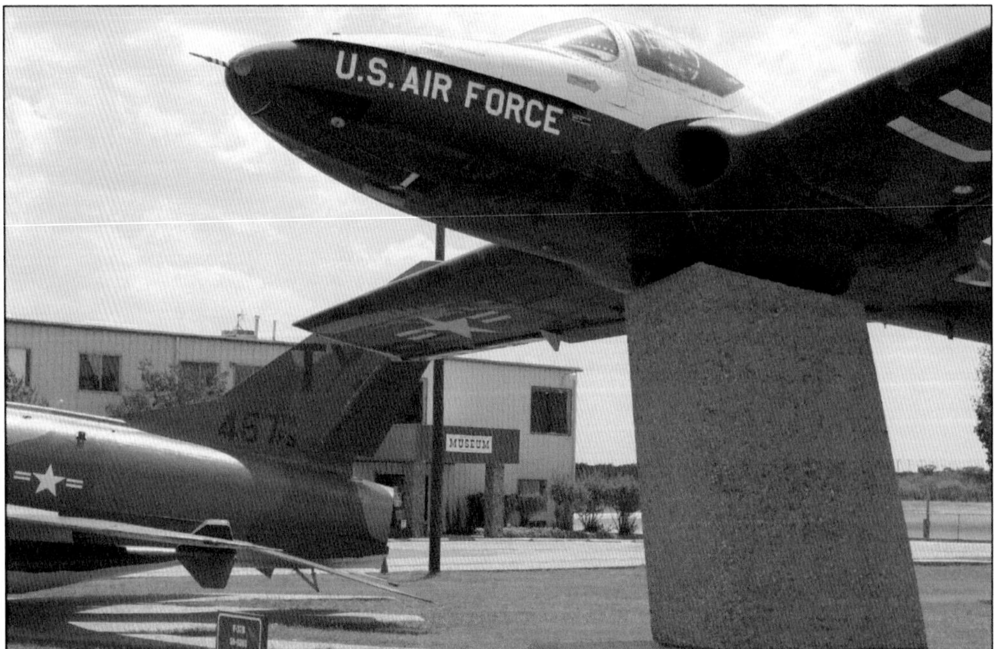

The Highland Lakes Air Museum on U.S. 281 South is the home of the Commemorative Air Force Show, held in conjunction with the Bluebonnet Festival. The museum houses both flying and static World War II war planes as well as World War II memorabilia.

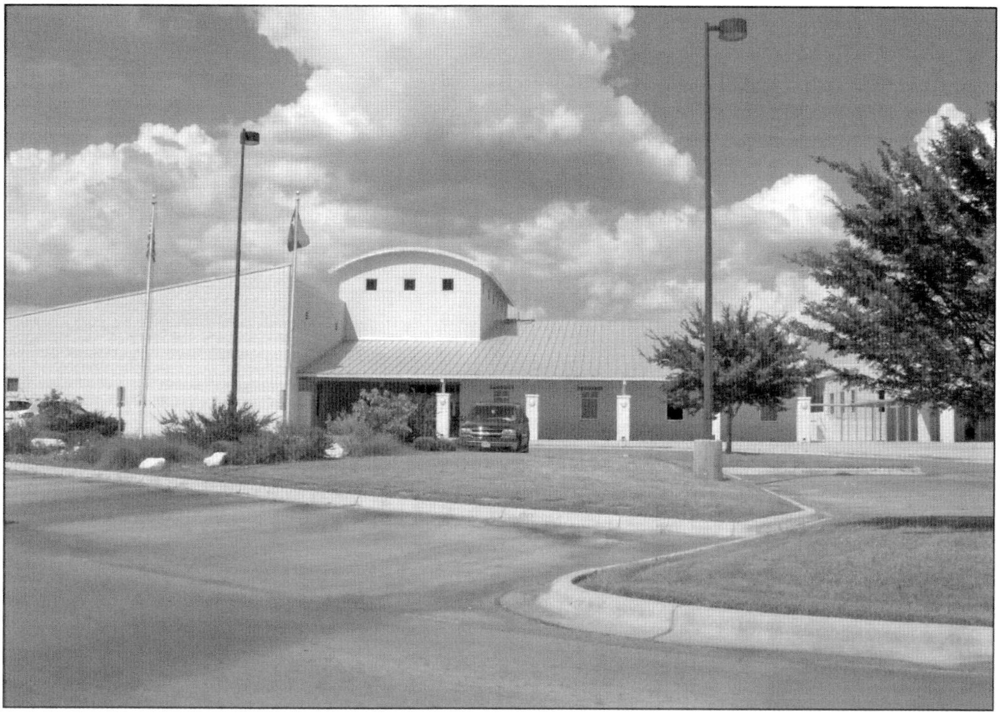

The Burnet High School is a state-of-the-art complex of buildings resembling a college campus. The Hill Country Foundation awards a scholarship to every graduate who is going to college. The R. J. Richey eighth-grade campus is seen in the picture below. These two schools have recently been completed and occupied. Burnet has six campuses.

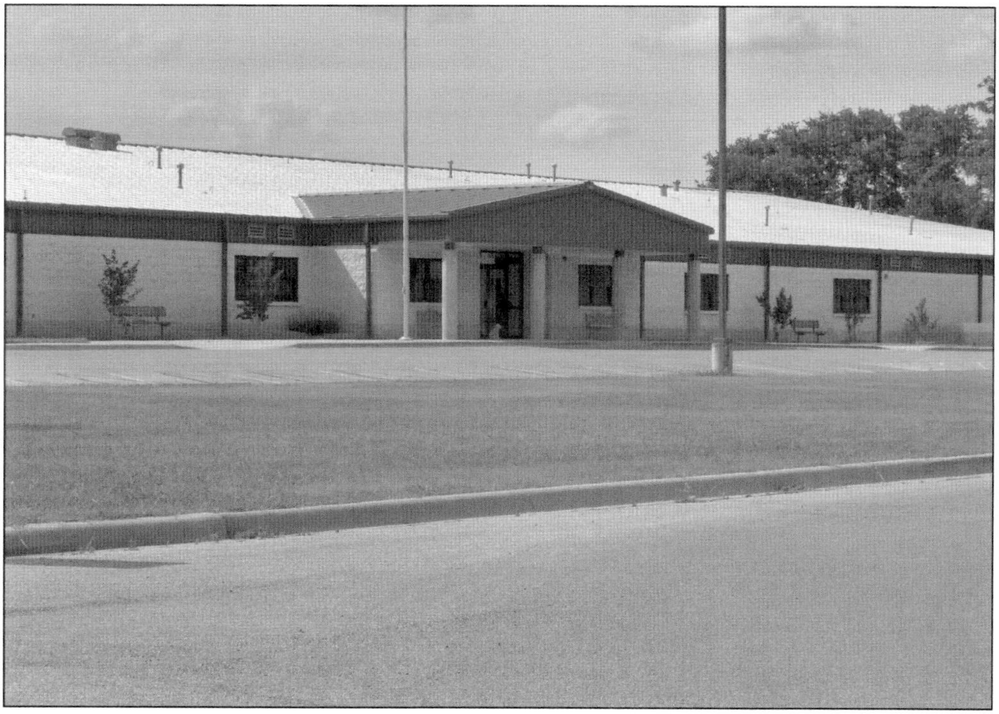

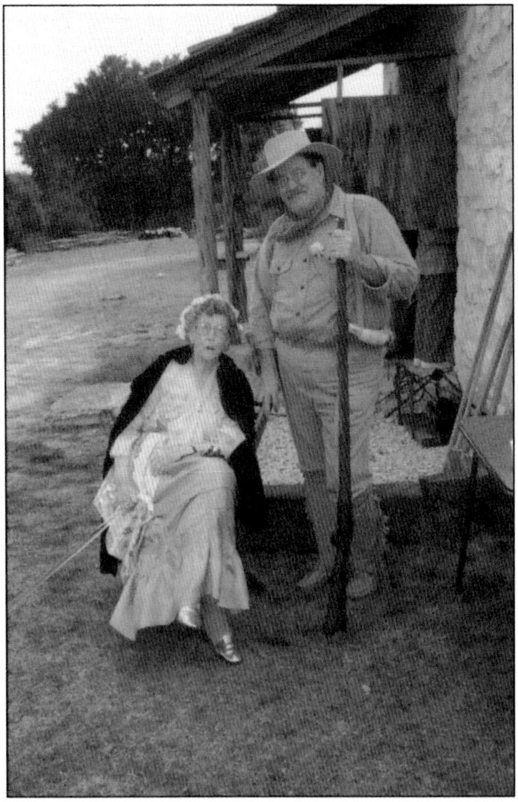

Lucile O'Donnell, shown in her Fort Croghan costume, was an early librarian, premier historian, community volunteer, writer, and friend to all. She made good things happen. The gentleman is unidentified. Below is how Fort Croghan looked soon after the first cabins were restored there. The Burnet County Heritage Society continues to improve the fort grounds for the enjoyment of visitors.

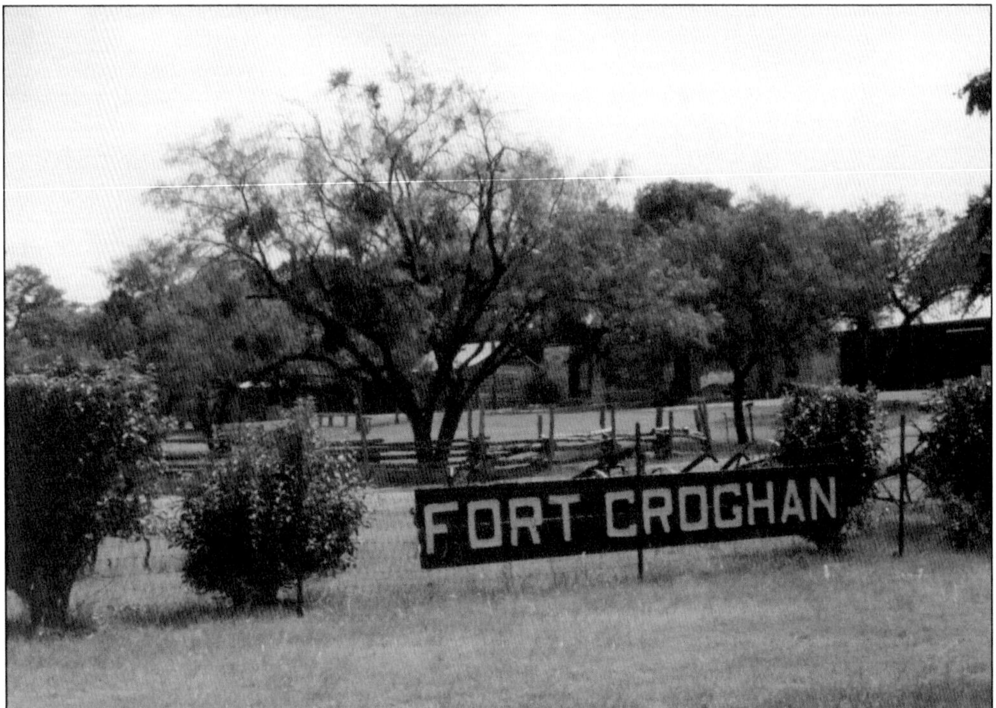

Former Burnet County judge Tommy Ferguson (1906–1991), a member of the National Trust for Historical Preservation and the Texas Historical Commission, organized the Burnet County Heritage Society and funded the creation of the Fort Croghan Museum. He and his wife, Vera, were diligent volunteers all of their lives, leaving an endowment for the acquisition of artifacts and maintenance of the fort. Ferguson, a World War II army veteran, was appointed to the first board of directors of the Lower Colorado River Authority in 1935. In honor of his long and dedicated service, the LCRA named a new steam generation plant, built in 1973 at Lake Lyndon B. Johnson, the Thomas C. Ferguson Plant.

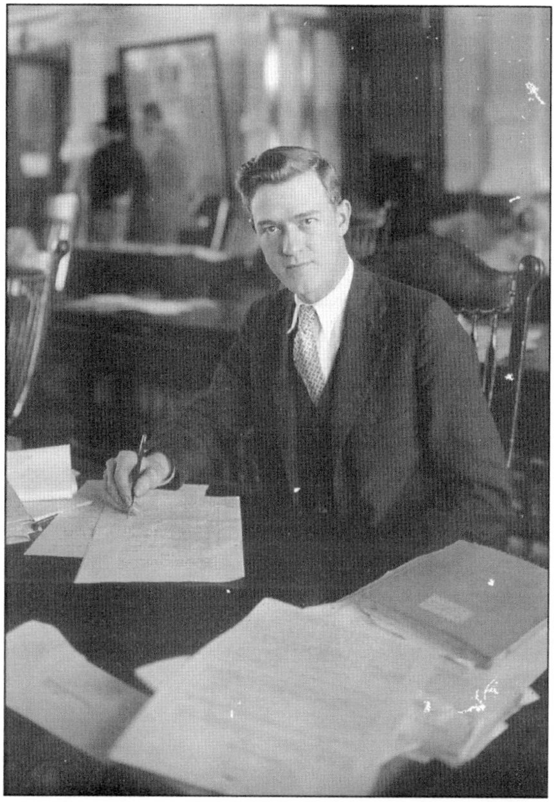

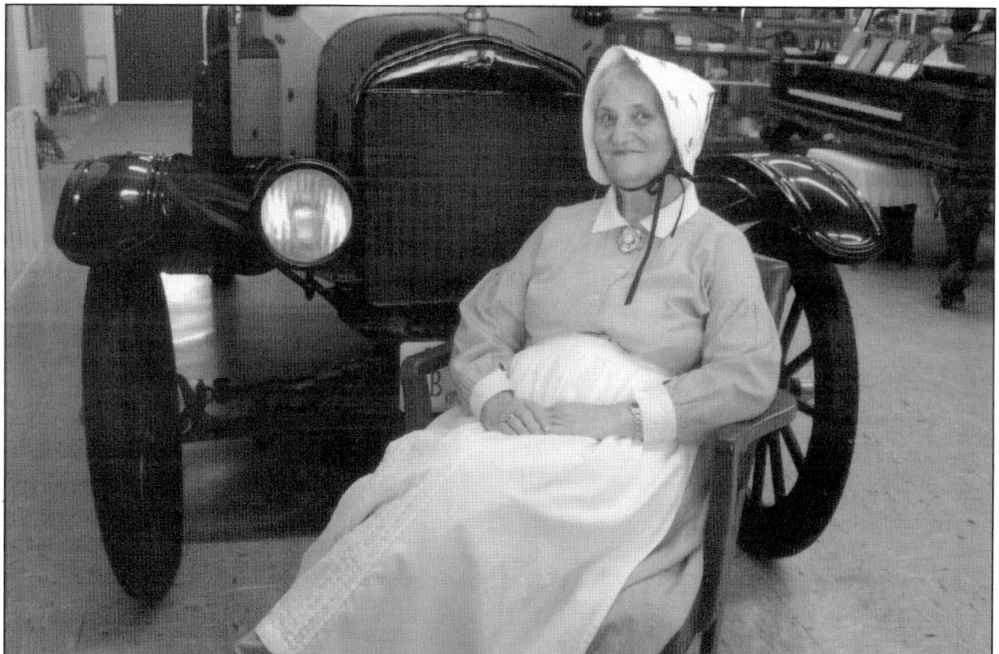

The author of this book relaxes after conducting a tour at the fort. More than 600 schoolchildren visit Fort Croghan every year, and it is a popular destination for summer visitors.